D0210531

32 STORIES

THE COMPLETE OPTIC NERVE MINI-COMICS

Adrian Tomine

DRAWN AND QUARTERLY PUBLICATIONS • MONTREAL

Publisher: Chris Oliveros
Publicity: Peggy Burns
Color separations/typesetting: John Kuramoto
Fifth Printing: December 2004
PRINTED IN CANADA

Softcover edition: ISBN 1-896597-00-9
Signed and numbered hardcover edition: ISBN 1-896597-01-7
10 9 8 7 6 5

Drawn & Quarterly Publications
PO Box 48056
Montreal, Quebec
H2V 4S8 Canada
www.drawnandquarterly.com

Distributed in the USA by:
Farrar, Straus and Giroux
19 Union Square West
New York, NY 10003
Orders: 888.330.8477

Distributed in Canada by:
Raincoast Books
9050 Shaughnessy Street
Vancouver, BC V6P 6E5
Orders: 800.663.5714

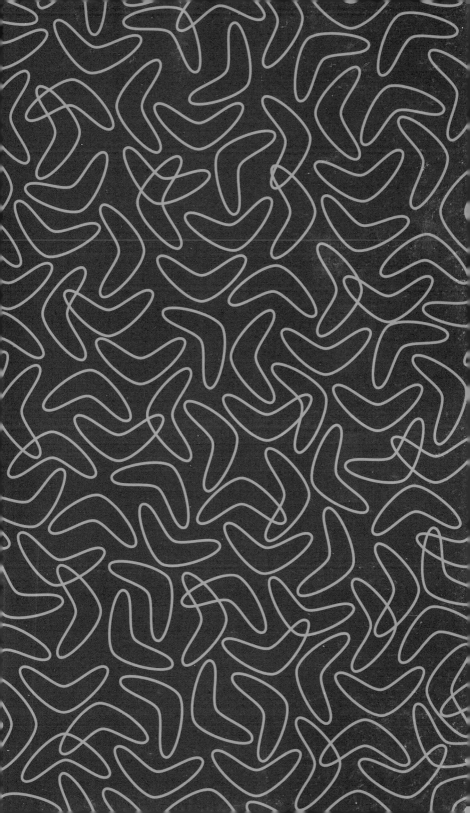

CONTENTS

INTRODUCTION

The book you hold in your hands would not exist had high school been a pleasant experience for me. Having moved to Sacramento, California just weeks before the first day of class, I became painfully aware of my detachment from any type of social interaction early into my freshman year. It was on those quiet weekend nights when even my parents were out having fun that I began making serious attempts to create stories in comics form. It was a cheap way to keep myself occupied, and when a strip started really coming together, I actually forgot that most of my peers were interacting and socializing. (The subject matter of these early strips, though, is rather telling: parties, friends, and dates figure prominently for some reason.)

Trust.
I SAT AT THAT TYPEWRITER FOR FIVE AND A HALF MONTHS... JUST SEARCHING FOR THE RIGHT WORDS.
FEVER
THE BEAT
Sketchbook drawing (1990)

optic · NERVE
NUMBER ONE
$1.00
words and pictures by ADRIAN TOMINE
Issue one, August 1991

I continued in this direction for about a year, filling up sketchbooks that I didn't intend for anyone to see. One holiday season, my older brother Dylan was back in town and he happened to take a peek into one of these secret tomes. I was initially furious with him for invading my privacy, but was quickly placated when he offered excessively complimentary feedback on my comics. He was the first person to read my writing, and his response encouraged me to do something with those stories.

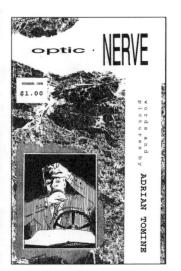

FRIDAY...
WELL, SHIT... IT'S LUNCH-TIME NOW.
FUCK, DON'T I HAVE THE BALLS TO SIT BY MYSELF AND EAT?
GUESS NOT.
SHIT!

*Excerpt from a pre-*Optic Nerve *strip entitled "Lonely Lunch" (1991)*

Around this same time, I had sent away for Terry LaBan and Julie Doucet's self-published mini-comics and was quickly inspired to put my own strips into a similar format. I carried a few of my sketchbooks down to the local Kinko's and made copies of what I thought were the least embarrassing stories of the batch. After several neophyte paste-up and stapling fiascoes, the first issue of *Optic Nerve* was thrust upon the world, with an optimistic print run of twenty-five.

optic NERVE
NUMBER TWO
$1.00
words and pictures by ADRIAN TOMINE

Issue two, November 1991

Aside from the kind encouragement of my family, this first effort was met with general disinterest. Most local comic stores didn't want to touch it, and the shop that did let me leave a few copies on consignment was absolutely unable to sell a single one. And rightfully so, I guess: one dollar is a lot to ask for a few pages of sloppy ball-point pen drawings.

I made a concerted effort to improve with issue two. Concentrating more on autobiography, I tried to accurately transcribe true experiences in a humorous tone. (I definitely got the "truth" part right; the "humor" is still debatable.) In this issue I also took my first serious stab at creating a realistic fictional character. Amy, the narrator of "Solitary Enjoyment," was inspired by a particular girl who seemed to be reading thick novels in the downtown Tower Books every time I went there late at night.

I enjoyed writing from this fictional point of view so much that I continued Amy's story in issue three. At this point, I learned the useful trick of taking a personal experience and veiling it with a sex change or two. The story "Patriotism is Alive and Kicking" is a forced attempt at "social commentary." By this time, I was getting a little bit of mail response, and this was the first strip that people bothered to criticize.

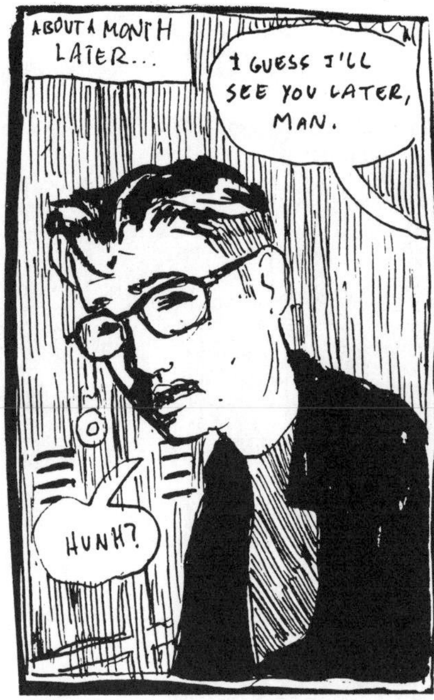
ABOUT A MONTH LATER...
I GUESS I'LL SEE YOU LATER, MAN.
HUNH?

From a 1991 sketchbook; a scene that would reappear in issue five

The best story in issue four is "Train I Ride," a one-pager that I hacked out at the last minute before dashing off to Kinko's. I wrote it as I was lettering it, thinking about someone I knew who had recently moved far away. Continuing my tradition of hit-or-miss experimentation, I tried my hand at biographical non-fiction with the Kerouac story. I have not attempted this again since.

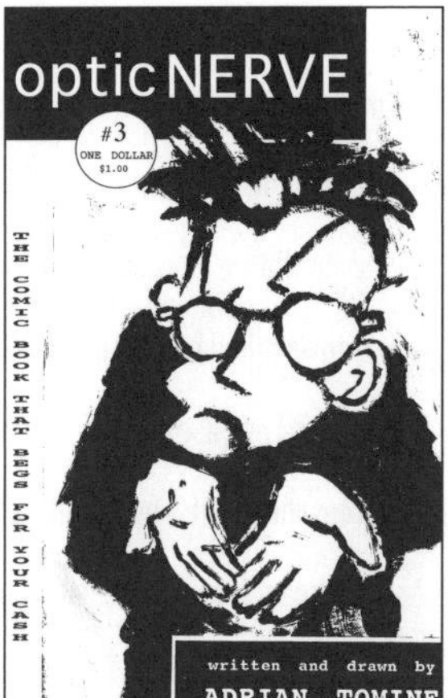
opticNERVE
#3
ONE DOLLAR
$1.00
THE COMIC BOOK THAT BEGS FOR YOUR CASH
written and drawn by
ADRIAN TOMINE

Issue three, January 1992

Between issues four and five, I graduated from high school and left home. I drew most of the pages in my college dormitory when I should have been studying, and in retrospect, the last panel of "Haircut" seems particularly relevant to my emotional state at the time. "Lifter" is important, if only because it taught me what type of shading film *not* to use. "Two in the Morning" is another Amy story, and a fantasy of sorts: wouldn't everyone like to be reunited with their unrequited love to talk things over?

With issue six, I decided to improve the production values on *Optic Nerve.* I made the leap from Xerox to offset printing and even sprung for a two-color cardstock cover. To afford this, I increased the

JANET MARKS WAS HER NAME. WHY THE HELL DID SHE HAVE TO INVADE MY LIFE?

WHEN I FIRST MET HER, SHE SEEMED PRETTY NORMAL. SHE JUST LOOKED LIKE THE AVERAGE RICH GIRL.

HI! MY NAMES JAN MARKS! WHAT'S YOURS?

MIKE.

SHE WAS REAL FRIENDLY AND OUTGOING, BUT AFTER AWHILE I BEGAN NOTICING SOME ANNOYING HABITS OF HERS.

HI!

HEY!

GETTING TO CLOSE TO MY FACE

NICE COAT!

TOUCHING ME TOO MUCH

WHAT'S THIS?

WHAT'S UP?

Excerpt from an unused story entitled "Crazy Girl" (1992)

cover price to two dollars, irritating several "small-press" purists in the process. "Leather Jacket" was the last Amy story, at least for now. Some people have told me that "Allergic" is "the funniest shit I've ever done," but I suspect that has more to do with the inherent humor of other people's suffering than anything else. "Smoke," like issue four's "Train I Ride," is the story I wrote and drew the quickest and have come to like the best. (The original, more pretentious title for this collection was *Smoke and Other Stories*.) The brush I used to draw this story was a very cheap #0, and I just gave up on trying to create any kind of precise line.

As I began work on issue seven, I received a Xeric grant, allowing me to make *Optic Nerve* a rather lavishly produced mini-comic with a huge print run. The "small-press" purists who were offended by the two-color cover on issue six probably gave up on me altogether when they saw the full-color cover on this one. At least two of the fictional stories in this issue are the result of taking an actual experience and rewriting it with my stand-in character behaving in an even more creepy or pathetic manner. I think with this issue, my artwork became a little stiff: I was whiting-out each brush stroke until it was "perfect" and I obsessively drew every straight line using a ruler. My dissatisfaction with the art was, nevertheless, highly educational. (Similarly, I learned an immeasurable amount from the stories in each issue in which my writing or drawing veered perilously close to the styles of my various comic book idols.)

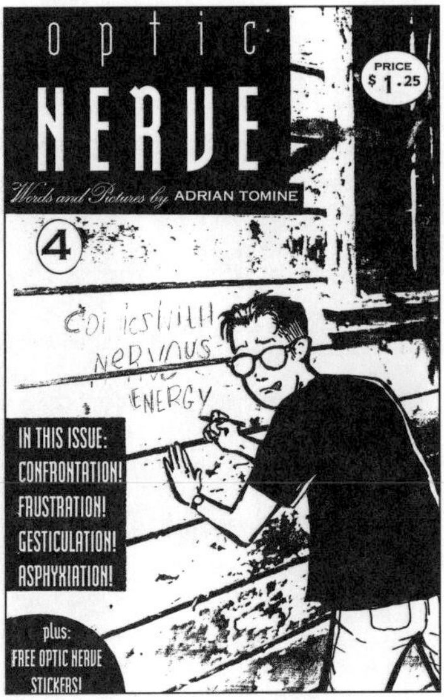
optic
NERVE
PRICE $1.25
Words and Pictures by ADRIAN TOMINE
4
ENERGY
IN THIS ISSUE:
CONFRONTATION!
FRUSTRATION!
GESTICULATION!
ASPHYXIATION!
plus:
FREE OPTIC NERVE
STICKERS!

Issue four, June 1992

Just prior to the release of issue seven, I received The Phone Call from Drawn and Quarterly's Chris Oliveros. I had been pestering him since issue three of *Optic Nerve*, so it was an indescribable thrill to hear him offer to publish my comic. I was completely fed up with the business side of producing a comic by that point . . . I felt like I was spending more time filling orders, hassling store owners for the five bucks they owed me, et cetera than actually writing and drawing. So, in late 1994 I signed a contract with Drawn and Quarterly, effectively ending the mini-comic incarnation of *Optic Nerve*.

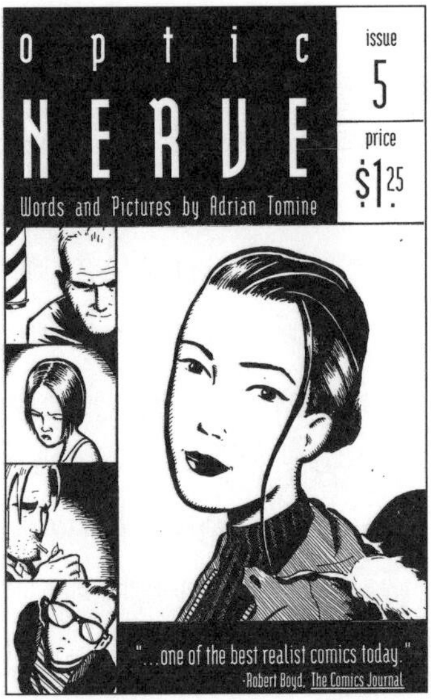
optic
NERVE
issue
5
price
$1.25
Words and Pictures by Adrian Tomine
"...one of the best realist comics today."
-Robert Boyd, The Comics Journal

Issue five, February 1993

My original plan for this book was to release a "best of"-type collection, allowing me to weed out the pieces that I found particularly embarrassing. However, as I began the selection process, I realized that the "to omit" pile was growing disproportionately large compared to the "to include" pile. I found I had reservations about the vast majority of this early stuff, and that I was about to offer my publisher a pretty slim collection. So I decided to give up on trying to discriminate and to just throw it all out there for people to see. I hope that this book offers some entertainment, if only in that it documents the "artistic development" of my teenage years.

(I should note that a few names have been changed for this edition. It's easy to be completely faithful to life when you think no one's going to see the story. In retrospect, I feel I was somewhat intrusive to others in a couple instances, and have tried to rectify that. I've since learned to be much more sneaky.)

optic NERVE
Words and Pictures by Adrian Tomine
issue 6 $2.00
Issue six, September 1993

If this book is the first example of my work that you've seen, I implore you to please seek out the more recent issues of *Optic Nerve*, available from Drawn and Quarterly. It's the work I'm proudest of, at least for the time being. Finally, if the tone of this exceedingly verbose introduction seems designed to make you feel like a fool for buying this book, a clarification is in order. There are some readers (maybe many) who swear that the stories contained here are the best work I've done and will ever do. They may be right . . . in which case, you're all set.

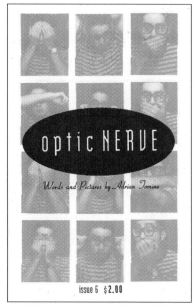

— ADRIAN TOMINE

November 1995

optic NERVE
by ADRIAN TOMINE
Number 7 • $2.00
"Stammer"
"Happy Anniversary"
"Laundry"
"Sleep = Waste"
"Dine and Dash"
"Grind"
Issue seven, August 1994

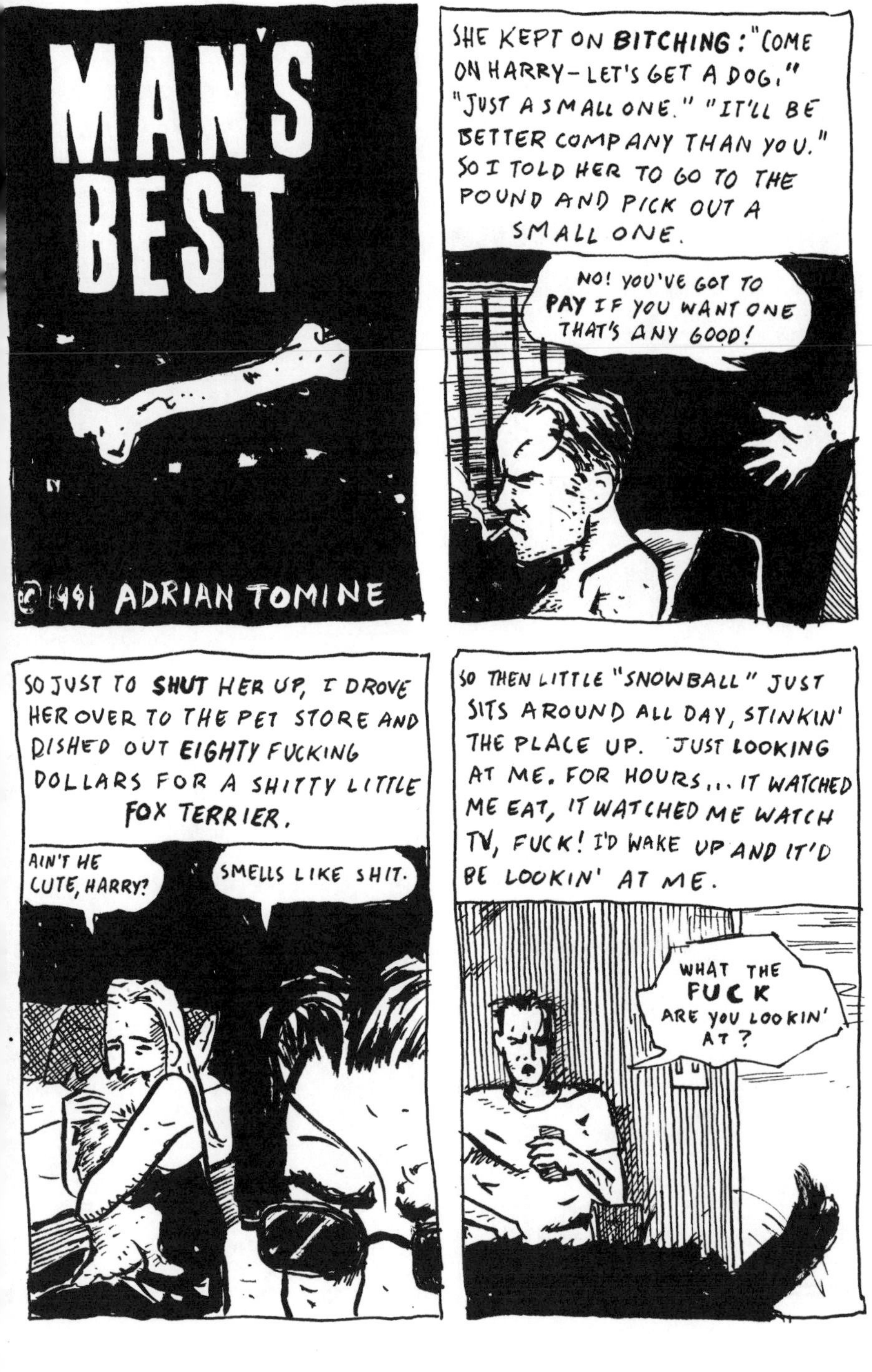
MAN'S BEST
©1991 ADRIAN TOMINE
SHE KEPT ON BITCHING: "COME ON HARRY— LET'S GET A DOG." "JUST A SMALL ONE." "IT'LL BE BETTER COMPANY THAN YOU." SO I TOLD HER TO GO TO THE POUND AND PICK OUT A SMALL ONE.
NO! YOU'VE GOT TO PAY IF YOU WANT ONE THAT'S ANY GOOD!
SO JUST TO SHUT HER UP, I DROVE HER OVER TO THE PET STORE AND DISHED OUT EIGHTY FUCKING DOLLARS FOR A SHITTY LITTLE FOX TERRIER.
AIN'T HE CUTE, HARRY?
SMELLS LIKE SHIT.
SO THEN LITTLE "SNOWBALL" JUST SITS AROUND ALL DAY, STINKIN' THE PLACE UP. JUST LOOKING AT ME. FOR HOURS... IT WATCHED ME EAT, IT WATCHED ME WATCH TV, FUCK! I'D WAKE UP AND IT'D BE LOOKIN' AT ME.
WHAT THE FUCK ARE YOU LOOKIN' AT?

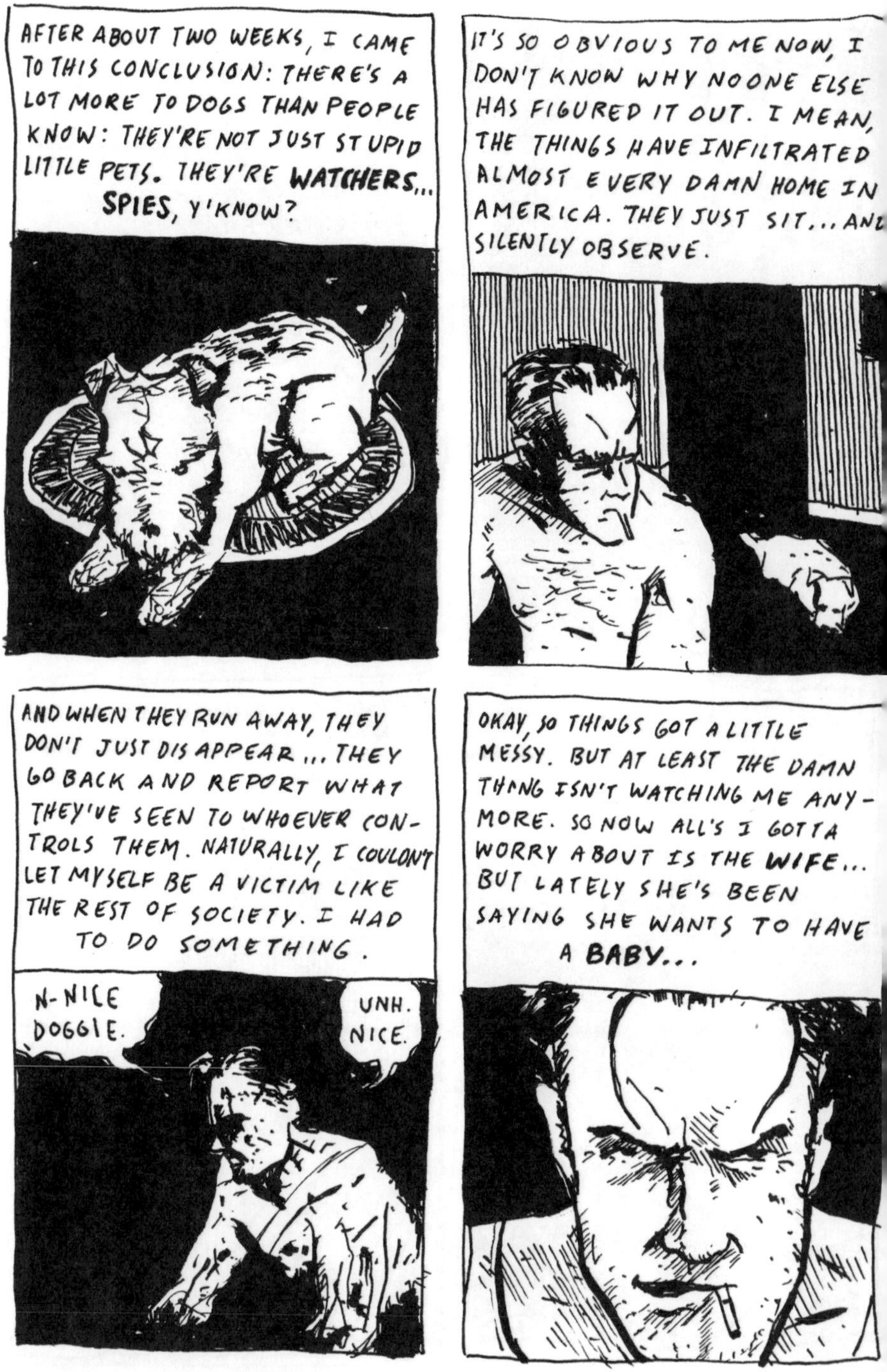
AFTER ABOUT TWO WEEKS, I CAME TO THIS CONCLUSION: THERE'S A LOT MORE TO DOGS THAN PEOPLE KNOW: THEY'RE NOT JUST STUPID LITTLE PETS. THEY'RE WATCHERS... SPIES, Y'KNOW?
IT'S SO OBVIOUS TO ME NOW, I DON'T KNOW WHY NOONE ELSE HAS FIGURED IT OUT. I MEAN, THE THINGS HAVE INFILTRATED ALMOST EVERY DAMN HOME IN AMERICA. THEY JUST SIT... AND SILENTLY OBSERVE.
AND WHEN THEY RUN AWAY, THEY DON'T JUST DISAPPEAR... THEY GO BACK AND REPORT WHAT THEY'VE SEEN TO WHOEVER CONTROLS THEM. NATURALLY, I COULDN'T LET MYSELF BE A VICTIM LIKE THE REST OF SOCIETY. I HAD TO DO SOMETHING.
N-NICE DOGGIE.
UNH. NICE.
OKAY, SO THINGS GOT A LITTLE MESSY. BUT AT LEAST THE DAMN THING ISN'T WATCHING ME ANYMORE. SO NOW ALL'S I GOTTA WORRY ABOUT IS THE WIFE... BUT LATELY SHE'S BEEN SAYING SHE WANTS TO HAVE A BABY...

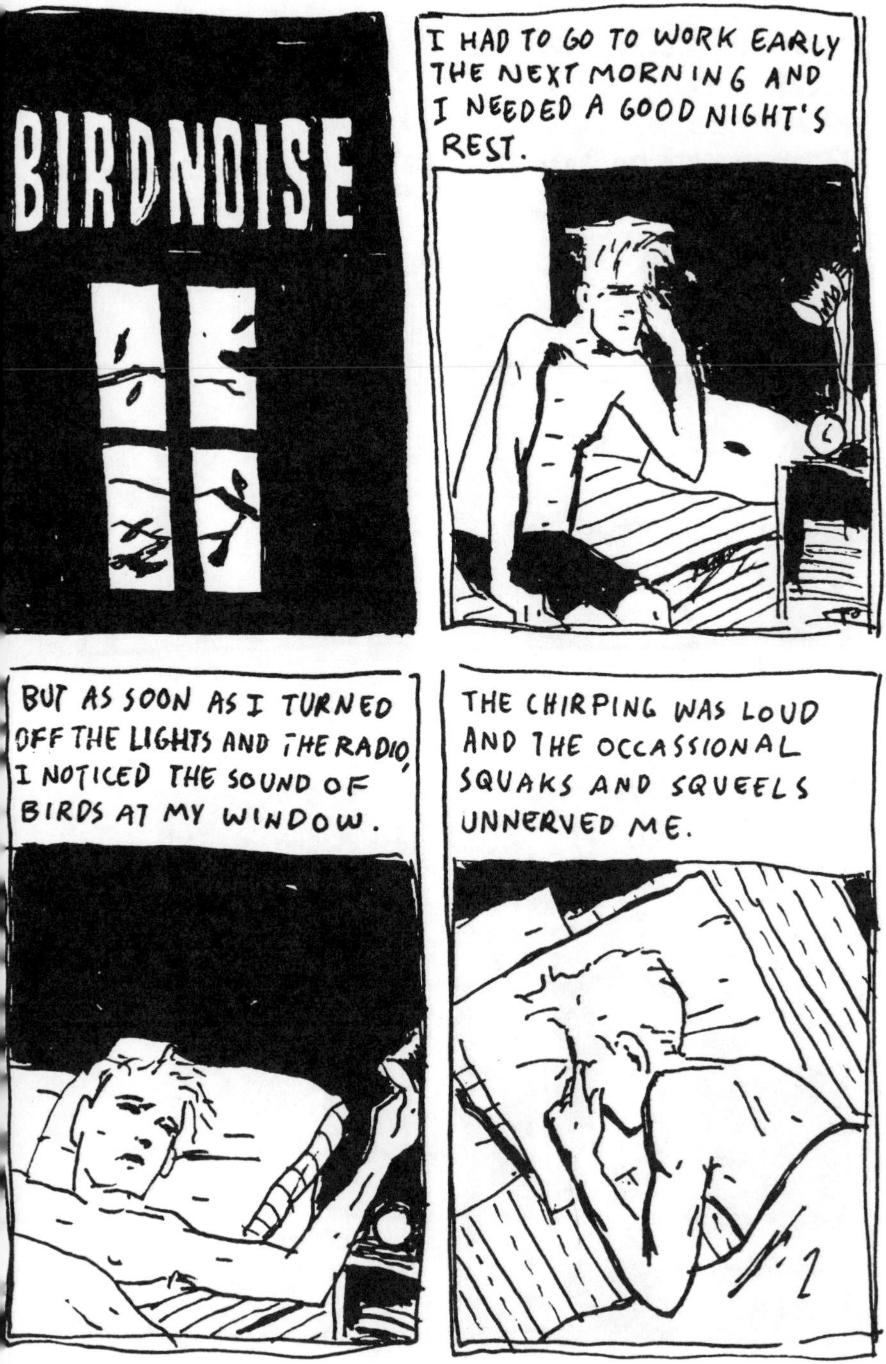
BIRDNOISE
I HAD TO GO TO WORK EARLY THE NEXT MORNING AND I NEEDED A GOOD NIGHT'S REST.
BUT AS SOON AS I TURNED OFF THE LIGHTS AND THE RADIO, I NOTICED THE SOUND OF BIRDS AT MY WINDOW.
THE CHIRPING WAS LOUD AND THE OCCASSIONAL SQUAKS AND SQUEELS UNNERVED ME.

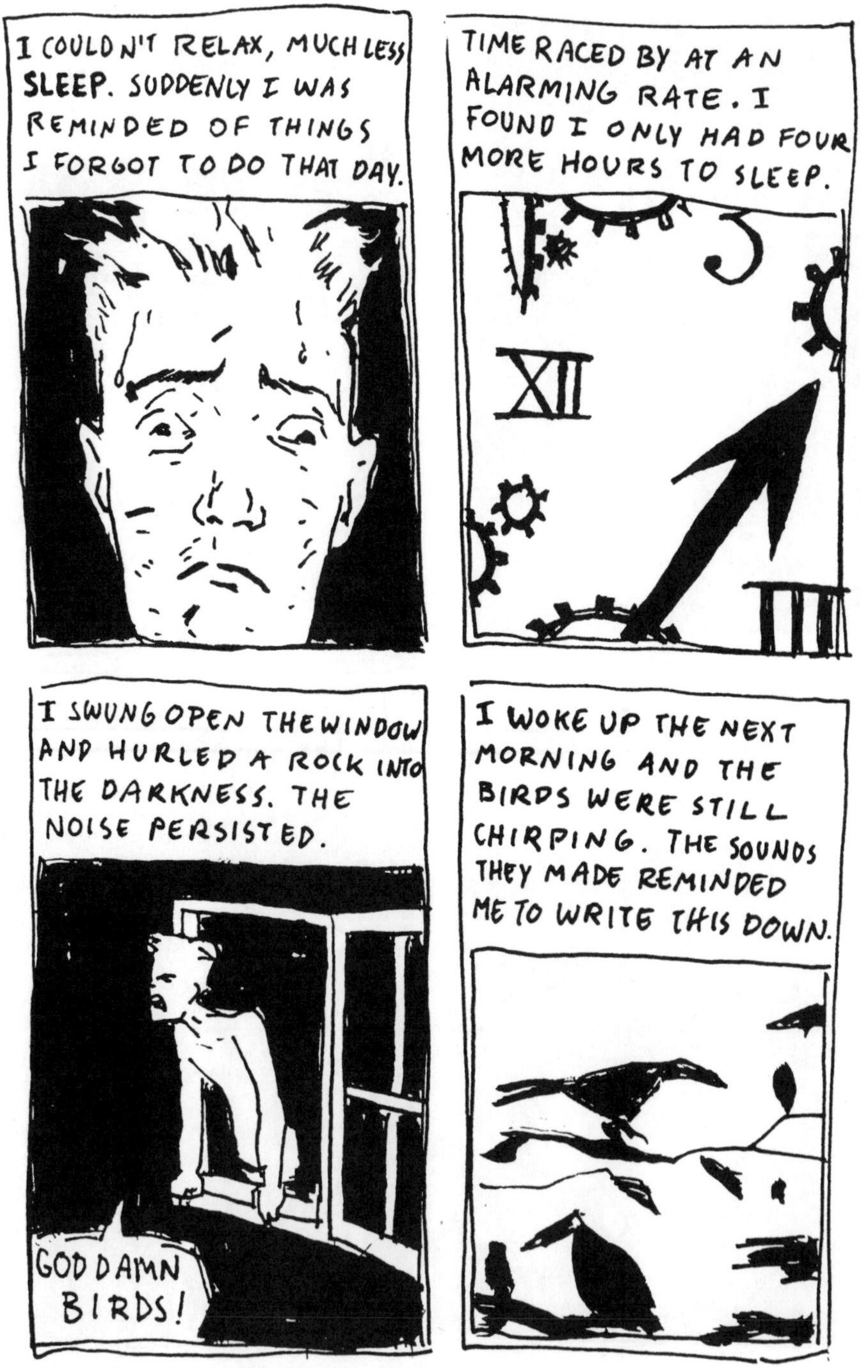
I COULDN'T RELAX, MUCH LESS SLEEP. SUDDENLY I WAS REMINDED OF THINGS I FORGOT TO DO THAT DAY.
TIME RACED BY AT AN ALARMING RATE. I FOUND I ONLY HAD FOUR MORE HOURS TO SLEEP.
XII
III
I SWUNG OPEN THE WINDOW AND HURLED A ROCK INTO THE DARKNESS. THE NOISE PERSISTED.
GOD DAMN BIRDS!
I WOKE UP THE NEXT MORNING AND THE BIRDS WERE STILL CHIRPING. THE SOUNDS THEY MADE REMINDED ME TO WRITE THIS DOWN.

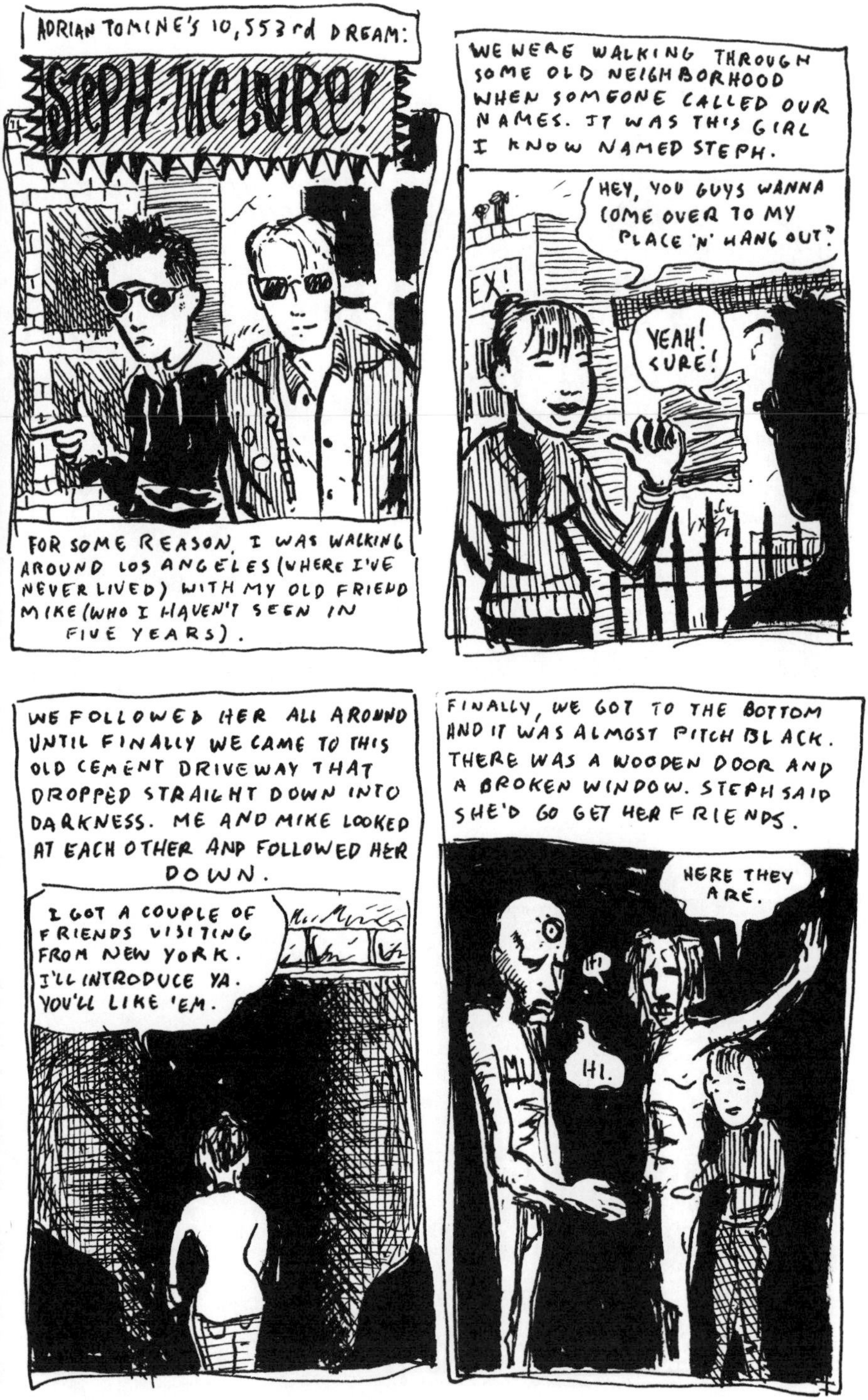
ADRIAN TOMINE'S 10,553rd DREAM:
STEPH-THE-LURE!
FOR SOME REASON, I WAS WALKING AROUND LOS ANGELES (WHERE I'VE NEVER LIVED) WITH MY OLD FRIEND MIKE (WHO I HAVEN'T SEEN IN FIVE YEARS).
WE WERE WALKING THROUGH SOME OLD NEIGHBORHOOD WHEN SOMEONE CALLED OUR NAMES. IT WAS THIS GIRL I KNOW NAMED STEPH.
HEY, YOU GUYS WANNA COME OVER TO MY PLACE 'N' HANG OUT?
YEAH! SURE!
WE FOLLOWED HER ALL AROUND UNTIL FINALLY WE CAME TO THIS OLD CEMENT DRIVEWAY THAT DROPPED STRAIGHT DOWN INTO DARKNESS. ME AND MIKE LOOKED AT EACH OTHER AND FOLLOWED HER DOWN.
I GOT A COUPLE OF FRIENDS VISITING FROM NEW YORK. I'LL INTRODUCE YA. YOU'LL LIKE 'EM.
FINALLY, WE GOT TO THE BOTTOM AND IT WAS ALMOST PITCH BLACK. THERE WAS A WOODEN DOOR AND A BROKEN WINDOW. STEPH SAID SHE'D GO GET HER FRIENDS.
HERE THEY ARE.
HI.
HI.

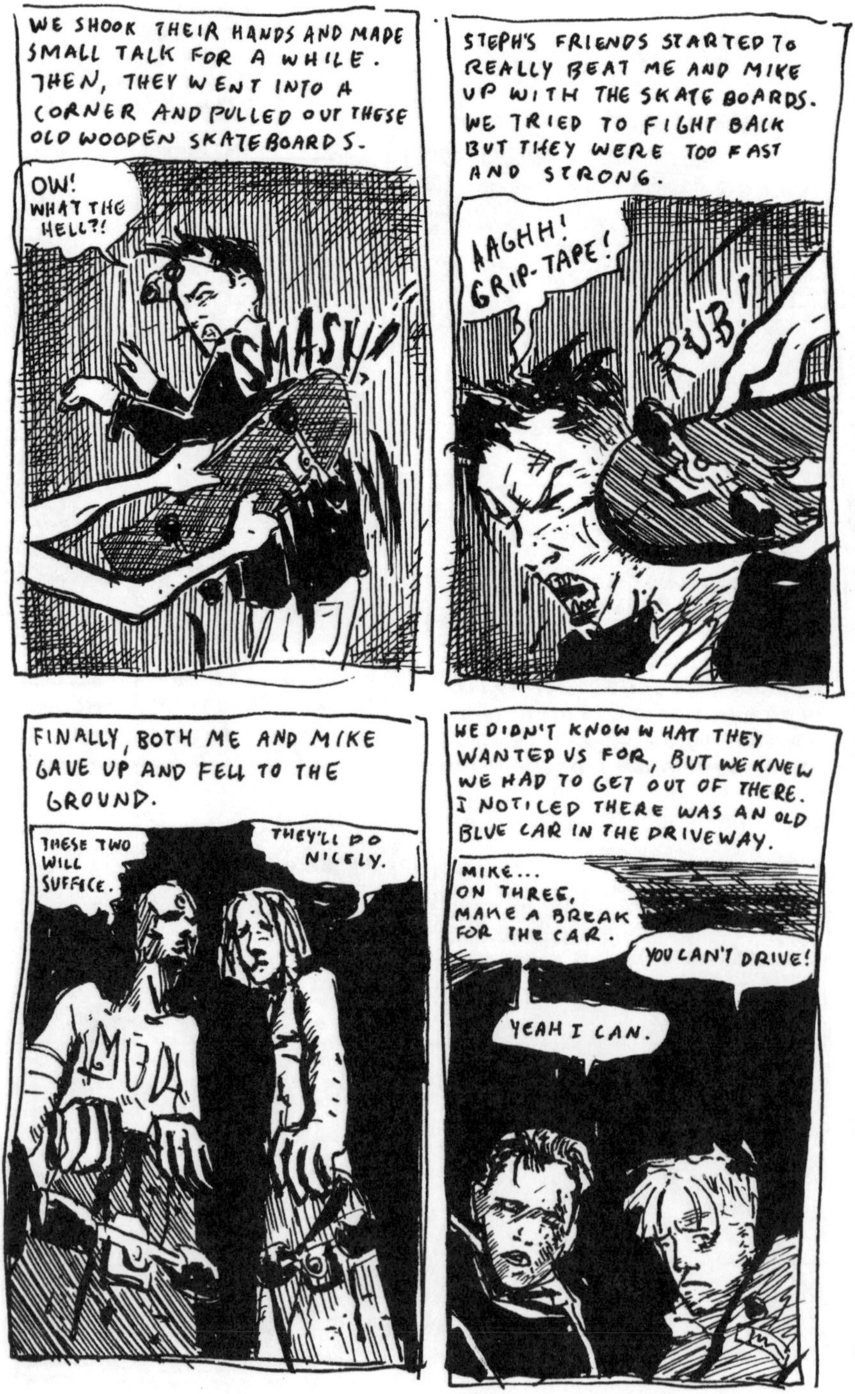
WE SHOOK THEIR HANDS AND MADE SMALL TALK FOR A WHILE. THEN, THEY WENT INTO A CORNER AND PULLED OUT THESE OLD WOODEN SKATEBOARDS.
OW! WHAT THE HELL?!
SMASH!
STEPH'S FRIENDS STARTED TO REALLY BEAT ME AND MIKE UP WITH THE SKATEBOARDS. WE TRIED TO FIGHT BACK BUT THEY WERE TOO FAST AND STRONG.
AAGHH! GRIP-TAPE!
RUB!
FINALLY, BOTH ME AND MIKE GAVE UP AND FELL TO THE GROUND.
THESE TWO WILL SUFFICE.
THEY'LL DO NICELY.
WE DIDN'T KNOW WHAT THEY WANTED US FOR, BUT WE KNEW WE HAD TO GET OUT OF THERE. I NOTICED THERE WAS AN OLD BLUE CAR IN THE DRIVEWAY.
MIKE... ON THREE, MAKE A BREAK FOR THE CAR.
YOU CAN'T DRIVE!
YEAH I CAN.

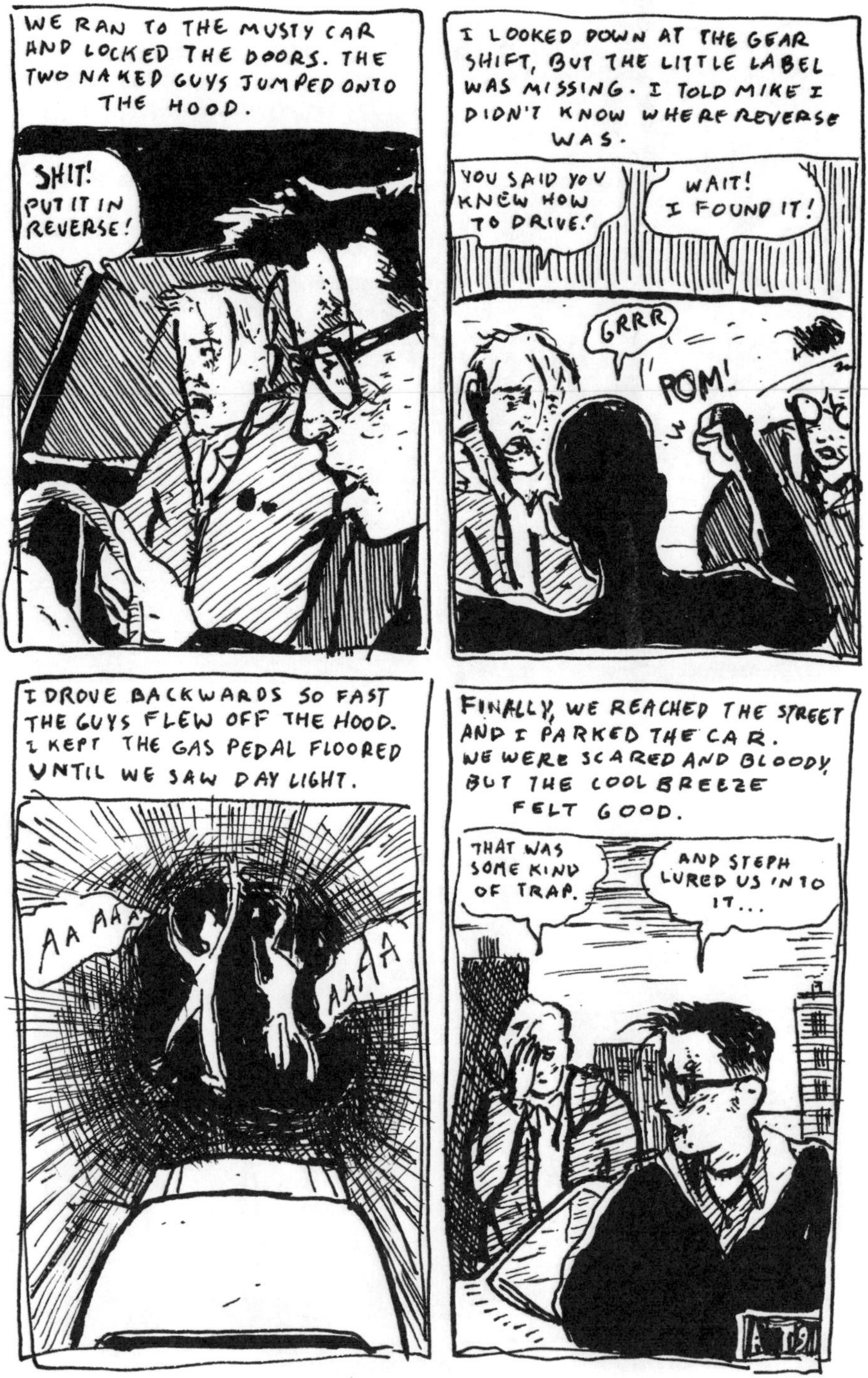
WE RAN TO THE MUSTY CAR AND LOCKED THE DOORS. THE TWO NAKED GUYS JUMPED ONTO THE HOOD.
SHIT! PUT IT IN REVERSE!
I LOOKED DOWN AT THE GEAR SHIFT, BUT THE LITTLE LABEL WAS MISSING. I TOLD MIKE I DIDN'T KNOW WHERE REVERSE WAS.
YOU SAID YOU KNEW HOW TO DRIVE!
WAIT! I FOUND IT!
GRRR
POM!
I DROVE BACKWARDS SO FAST THE GUYS FLEW OFF THE HOOD. I KEPT THE GAS PEDAL FLOORED UNTIL WE SAW DAY LIGHT.
AA AAA
AAAA
FINALLY, WE REACHED THE STREET AND I PARKED THE CAR. WE WERE SCARED AND BLOODY, BUT THE COOL BREEZE FELT GOOD.
THAT WAS SOME KIND OF TRAP.
AND STEPH LURED US INTO IT...

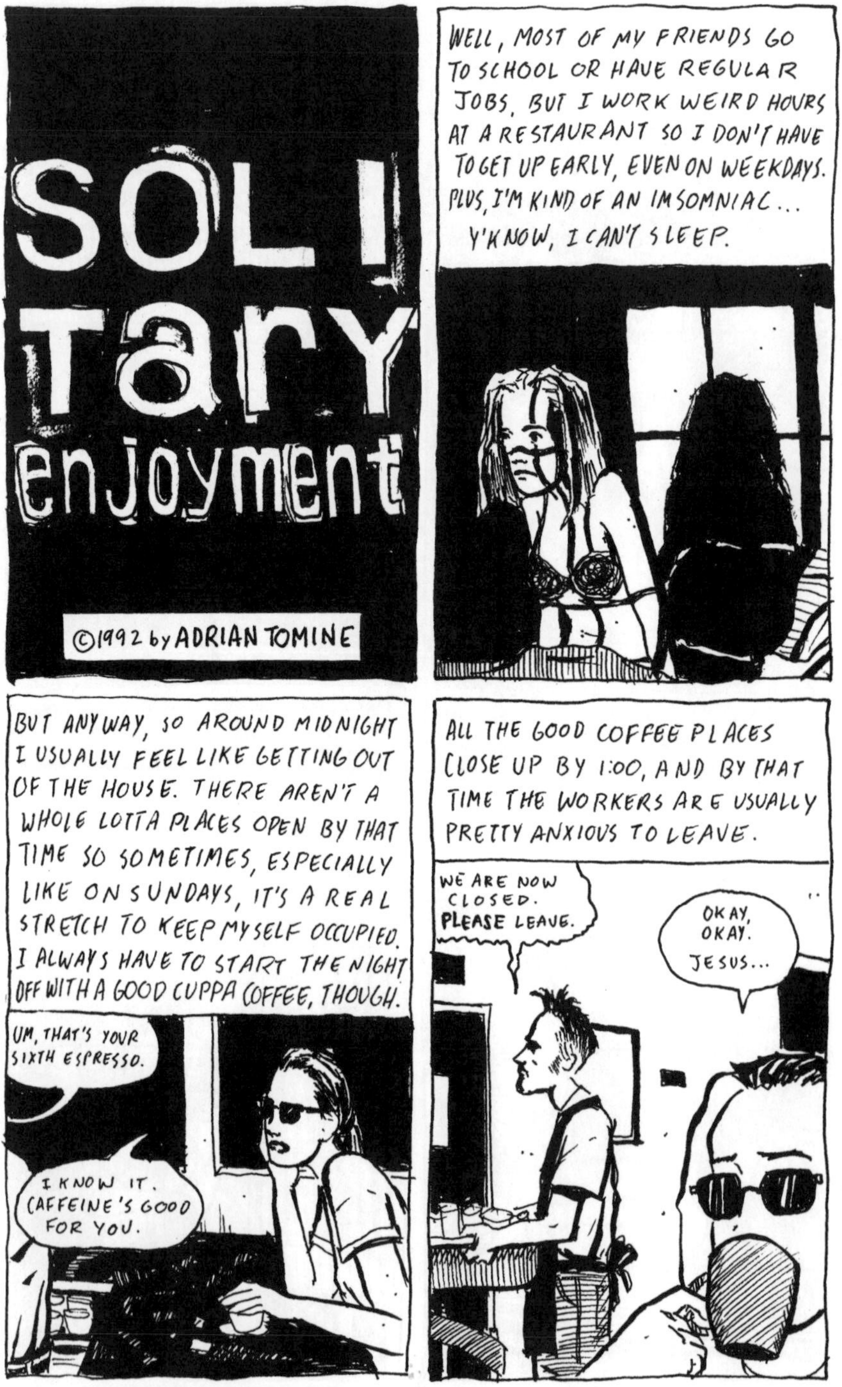
SOLI
TARY
ENJOYMENT
©1992 by ADRIAN TOMINE
WELL, MOST OF MY FRIENDS GO TO SCHOOL OR HAVE REGULAR JOBS, BUT I WORK WEIRD HOURS AT A RESTAURANT SO I DON'T HAVE TO GET UP EARLY, EVEN ON WEEKDAYS. PLUS, I'M KIND OF AN IMSOMNIAC... Y'KNOW, I CAN'T SLEEP.
BUT ANYWAY, SO AROUND MIDNIGHT I USUALLY FEEL LIKE GETTING OUT OF THE HOUSE. THERE AREN'T A WHOLE LOTTA PLACES OPEN BY THAT TIME SO SOMETIMES, ESPECIALLY LIKE ON SUNDAYS, IT'S A REAL STRETCH TO KEEP MYSELF OCCUPIED. I ALWAYS HAVE TO START THE NIGHT OFF WITH A GOOD CUPPA COFFEE, THOUGH.
UM, THAT'S YOUR SIXTH ESPRESSO.
I KNOW IT. CAFFEINE'S GOOD FOR YOU.
ALL THE GOOD COFFEE PLACES CLOSE UP BY 1:00, AND BY THAT TIME THE WORKERS ARE USUALLY PRETTY ANXIOUS TO LEAVE.
WE ARE NOW CLOSED. PLEASE LEAVE.
OKAY, OKAY. JESUS...

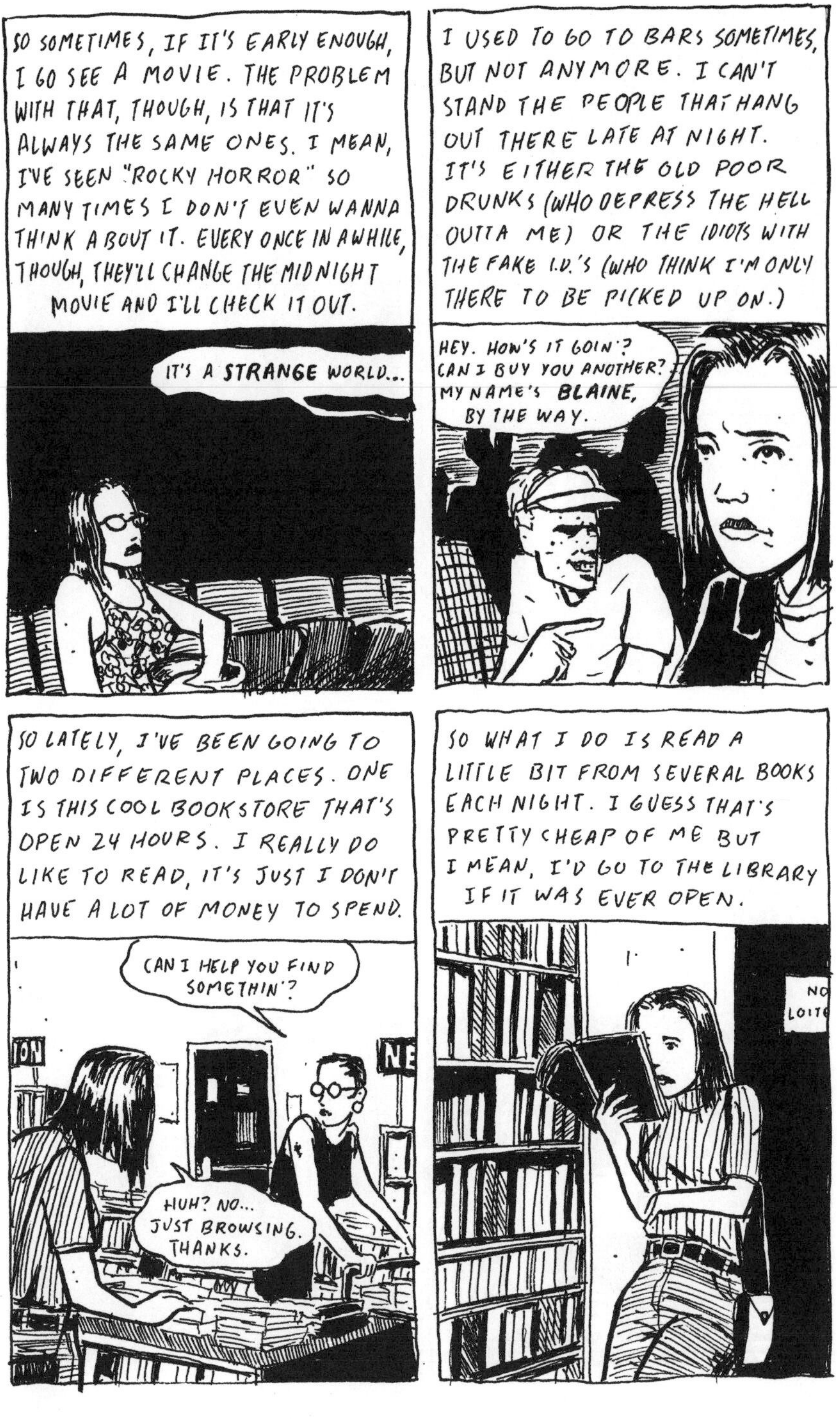
SO SOMETIMES, IF IT'S EARLY ENOUGH, I GO SEE A MOVIE. THE PROBLEM WITH THAT, THOUGH, IS THAT IT'S ALWAYS THE SAME ONES. I MEAN, I'VE SEEN "ROCKY HORROR" SO MANY TIMES I DON'T EVEN WANNA THINK ABOUT IT. EVERY ONCE IN AWHILE, THOUGH, THEY'LL CHANGE THE MIDNIGHT MOVIE AND I'LL CHECK IT OUT.
IT'S A STRANGE WORLD...
I USED TO GO TO BARS SOMETIMES, BUT NOT ANYMORE. I CAN'T STAND THE PEOPLE THAT HANG OUT THERE LATE AT NIGHT. IT'S EITHER THE OLD POOR DRUNKS (WHO DEPRESS THE HELL OUTTA ME) OR THE IDIOTS WITH THE FAKE I.D.'S (WHO THINK I'M ONLY THERE TO BE PICKED UP ON.)
HEY. HOW'S IT GOIN'? CAN I BUY YOU ANOTHER? MY NAME'S BLAINE, BY THE WAY.
SO LATELY, I'VE BEEN GOING TO TWO DIFFERENT PLACES. ONE IS THIS COOL BOOKSTORE THAT'S OPEN 24 HOURS. I REALLY DO LIKE TO READ, IT'S JUST I DON'T HAVE A LOT OF MONEY TO SPEND.
CAN I HELP YOU FIND SOMETHIN'?
HUH? NO... JUST BROWSING. THANKS.
SO WHAT I DO IS READ A LITTLE BIT FROM SEVERAL BOOKS EACH NIGHT. I GUESS THAT'S PRETTY CHEAP OF ME BUT I MEAN, I'D GO TO THE LIBRARY IF IT WAS EVER OPEN.

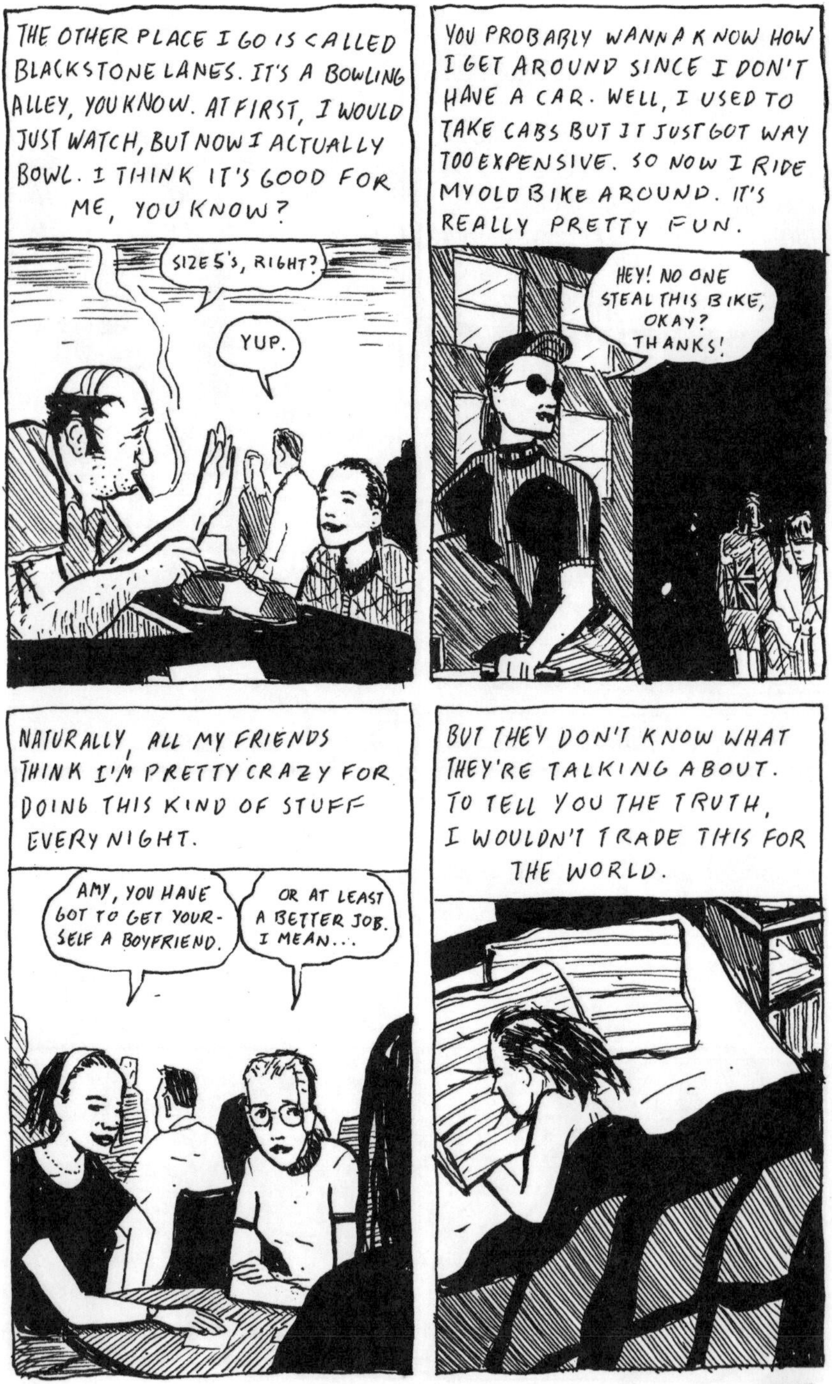
THE OTHER PLACE I GO IS CALLED BLACKSTONE LANES. IT'S A BOWLING ALLEY, YOU KNOW. AT FIRST, I WOULD JUST WATCH, BUT NOW I ACTUALLY BOWL. I THINK IT'S GOOD FOR ME, YOU KNOW?
SIZE 5'S, RIGHT?
YUP.
YOU PROBABLY WANNA KNOW HOW I GET AROUND SINCE I DON'T HAVE A CAR. WELL, I USED TO TAKE CABS BUT IT JUST GOT WAY TOO EXPENSIVE. SO NOW I RIDE MY OLD BIKE AROUND. IT'S REALLY PRETTY FUN.
HEY! NO ONE STEAL THIS BIKE, OKAY? THANKS!
NATURALLY, ALL MY FRIENDS THINK I'M PRETTY CRAZY FOR DOING THIS KIND OF STUFF EVERY NIGHT.
AMY, YOU HAVE GOT TO GET YOURSELF A BOYFRIEND.
OR AT LEAST A BETTER JOB. I MEAN...
BUT THEY DON'T KNOW WHAT THEY'RE TALKING ABOUT. TO TELL YOU THE TRUTH, I WOULDN'T TRADE THIS FOR THE WORLD.
AT

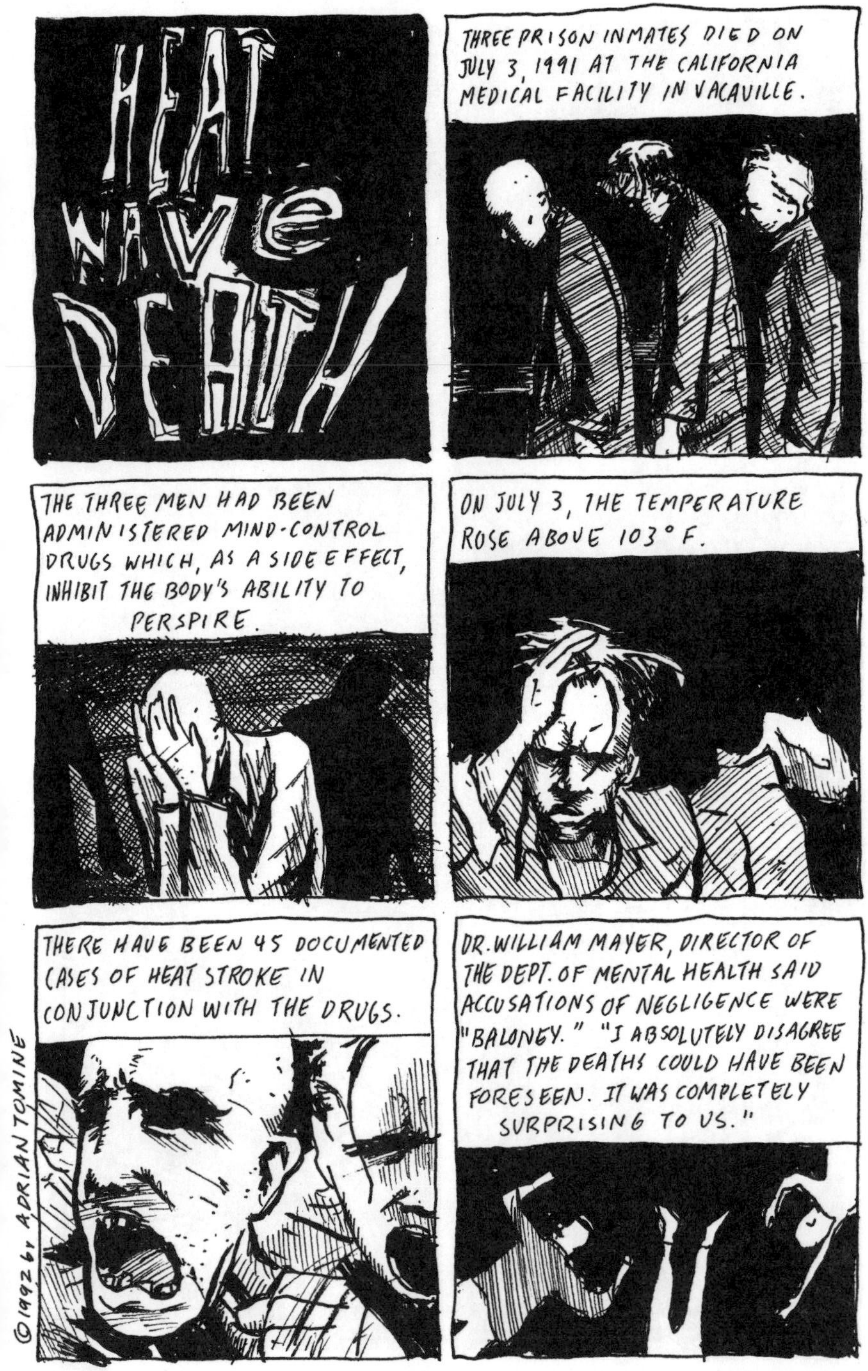
HEAT WAVE DEATH
THREE PRISON INMATES DIED ON JULY 3, 1991 AT THE CALIFORNIA MEDICAL FACILITY IN VACAVILLE.
THE THREE MEN HAD BEEN ADMINISTERED MIND-CONTROL DRUGS WHICH, AS A SIDE EFFECT, INHIBIT THE BODY'S ABILITY TO PERSPIRE.
ON JULY 3, THE TEMPERATURE ROSE ABOVE 103° F.
THERE HAVE BEEN 45 DOCUMENTED CASES OF HEAT STROKE IN CONJUNCTION WITH THE DRUGS.
DR. WILLIAM MAYER, DIRECTOR OF THE DEPT. OF MENTAL HEALTH SAID ACCUSATIONS OF NEGLIGENCE WERE "BALONEY." "I ABSOLUTELY DISAGREE THAT THE DEATHS COULD HAVE BEEN FORESEEN. IT WAS COMPLETELY SURPRISING TO US."
©1992 by ADRIAN TOMINE

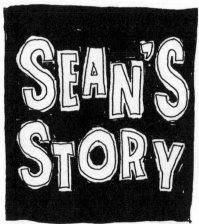

SEAN'S STORY

MAN... THE OTHER DAY I WAS RIDING MY BIKE DOWNTOWN AND I SAW THESE TWO BIG GUYS WALKING AROUND WITH NO SHIRTS ON AND HAIR THAT'S LIKE, SHORT ON TOP AND LONG IN BACK.

AND MY FIRST THOUGHT WAS, "MAN, LOOK AT THOSE GOONS," Y'KNOW?

HAHA... YEAH.

AND THEN I THOUGHT, "HEY! I SHOULDN'T THINK THAT! I MEAN THEY **MIGHT** BE REALLY NICE GUYS!"

UH HUH...

SO I RIDE BY AND ONE OF THEM SHOUTS OUT "**FAGGOT!!!**"

HAW HAW HAW

GUESS I LEARNED MY LESSON!

HA HA... YEAH, I GUESS...

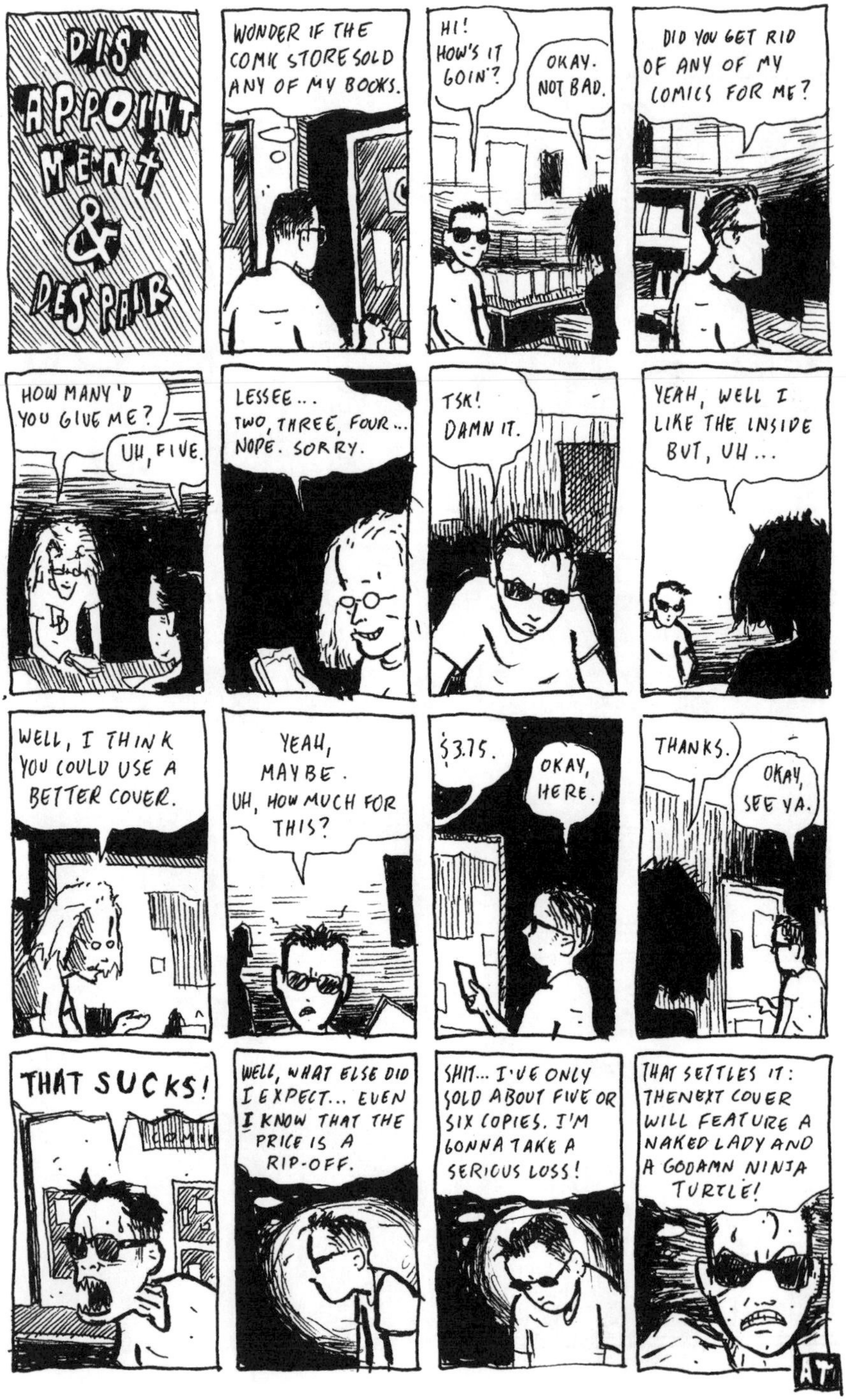
DIS APPOINT MENT & DESPAIR
WONDER IF THE COMIC STORE SOLD ANY OF MY BOOKS.
HI! HOW'S IT GOIN'?
OKAY. NOT BAD.
DID YOU GET RID OF ANY OF MY COMICS FOR ME?
HOW MANY'D YOU GIVE ME?
UH, FIVE.
LESSEE... TWO, THREE, FOUR... NOPE. SORRY.
TSK! DAMN IT.
YEAH, WELL I LIKE THE INSIDE BUT, UH...
WELL, I THINK YOU COULD USE A BETTER COVER.
YEAH, MAYBE. UH, HOW MUCH FOR THIS?
$3.75.
OKAY, HERE.
THANKS.
OKAY, SEE YA.
THAT SUCKS!
WELL, WHAT ELSE DID I EXPECT... EVEN I KNOW THAT THE PRICE IS A RIP-OFF.
SHIT... I'VE ONLY SOLD ABOUT FIVE OR SIX COPIES. I'M GONNA TAKE A SERIOUS LOSS!
THAT SETTLES IT: THE NEXT COVER WILL FEATURE A NAKED LADY AND A GODAMN NINJA TURTLE!
AT

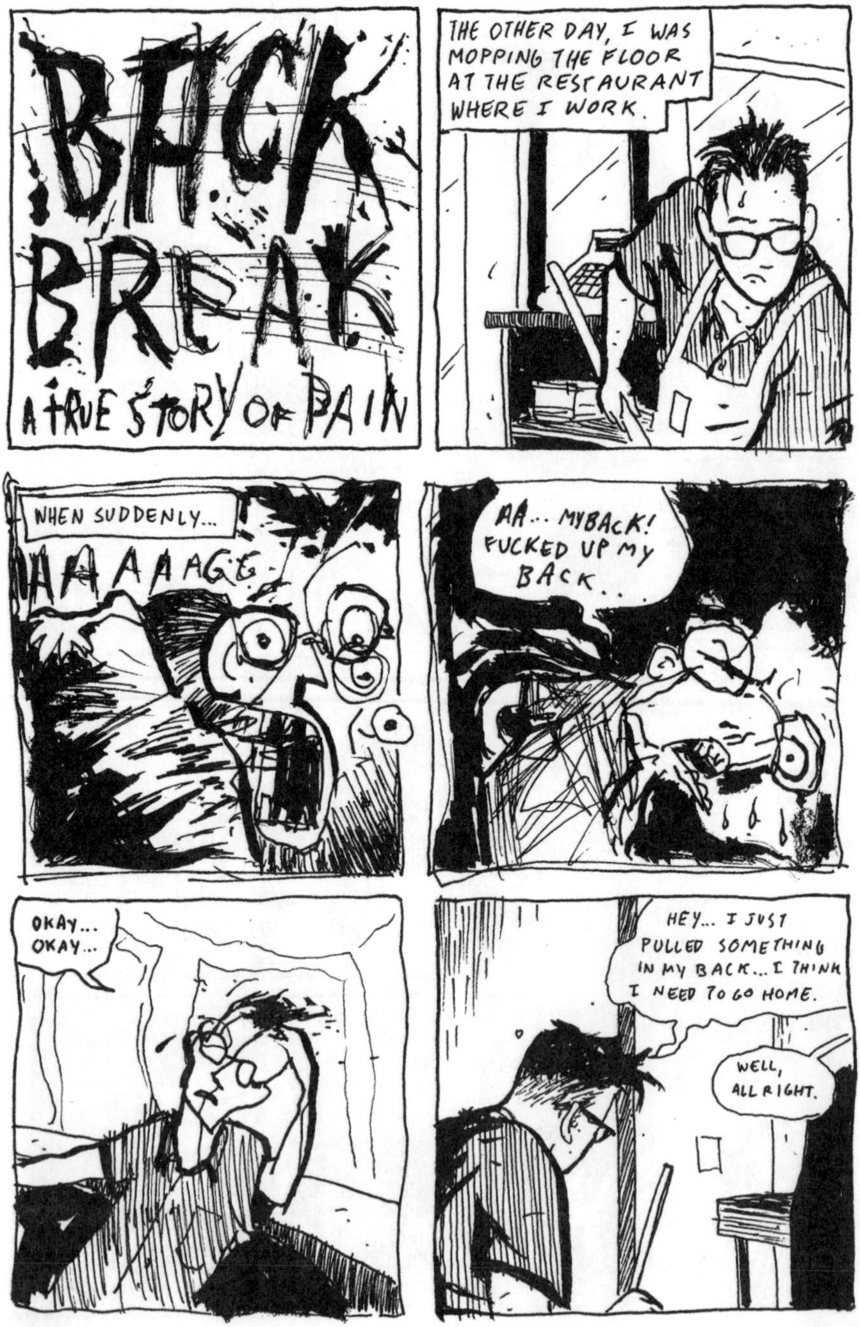
BACK BREAK
A TRUE STORY OF PAIN
THE OTHER DAY, I WAS MOPPING THE FLOOR AT THE RESTAURANT WHERE I WORK.
WHEN SUDDENLY...
AAAAAAGE
AA... MY BACK! FUCKED UP MY BACK..
OKAY... OKAY...
HEY... I JUST PULLED SOMETHING IN MY BACK... I THINK I NEED TO GO HOME.
WELL, ALL RIGHT.

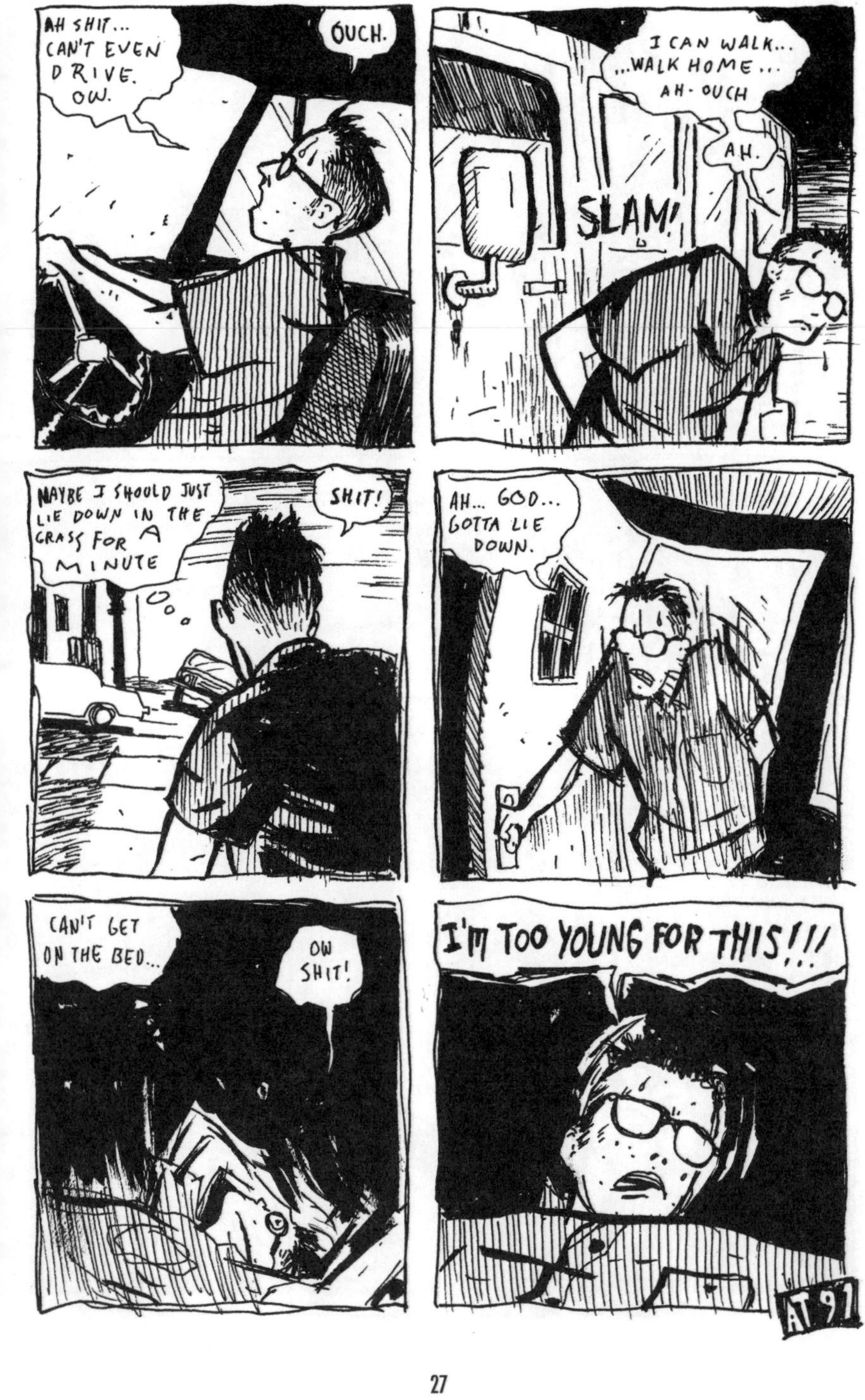
AH SHIT... CAN'T EVEN DRIVE. OW.
OUCH.
I CAN WALK... ...WALK HOME... AH-OUCH
AH.
SLAM!
MAYBE I SHOULD JUST LIE DOWN IN THE GRASS FOR A MINUTE
SHIT!
AH... GOD... GOTTA LIE DOWN.
CAN'T GET ON THE BED...
OW SHIT!
I'M TOO YOUNG FOR THIS!!!
AT 97

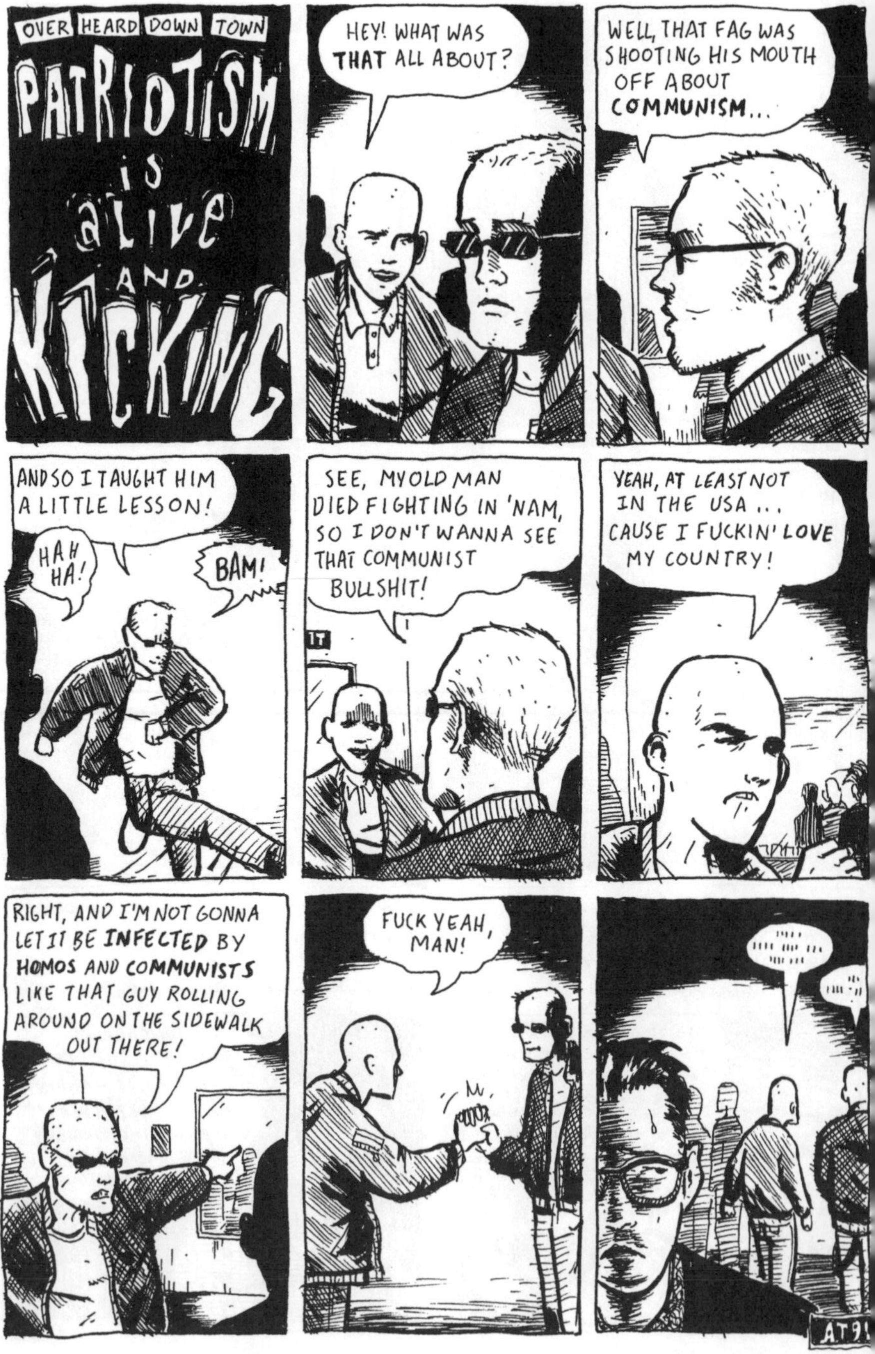
OVER HEARD DOWN TOWN
PATRIOTISM is alive AND KICKING
HEY! WHAT WAS THAT ALL ABOUT?
WELL, THAT FAG WAS SHOOTING HIS MOUTH OFF ABOUT COMMUNISM...
AND SO I TAUGHT HIM A LITTLE LESSON!
HAH HA!
BAM!
SEE, MY OLD MAN DIED FIGHTING IN 'NAM, SO I DON'T WANNA SEE THAT COMMUNIST BULLSHIT!
YEAH, AT LEAST NOT IN THE USA... CAUSE I FUCKIN' LOVE MY COUNTRY!
RIGHT, AND I'M NOT GONNA LET IT BE INFECTED BY HOMOS AND COMMUNISTS LIKE THAT GUY ROLLING AROUND ON THE SIDEWALK OUT THERE!
FUCK YEAH, MAN!
AT 9

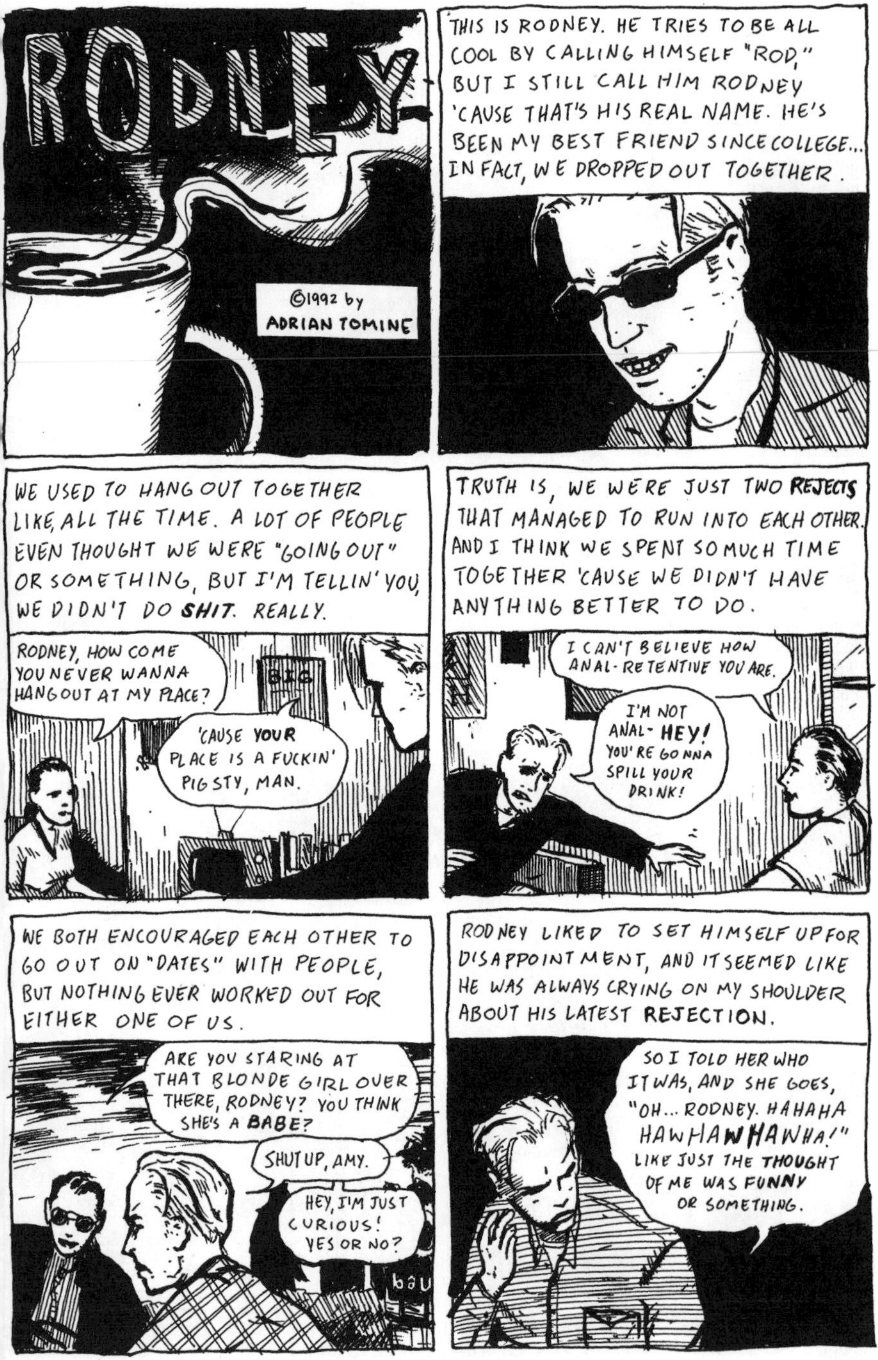
RODNEY
©1992 by ADRIAN TOMINE
THIS IS RODNEY. HE TRIES TO BE ALL COOL BY CALLING HIMSELF "ROD," BUT I STILL CALL HIM RODNEY 'CAUSE THAT'S HIS REAL NAME. HE'S BEEN MY BEST FRIEND SINCE COLLEGE... IN FACT, WE DROPPED OUT TOGETHER.
WE USED TO HANG OUT TOGETHER LIKE, ALL THE TIME. A LOT OF PEOPLE EVEN THOUGHT WE WERE "GOING OUT" OR SOMETHING, BUT I'M TELLIN' YOU, WE DIDN'T DO SHIT. REALLY.
RODNEY, HOW COME YOU NEVER WANNA HANG OUT AT MY PLACE?
'CAUSE YOUR PLACE IS A FUCKIN' PIG STY, MAN.
TRUTH IS, WE WERE JUST TWO REJECTS THAT MANAGED TO RUN INTO EACH OTHER. AND I THINK WE SPENT SO MUCH TIME TOGETHER 'CAUSE WE DIDN'T HAVE ANYTHING BETTER TO DO.
I CAN'T BELIEVE HOW ANAL-RETENTIVE YOU ARE.
I'M NOT ANAL- HEY! YOU'RE GONNA SPILL YOUR DRINK!
WE BOTH ENCOURAGED EACH OTHER TO GO OUT ON "DATES" WITH PEOPLE, BUT NOTHING EVER WORKED OUT FOR EITHER ONE OF US.
ARE YOU STARING AT THAT BLONDE GIRL OVER THERE, RODNEY? YOU THINK SHE'S A BABE?
SHUT UP, AMY.
HEY, I'M JUST CURIOUS! YES OR NO?
RODNEY LIKED TO SET HIMSELF UP FOR DISAPPOINTMENT, AND IT SEEMED LIKE HE WAS ALWAYS CRYING ON MY SHOULDER ABOUT HIS LATEST REJECTION.
SO I TOLD HER WHO IT WAS, AND SHE GOES, "OH... RODNEY. HAHAHA HAWHAWHAWHA!" LIKE JUST THE THOUGHT OF ME WAS FUNNY OR SOMETHING.

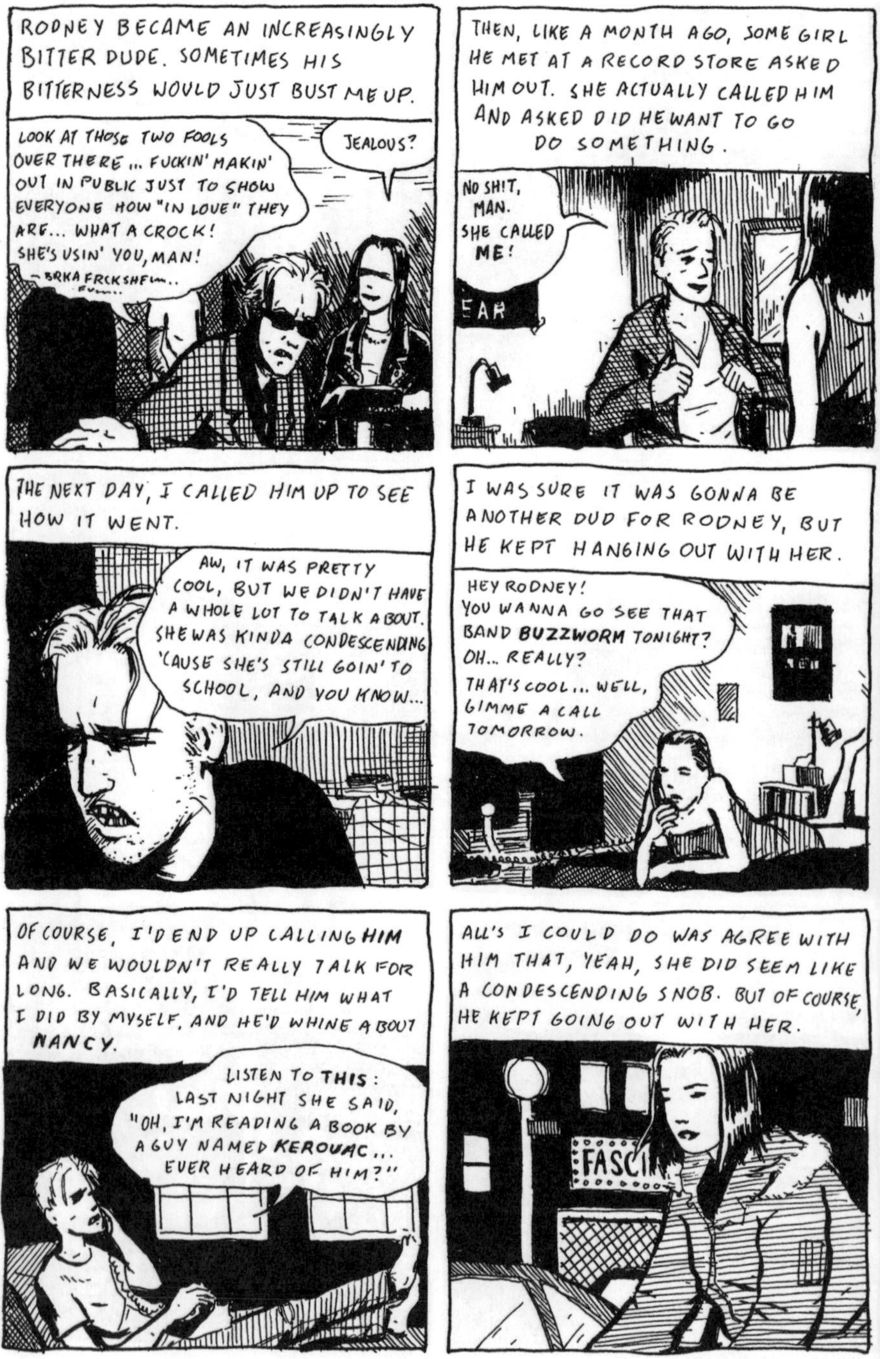
RODNEY BECAME AN INCREASINGLY BITTER DUDE. SOMETIMES HIS BITTERNESS WOULD JUST BUST ME UP.
LOOK AT THOSE TWO FOOLS OVER THERE ... FUCKIN' MAKIN' OUT IN PUBLIC JUST TO SHOW EVERYONE HOW "IN LOVE" THEY ARE... WHAT A CROCK! SHE'S USIN' YOU, MAN!
JEALOUS?
THEN, LIKE A MONTH AGO, SOME GIRL HE MET AT A RECORD STORE ASKED HIM OUT. SHE ACTUALLY CALLED HIM AND ASKED DID HE WANT TO GO DO SOMETHING.
NO SHIT, MAN. SHE CALLED ME!
THE NEXT DAY, I CALLED HIM UP TO SEE HOW IT WENT.
AW, IT WAS PRETTY COOL, BUT WE DIDN'T HAVE A WHOLE LOT TO TALK ABOUT. SHE WAS KINDA CONDESCENDING 'CAUSE SHE'S STILL GOIN' TO SCHOOL, AND YOU KNOW...
I WAS SURE IT WAS GONNA BE ANOTHER DUD FOR RODNEY, BUT HE KEPT HANGING OUT WITH HER.
HEY RODNEY! YOU WANNA GO SEE THAT BAND BUZZWORM TONIGHT? OH... REALLY? THAT'S COOL... WELL, GIMME A CALL TOMORROW.
OF COURSE, I'D END UP CALLING HIM AND WE WOULDN'T REALLY TALK FOR LONG. BASICALLY, I'D TELL HIM WHAT I DID BY MYSELF, AND HE'D WHINE ABOUT NANCY.
LISTEN TO THIS: LAST NIGHT SHE SAID, "OH, I'M READING A BOOK BY A GUY NAMED KEROUAC... EVER HEARD OF HIM?"
ALL'S I COULD DO WAS AGREE WITH HIM THAT, YEAH, SHE DID SEEM LIKE A CONDESCENDING SNOB. BUT OF COURSE, HE KEPT GOING OUT WITH HER.
FASCI

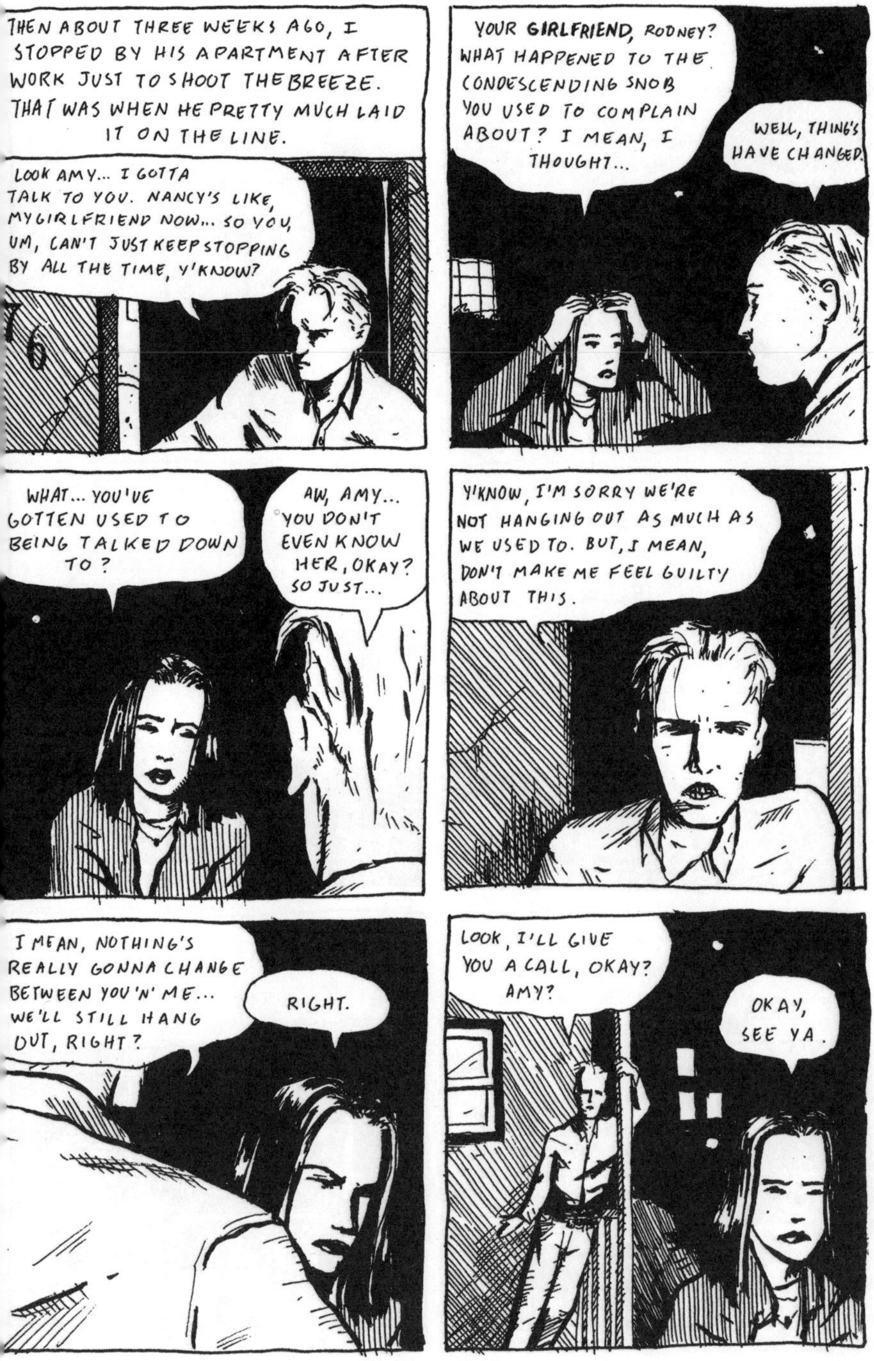
THEN ABOUT THREE WEEKS AGO, I STOPPED BY HIS APARTMENT AFTER WORK JUST TO SHOOT THE BREEZE. THAT WAS WHEN HE PRETTY MUCH LAID IT ON THE LINE.
LOOK AMY... I GOTTA TALK TO YOU. NANCY'S LIKE, MY GIRLFRIEND NOW... SO YOU, UM, CAN'T JUST KEEP STOPPING BY ALL THE TIME, Y'KNOW?
76
YOUR **GIRLFRIEND**, RODNEY? WHAT HAPPENED TO THE CONDESCENDING SNOB YOU USED TO COMPLAIN ABOUT? I MEAN, I THOUGHT...
WELL, THING'S HAVE CHANGED.
WHAT... YOU'VE GOTTEN USED TO BEING TALKED DOWN TO?
AW, AMY... YOU DON'T EVEN KNOW HER, OKAY? SO JUST...
Y'KNOW, I'M SORRY WE'RE NOT HANGING OUT AS MUCH AS WE USED TO. BUT, I MEAN, DON'T MAKE ME FEEL GUILTY ABOUT THIS.
I MEAN, NOTHING'S REALLY GONNA CHANGE BETWEEN YOU 'N' ME... WE'LL STILL HANG OUT, RIGHT?
RIGHT.
LOOK, I'LL GIVE YOU A CALL, OKAY? AMY?
OKAY, SEE YA.

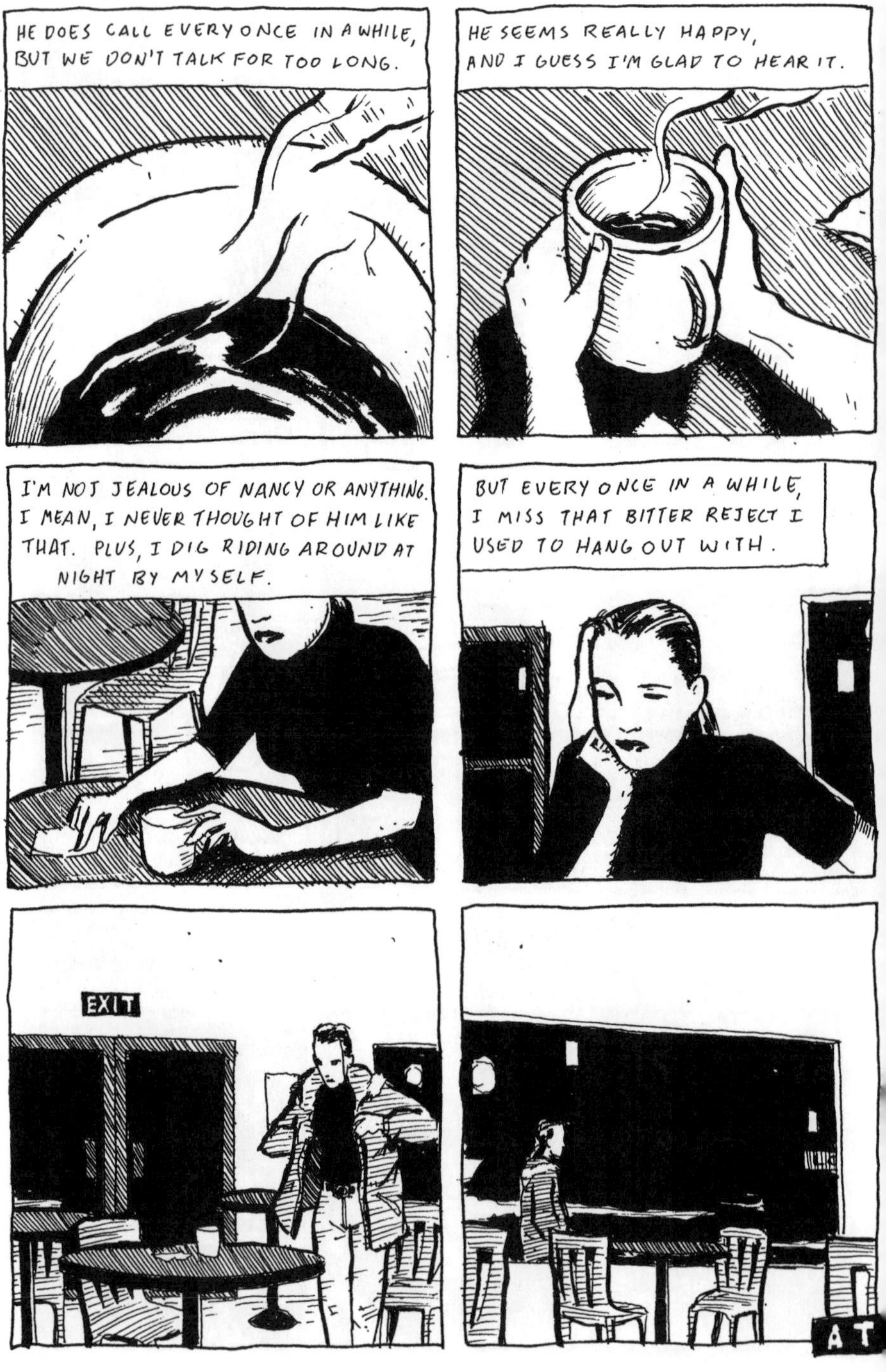
HE DOES CALL EVERY ONCE IN A WHILE, BUT WE DON'T TALK FOR TOO LONG.
HE SEEMS REALLY HAPPY, AND I GUESS I'M GLAD TO HEAR IT.
I'M NOT JEALOUS OF NANCY OR ANYTHING. I MEAN, I NEVER THOUGHT OF HIM LIKE THAT. PLUS, I DIG RIDING AROUND AT NIGHT BY MYSELF.
BUT EVERY ONCE IN A WHILE, I MISS THAT BITTER REJECT I USED TO HANG OUT WITH.
EXIT
AT

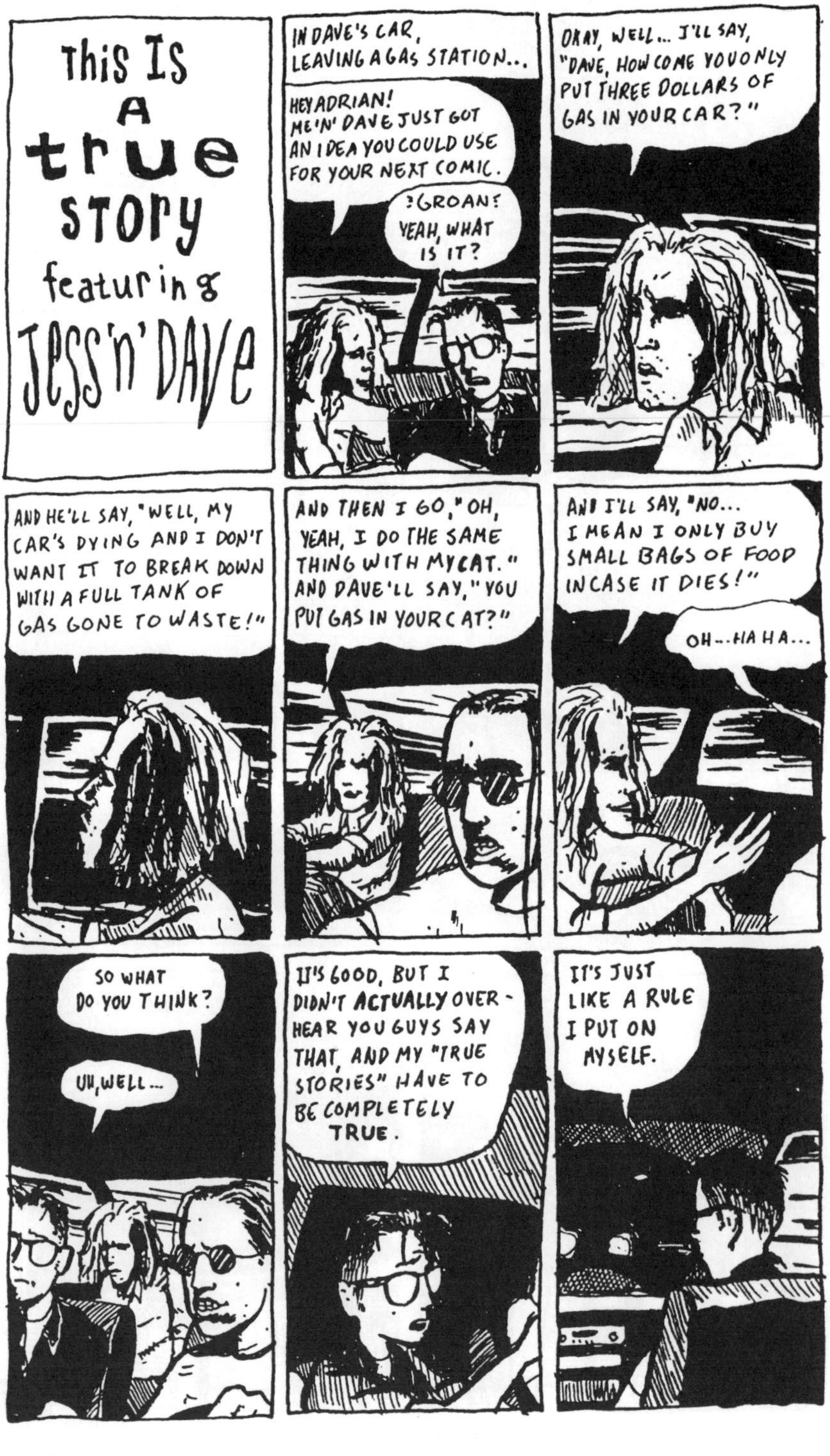
This Is a true story featuring Jess'n'Dave
IN DAVE'S CAR, LEAVING A GAS STATION...
HEY ADRIAN! ME'N' DAVE JUST GOT AN IDEA YOU COULD USE FOR YOUR NEXT COMIC.
?GROAN? YEAH, WHAT IS IT?
OKAY, WELL... I'LL SAY, "DAVE, HOW COME YOU ONLY PUT THREE DOLLARS OF GAS IN YOUR CAR?"
AND HE'LL SAY, "WELL, MY CAR'S DYING AND I DON'T WANT IT TO BREAK DOWN WITH A FULL TANK OF GAS GONE TO WASTE!"
AND THEN I GO, "OH, YEAH, I DO THE SAME THING WITH MY CAT." AND DAVE'LL SAY, "YOU PUT GAS IN YOUR CAT?"
AND I'LL SAY, "NO... I MEAN I ONLY BUY SMALL BAGS OF FOOD INCASE IT DIES!"
OH...HA HA...
SO WHAT DO YOU THINK?
UH, WELL...
IT'S GOOD, BUT I DIDN'T ACTUALLY OVER-HEAR YOU GUYS SAY THAT, AND MY "TRUE STORIES" HAVE TO BE COMPLETELY TRUE.
IT'S JUST LIKE A RULE I PUT ON MYSELF.

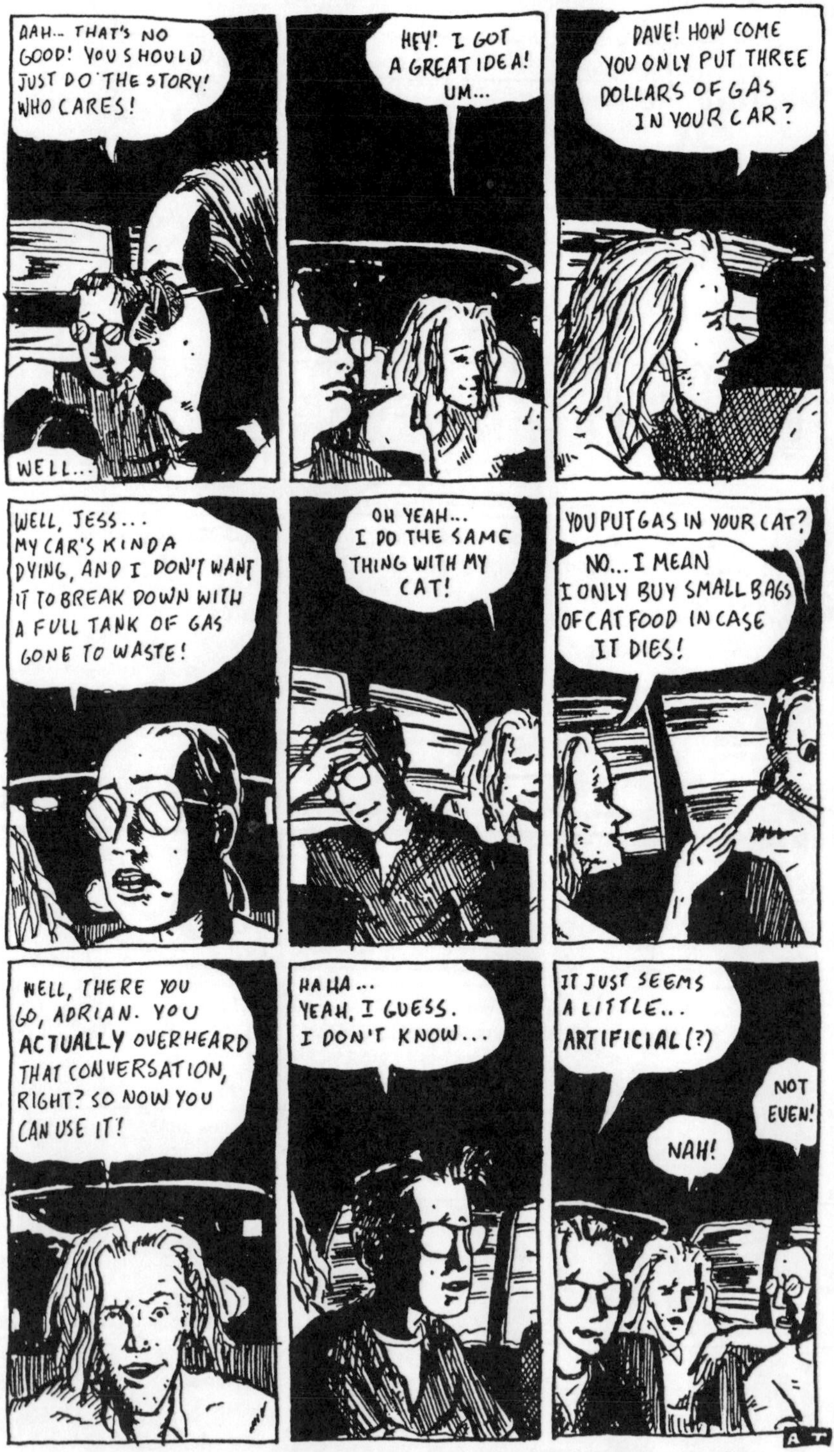
AAH... THAT'S NO GOOD! YOU SHOULD JUST DO THE STORY! WHO CARES!
WELL...
HEY! I GOT A GREAT IDEA! UM...
DAVE! HOW COME YOU ONLY PUT THREE DOLLARS OF GAS IN YOUR CAR?
WELL, JESS... MY CAR'S KINDA DYING, AND I DON'T WANT IT TO BREAK DOWN WITH A FULL TANK OF GAS GONE TO WASTE!
OH YEAH... I DO THE SAME THING WITH MY CAT!
YOU PUT GAS IN YOUR CAT?
NO... I MEAN I ONLY BUY SMALL BAGS OF CAT FOOD IN CASE IT DIES!
WELL, THERE YOU GO, ADRIAN. YOU ACTUALLY OVERHEARD THAT CONVERSATION, RIGHT? SO NOW YOU CAN USE IT!
HA HA... YEAH, I GUESS. I DON'T KNOW...
IT JUST SEEMS A LITTLE... ARTIFICIAL (?)
NOT EVEN!
NAH!
A.T.

P.S: I JUST REALIZED THAT DAVE WASN'T ACTUALLY WEARING THOSE SUNGLASSES THAT NIGHT (THEY WERE JUST EASIER TO DRAW THAN HIS EYES)... SO MUCH FOR MY BIG "RULE."

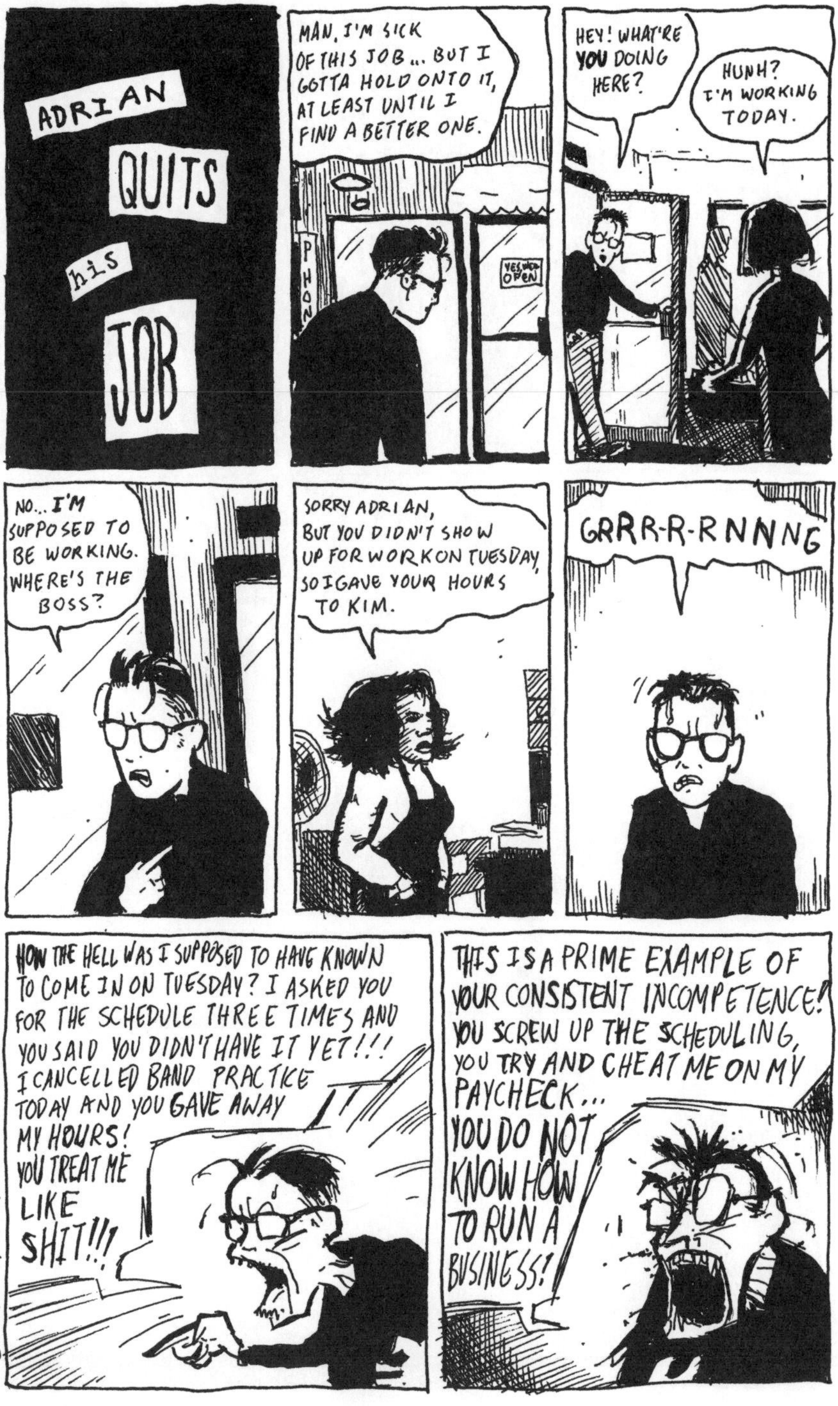
ADRIAN
QUITS
his
JOB
MAN, I'M SICK OF THIS JOB... BUT I GOTTA HOLD ONTO IT, AT LEAST UNTIL I FIND A BETTER ONE.
PHON
YES WE'RE OPEN
HEY! WHAT'RE YOU DOING HERE?
HUNH? I'M WORKING TODAY.
NO... I'M SUPPOSED TO BE WORKING. WHERE'S THE BOSS?
SORRY ADRIAN, BUT YOU DIDN'T SHOW UP FOR WORK ON TUESDAY, SO I GAVE YOUR HOURS TO KIM.
GRRR-R-RNNNG
HOW THE HELL WAS I SUPPOSED TO HAVE KNOWN TO COME IN ON TUESDAY? I ASKED YOU FOR THE SCHEDULE THREE TIMES AND YOU SAID YOU DIDN'T HAVE IT YET!!! I CANCELLED BAND PRACTICE TODAY AND YOU GAVE AWAY MY HOURS! YOU TREAT ME LIKE SHIT!!!
THIS IS A PRIME EXAMPLE OF YOUR CONSISTENT INCOMPETENCE! YOU SCREW UP THE SCHEDULING, YOU TRY AND CHEAT ME ON MY PAYCHECK... YOU DO NOT KNOW HOW TO RUN A BUSINESS!

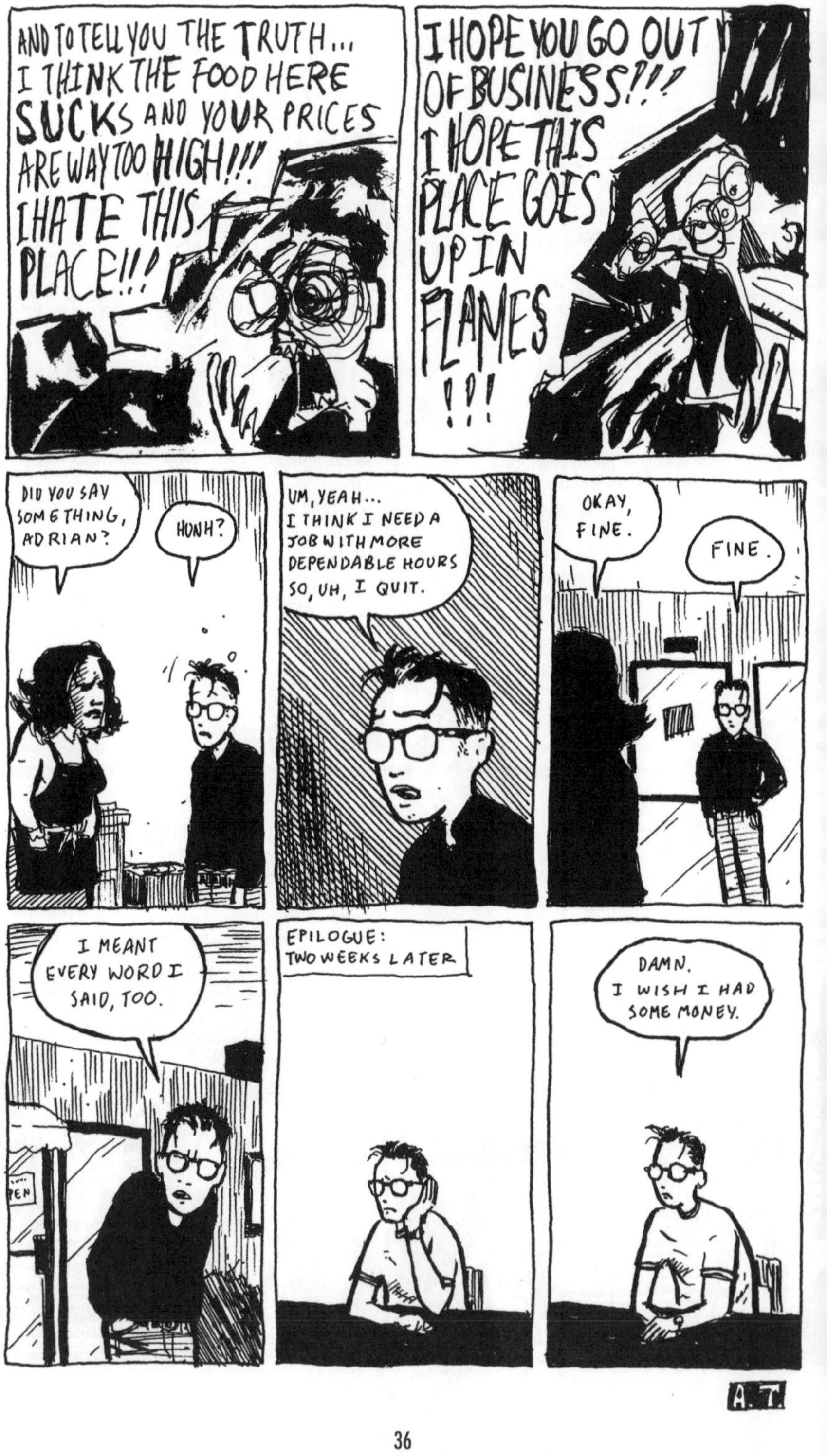
AND TO TELL YOU THE TRUTH... I THINK THE FOOD HERE SUCKS AND YOUR PRICES ARE WAY TOO HIGH!!! I HATE THIS PLACE!!!
I HOPE YOU GO OUT OF BUSINESS!!! I HOPE THIS PLACE GOES UP IN FLAMES!!!
DID YOU SAY SOMETHING, ADRIAN?
HUNH?
UM, YEAH... I THINK I NEED A JOB WITH MORE DEPENDABLE HOURS SO, UH, I QUIT.
OKAY, FINE.
FINE.
I MEANT EVERY WORD I SAID, TOO.
EPILOGUE: TWO WEEKS LATER
DAMN. I WISH I HAD SOME MONEY.
A.T.

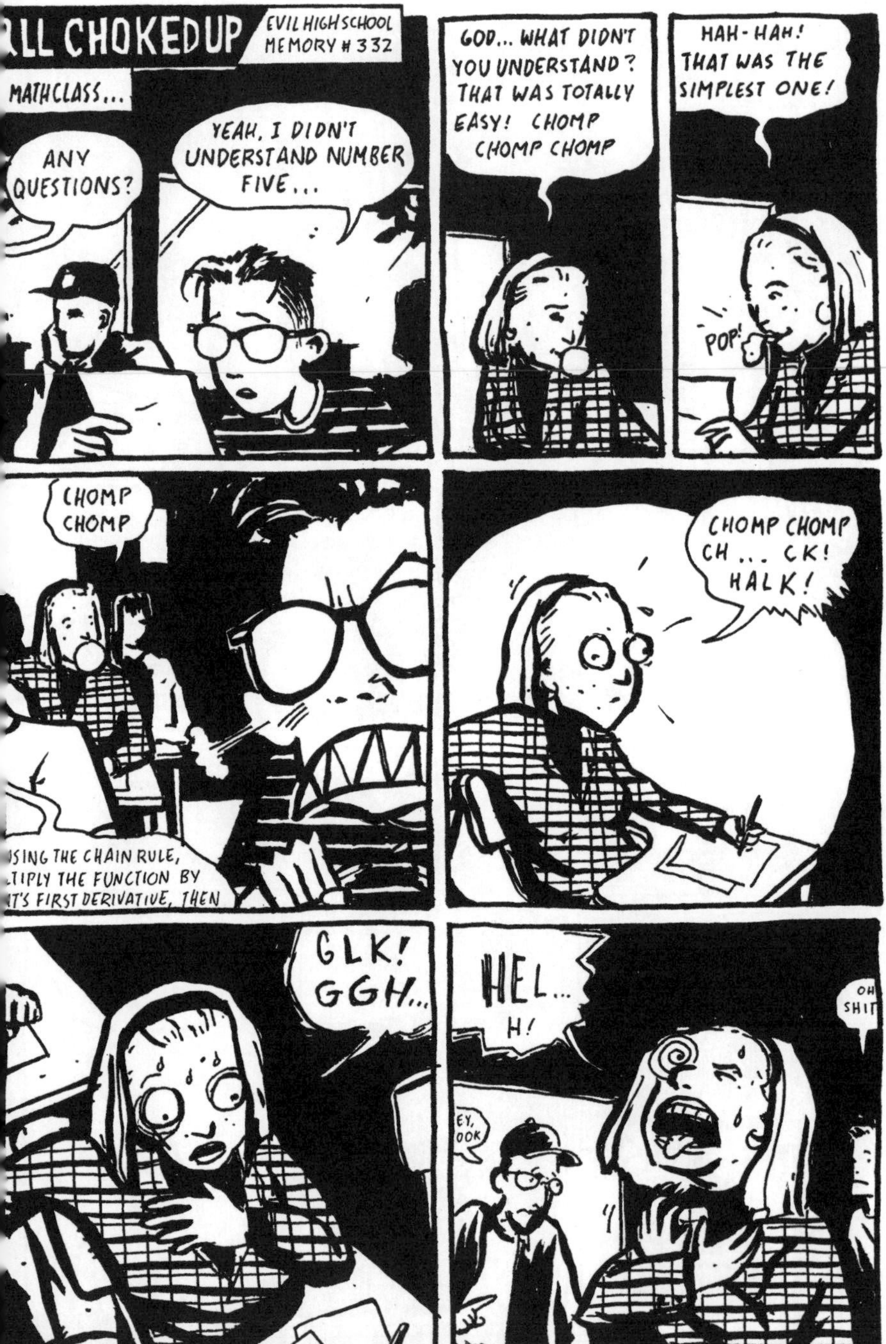

ALL CHOKEDUP
EVIL HIGHSCHOOL MEMORY # 332
MATHCLASS...
ANY QUESTIONS?
YEAH, I DIDN'T UNDERSTAND NUMBER FIVE...
GOD... WHAT DIDN'T YOU UNDERSTAND? THAT WAS TOTALLY EASY! CHOMP CHOMP CHOMP
HAH-HAH! THAT WAS THE SIMPLEST ONE!
POP!
CHOMP CHOMP
USING THE CHAIN RULE, TIPLY THE FUNCTION BY IT'S FIRST DERIVATIVE, THEN
CHOMP CHOMP CH... CK! HALK!
GLK! GGH...
HEL... H!
OH SHIT
EY, OOK

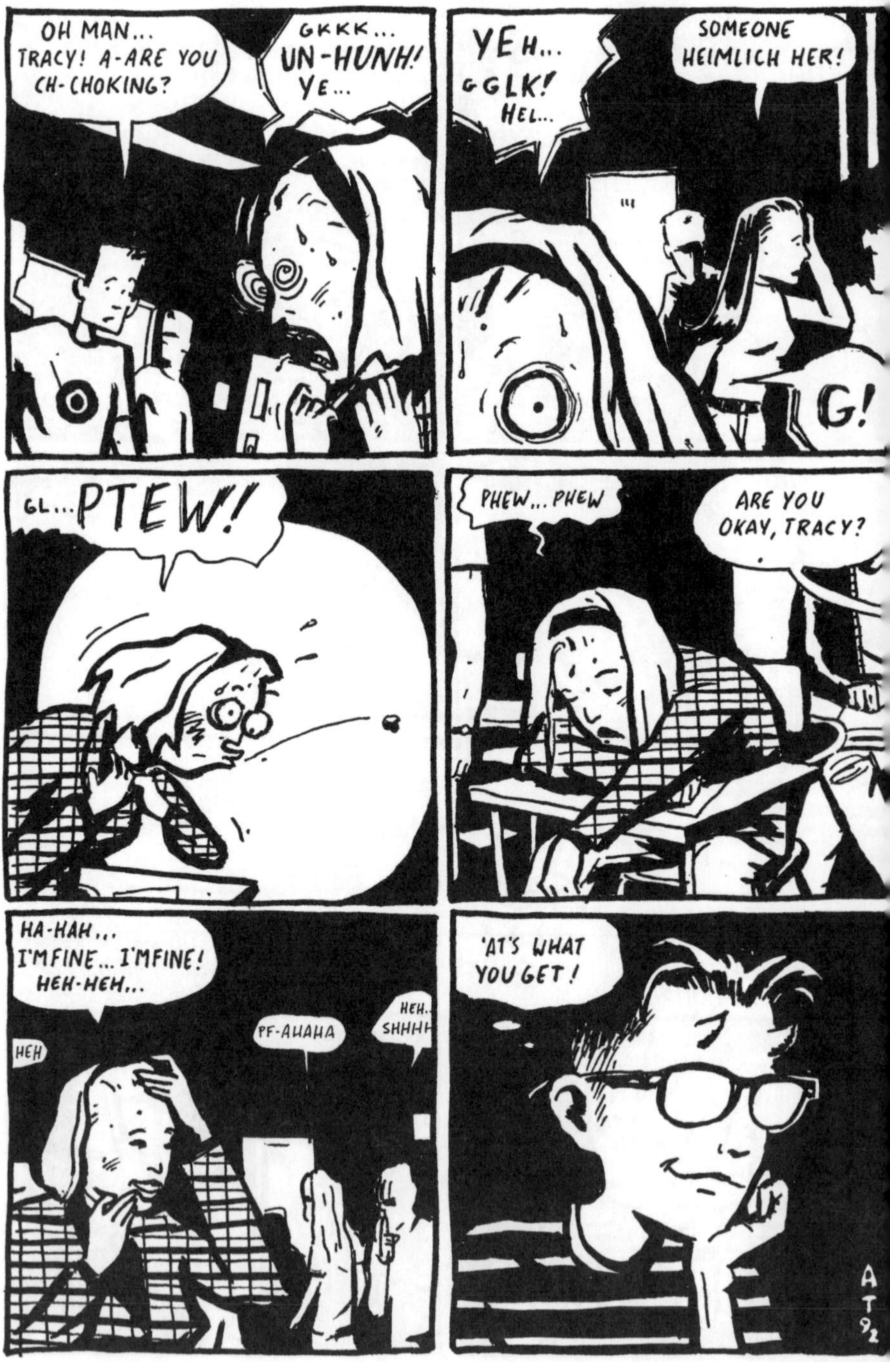

OH MAN... TRACY! A-ARE YOU CH-CHOKING?
GKKK... UN-HUNH! YE...
YEH... GGLK! HEL...
SOMEONE HEIMLICH HER!
G!
GL...PTEW!
PHEW... PHEW
ARE YOU OKAY, TRACY?
HA-HAH... I'MFINE... I'MFINE! HEH-HEH...
HEH
PF-AHAHA
HEH.. SHHHH
'AT'S WHAT YOU GET!
AT 92

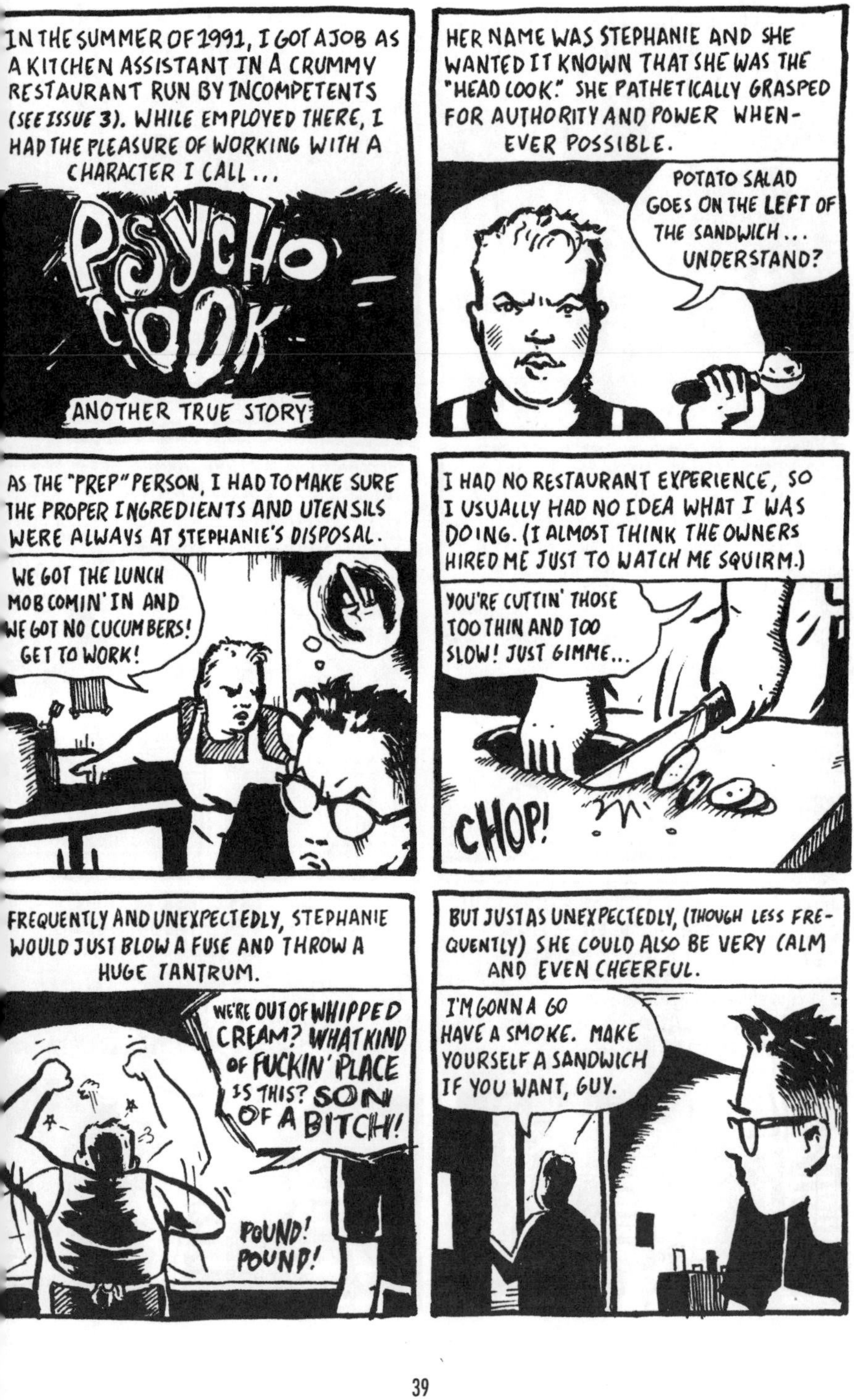
IN THE SUMMER OF 1991, I GOT A JOB AS A KITCHEN ASSISTANT IN A CRUMMY RESTAURANT RUN BY INCOMPETENTS (SEE ISSUE 3). WHILE EMPLOYED THERE, I HAD THE PLEASURE OF WORKING WITH A CHARACTER I CALL...
PSYCHO COOK
ANOTHER TRUE STORY
HER NAME WAS STEPHANIE AND SHE WANTED IT KNOWN THAT SHE WAS THE "HEAD COOK." SHE PATHETICALLY GRASPED FOR AUTHORITY AND POWER WHENEVER POSSIBLE.
POTATO SALAD GOES ON THE LEFT OF THE SANDWICH... UNDERSTAND?
AS THE "PREP" PERSON, I HAD TO MAKE SURE THE PROPER INGREDIENTS AND UTENSILS WERE ALWAYS AT STEPHANIE'S DISPOSAL.
WE GOT THE LUNCH MOB COMIN' IN AND WE GOT NO CUCUMBERS! GET TO WORK!
I HAD NO RESTAURANT EXPERIENCE, SO I USUALLY HAD NO IDEA WHAT I WAS DOING. (I ALMOST THINK THE OWNERS HIRED ME JUST TO WATCH ME SQUIRM.)
YOU'RE CUTTIN' THOSE TOO THIN AND TOO SLOW! JUST GIMME...
CHOP!
FREQUENTLY AND UNEXPECTEDLY, STEPHANIE WOULD JUST BLOW A FUSE AND THROW A HUGE TANTRUM.
WE'RE OUT OF WHIPPED CREAM? WHAT KIND OF FUCKIN' PLACE IS THIS? SON OF A BITCH!
POUND! POUND!
BUT JUST AS UNEXPECTEDLY, (THOUGH LESS FREQUENTLY) SHE COULD ALSO BE VERY CALM AND EVEN CHEERFUL.
I'M GONNA GO HAVE A SMOKE. MAKE YOURSELF A SANDWICH IF YOU WANT, GUY.

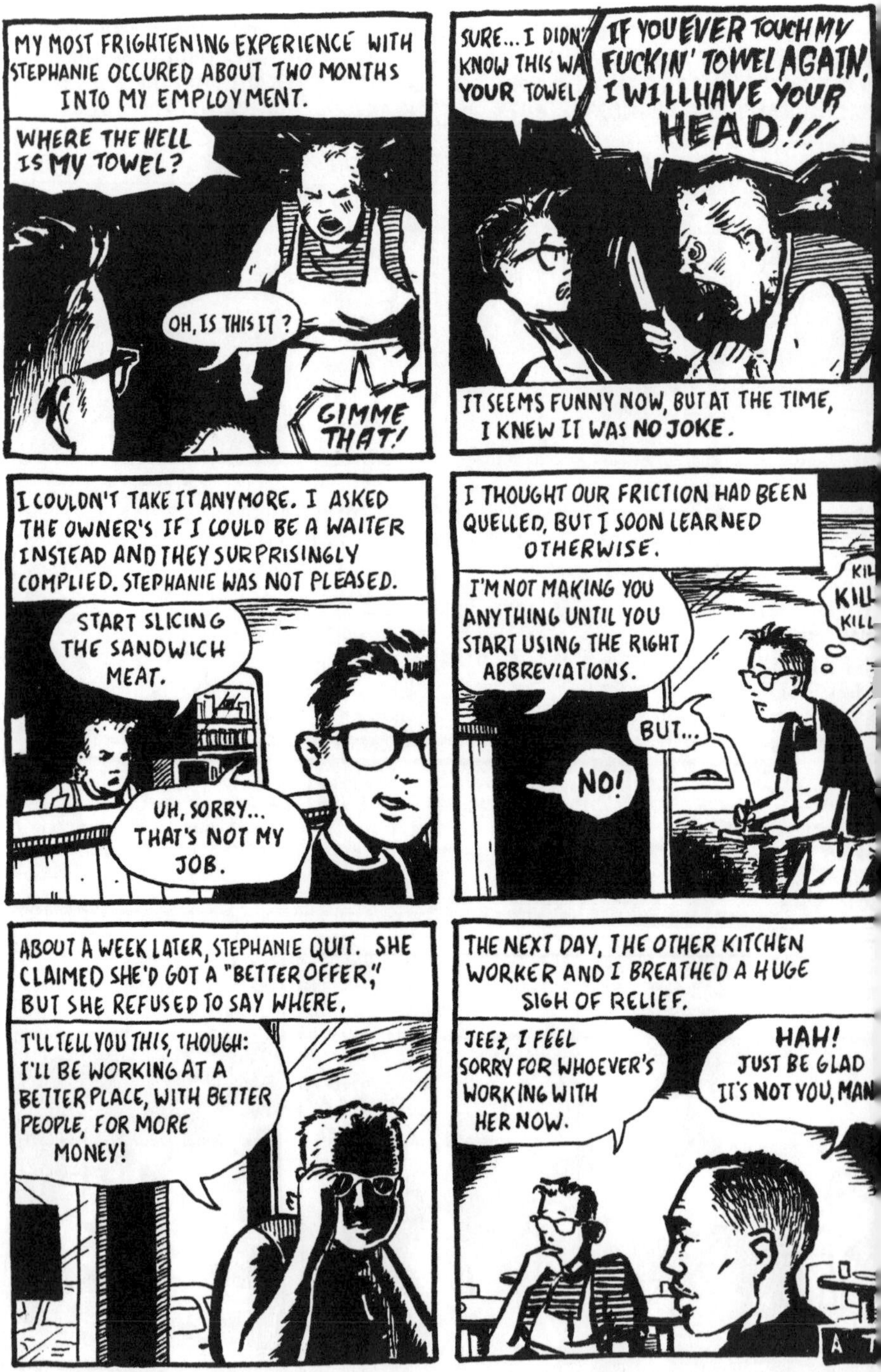
MY MOST FRIGHTENING EXPERIENCE WITH STEPHANIE OCCURED ABOUT TWO MONTHS INTO MY EMPLOYMENT.
WHERE THE HELL IS MY TOWEL?
OH, IS THIS IT?
GIMME THAT!
SURE... I DIDN' KNOW THIS WA YOUR TOWEL
IF YOU EVER TOUCH MY FUCKIN' TOWEL AGAIN, I WILL HAVE YOUR HEAD!!!
IT SEEMS FUNNY NOW, BUT AT THE TIME, I KNEW IT WAS NO JOKE.
I COULDN'T TAKE IT ANYMORE. I ASKED THE OWNER'S IF I COULD BE A WAITER INSTEAD AND THEY SURPRISINGLY COMPLIED. STEPHANIE WAS NOT PLEASED.
START SLICING THE SANDWICH MEAT.
UH, SORRY... THAT'S NOT MY JOB.
I THOUGHT OUR FRICTION HAD BEEN QUELLED, BUT I SOON LEARNED OTHERWISE.
I'M NOT MAKING YOU ANYTHING UNTIL YOU START USING THE RIGHT ABBREVIATIONS.
BUT...
NO!
ABOUT A WEEK LATER, STEPHANIE QUIT. SHE CLAIMED SHE'D GOT A "BETTER OFFER," BUT SHE REFUSED TO SAY WHERE.
I'LL TELL YOU THIS, THOUGH: I'LL BE WORKING AT A BETTER PLACE, WITH BETTER PEOPLE, FOR MORE MONEY!
THE NEXT DAY, THE OTHER KITCHEN WORKER AND I BREATHED A HUGE SIGH OF RELIEF.
JEEZ, I FEEL SORRY FOR WHOEVER'S WORKING WITH HER NOW.
HAH! JUST BE GLAD IT'S NOT YOU, MAN

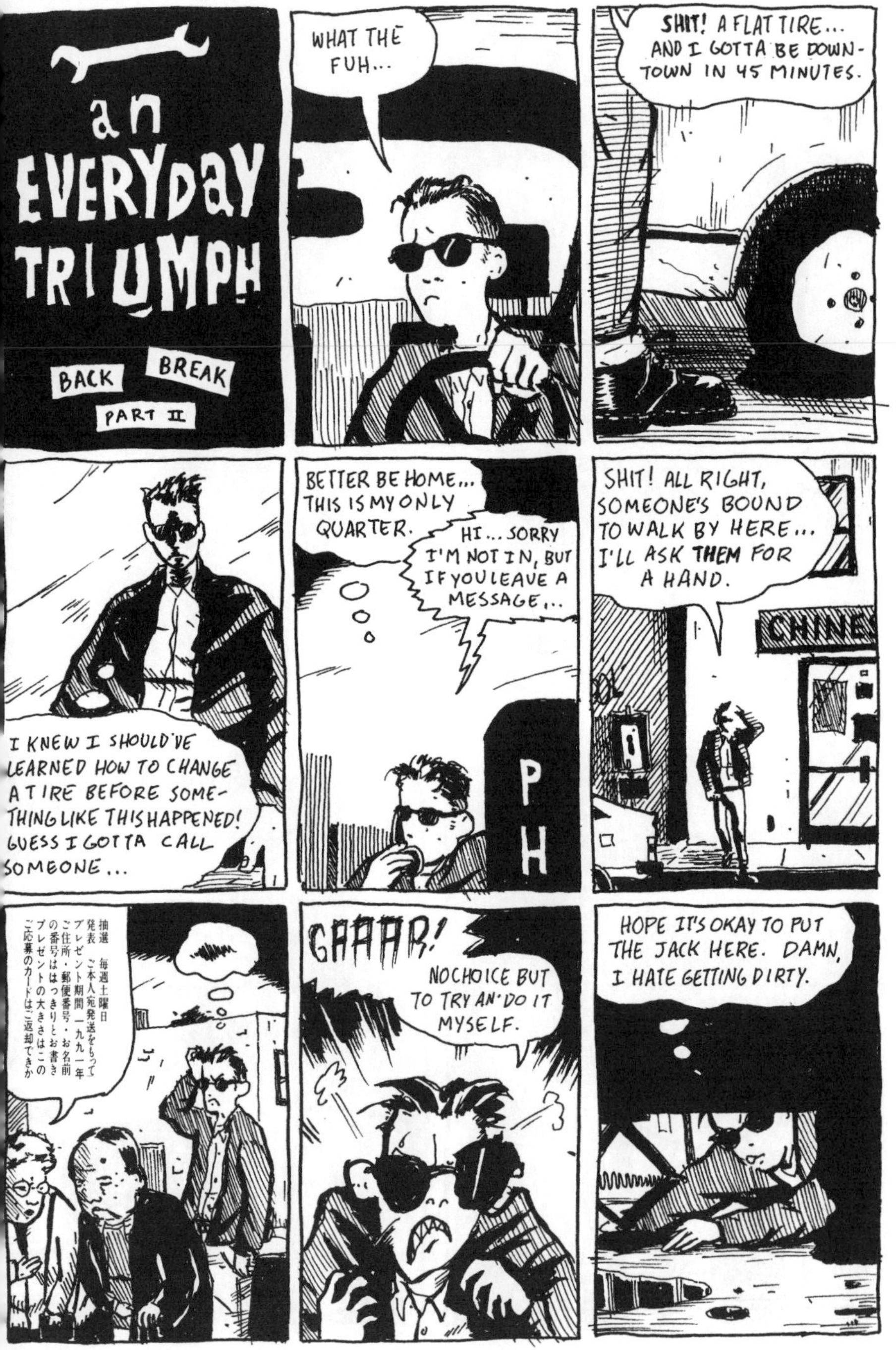
an EVERYDAY TRIUMPH
BACK BREAK
PART II
WHAT THE FUH...
SHIT! A FLAT TIRE... AND I GOTTA BE DOWNTOWN IN 45 MINUTES.
I KNEW I SHOULD'VE LEARNED HOW TO CHANGE A TIRE BEFORE SOMETHING LIKE THIS HAPPENED! GUESS I GOTTA CALL SOMEONE...
BETTER BE HOME... THIS IS MY ONLY QUARTER.
HI... SORRY I'M NOT IN, BUT IF YOU LEAVE A MESSAGE...
PH
SHIT! ALL RIGHT, SOMEONE'S BOUND TO WALK BY HERE... I'LL ASK THEM FOR A HAND.
CHINE
抽選　毎週土曜日
発表　ご本人宛発送をもって
プレゼント期間　一九九一年
ご住所・郵便番号・お名前
の番号ははっきりとお書き
プレゼントの大きさはこの
ご応募のカードはご返却できか
GAAAR!
NO CHOICE BUT TO TRY AN' DO IT MYSELF.
HOPE IT'S OKAY TO PUT THE JACK HERE. DAMN, I HATE GETTING DIRTY.

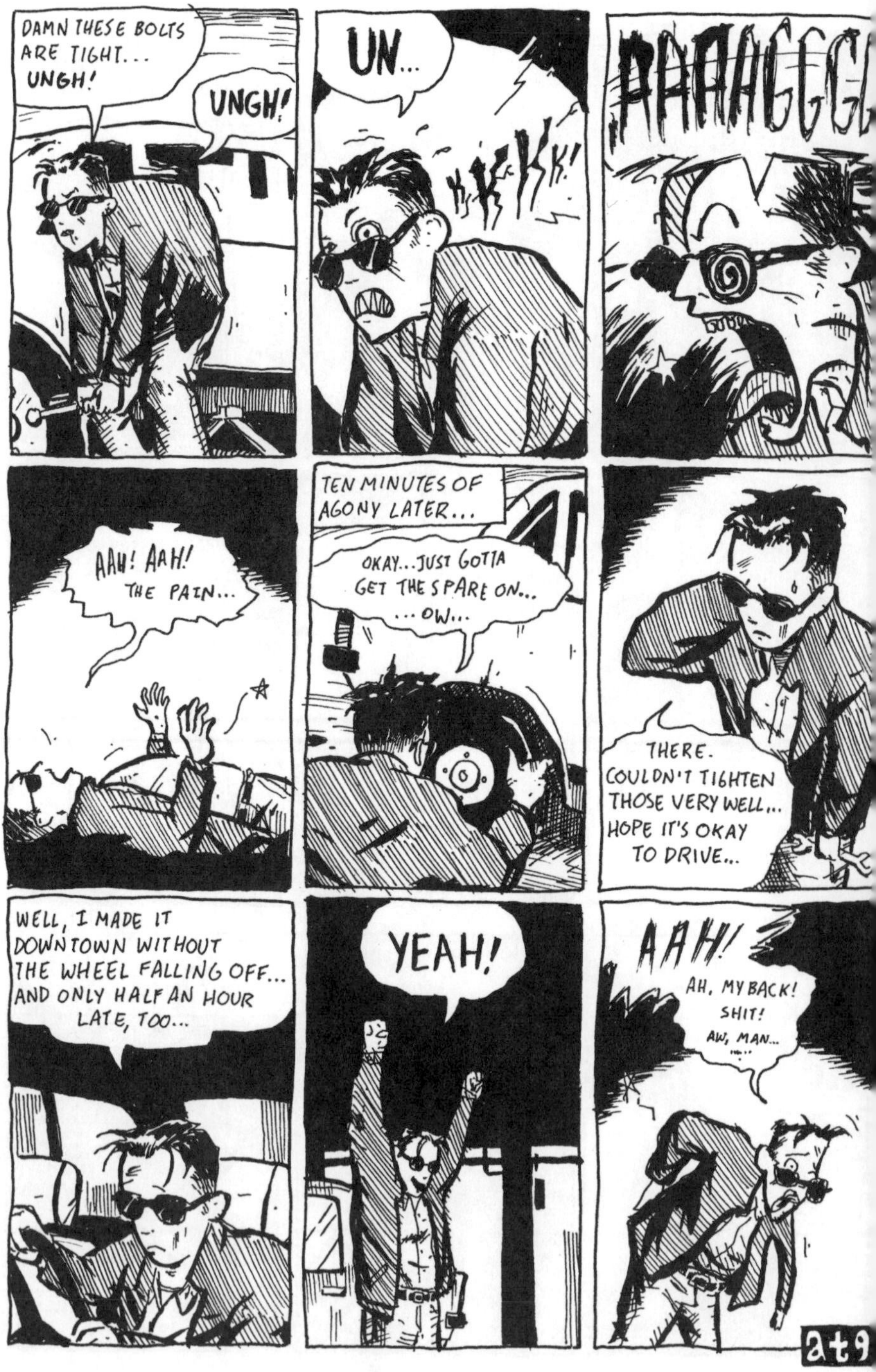
DAMN THESE BOLTS ARE TIGHT... UNGH!
UNGH!
UN...
KKKK!
AAAAGGG
AAH! AAH! THE PAIN...
TEN MINUTES OF AGONY LATER...
OKAY...JUST GOTTA GET THE SPARE ON... ...OW...
THERE. COULDN'T TIGHTEN THOSE VERY WELL... HOPE IT'S OKAY TO DRIVE...
WELL, I MADE IT DOWNTOWN WITHOUT THE WHEEL FALLING OFF... AND ONLY HALF AN HOUR LATE, TOO...
YEAH!
AAH!
AH, MY BACK! SHIT! AW, MAN...
at9

Kerouac's life with comics

A TRUE STORY ABOUT THE AUTHOR OF ON THE ROAD & THE DHARMA BUMS

AROUND THE AGE OF TEN, JACK KEROUAC DISCOVERED COMIC BOOKS. SOMEWHAT OF A LONER, HE'D SPEND MANY AFTERNOONS READING *THE GREEN HORNET* AND *THE SHADOW*, OR SEARCHING THE MAGAZINE RACKS AT THE CANDY STORE FOR A NEW ISSUE.

ALONG WITH HIS NEIGHBORS, KEROUAC TOOK TO RUNNING IN THE STREETS AT NIGHT DRESSED IN HOME-MADE COSTUMES, PRETENDING TO BE HIS CARTOON HEROES. HE EVEN WENT SO FAR AS TO PERFECT HIS OWN "SUPER-POWER."

SPITTING KEROSENE ACROSS A MATCH

INSTRUCTED AND INSPIRED BY HIS OLDER BROTHER GERARD, KEROUAC BEGAN DRAWING HIS OWN COMICS. HE FIRST COPIED THE SHADOW, AND LATER CREATED HIS OWN CHARACTERS, COUNT CONDU AND DR. SAX.

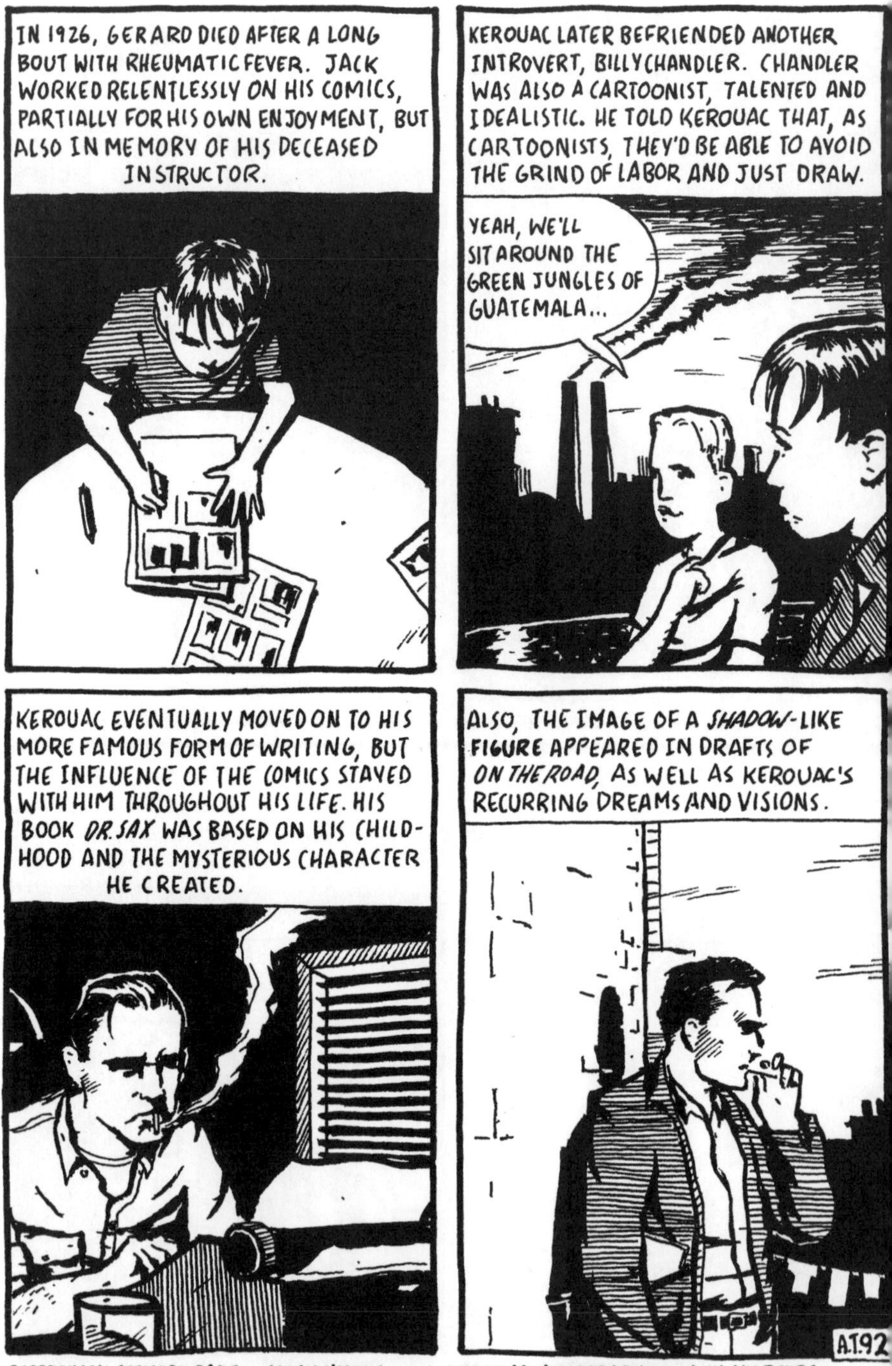
IN 1926, GERARD DIED AFTER A LONG BOUT WITH RHEUMATIC FEVER. JACK WORKED RELENTLESSLY ON HIS COMICS, PARTIALLY FOR HIS OWN ENJOYMENT, BUT ALSO IN MEMORY OF HIS DECEASED INSTRUCTOR.
KEROUAC LATER BEFRIENDED ANOTHER INTROVERT, BILLY CHANDLER. CHANDLER WAS ALSO A CARTOONIST, TALENTED AND IDEALISTIC. HE TOLD KEROUAC THAT, AS CARTOONISTS, THEY'D BE ABLE TO AVOID THE GRIND OF LABOR AND JUST DRAW.
YEAH, WE'LL SIT AROUND THE GREEN JUNGLES OF GUATEMALA...
KEROUAC EVENTUALLY MOVED ON TO HIS MORE FAMOUS FORM OF WRITING, BUT THE INFLUENCE OF THE COMICS STAYED WITH HIM THROUGHOUT HIS LIFE. HIS BOOK *DR. SAX* WAS BASED ON HIS CHILDHOOD AND THE MYSTERIOUS CHARACTER HE CREATED.
ALSO, THE IMAGE OF A *SHADOW*-LIKE FIGURE APPEARED IN DRAFTS OF *ON THE ROAD*, AS WELL AS KEROUAC'S RECURRING DREAMS AND VISIONS.
A.T.92

REFERENCES: *MEMORY BABE* by GERALD NICOSIA, and *KEROUAC: A BIOGRAPHY* by ANN CHARTERS.

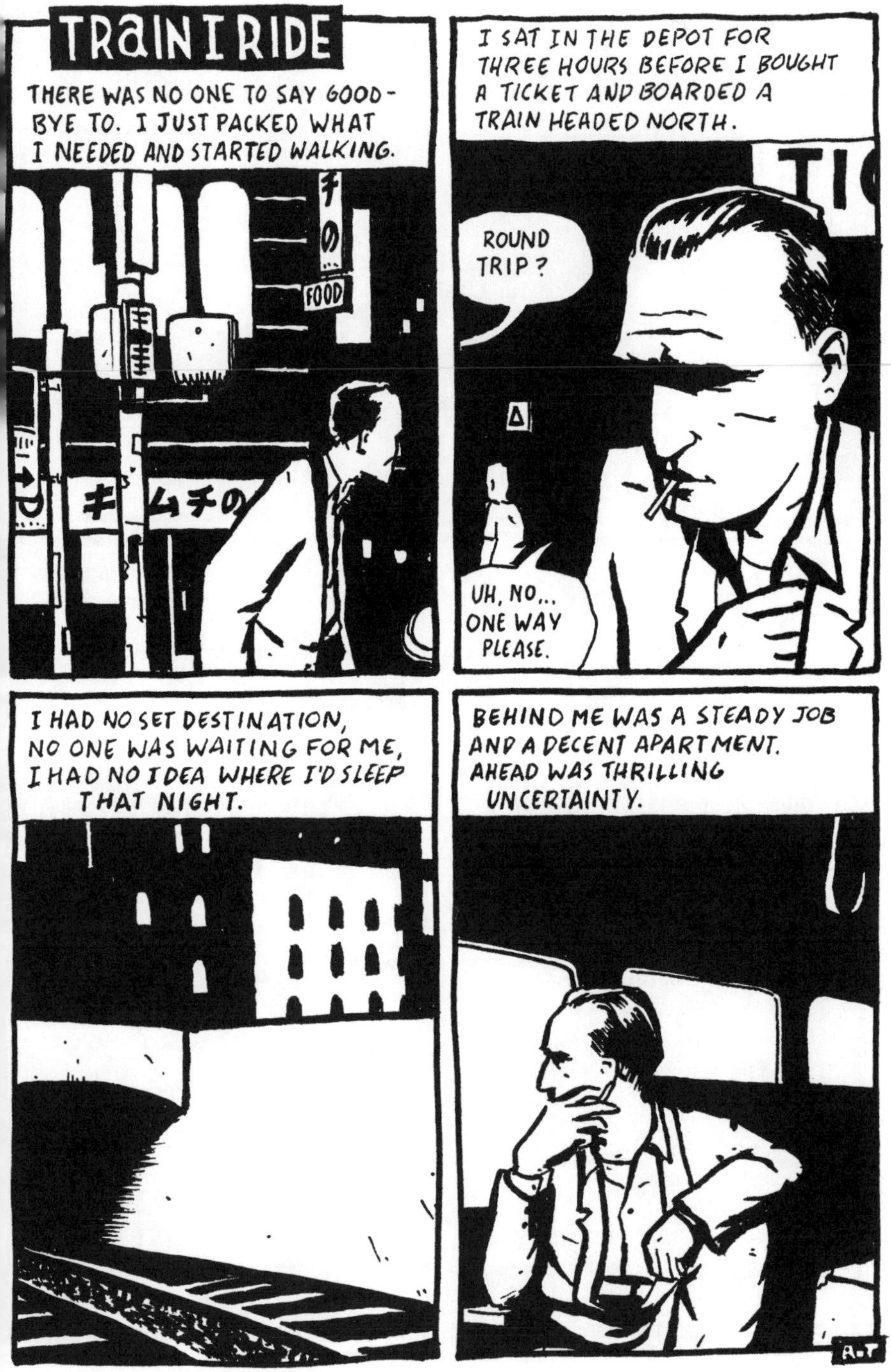
TRAIN I RIDE
THERE WAS NO ONE TO SAY GOOD-BYE TO. I JUST PACKED WHAT I NEEDED AND STARTED WALKING.
FOOD
I SAT IN THE DEPOT FOR THREE HOURS BEFORE I BOUGHT A TICKET AND BOARDED A TRAIN HEADED NORTH.
ROUND TRIP?
UH, NO... ONE WAY PLEASE.
I HAD NO SET DESTINATION, NO ONE WAS WAITING FOR ME, I HAD NO IDEA WHERE I'D SLEEP THAT NIGHT.
BEHIND ME WAS A STEADY JOB AND A DECENT APARTMENT. AHEAD WAS THRILLING UNCERTAINTY.
A.T

HAIRCUT

(An actual dream I had on December 15th, 1992.)

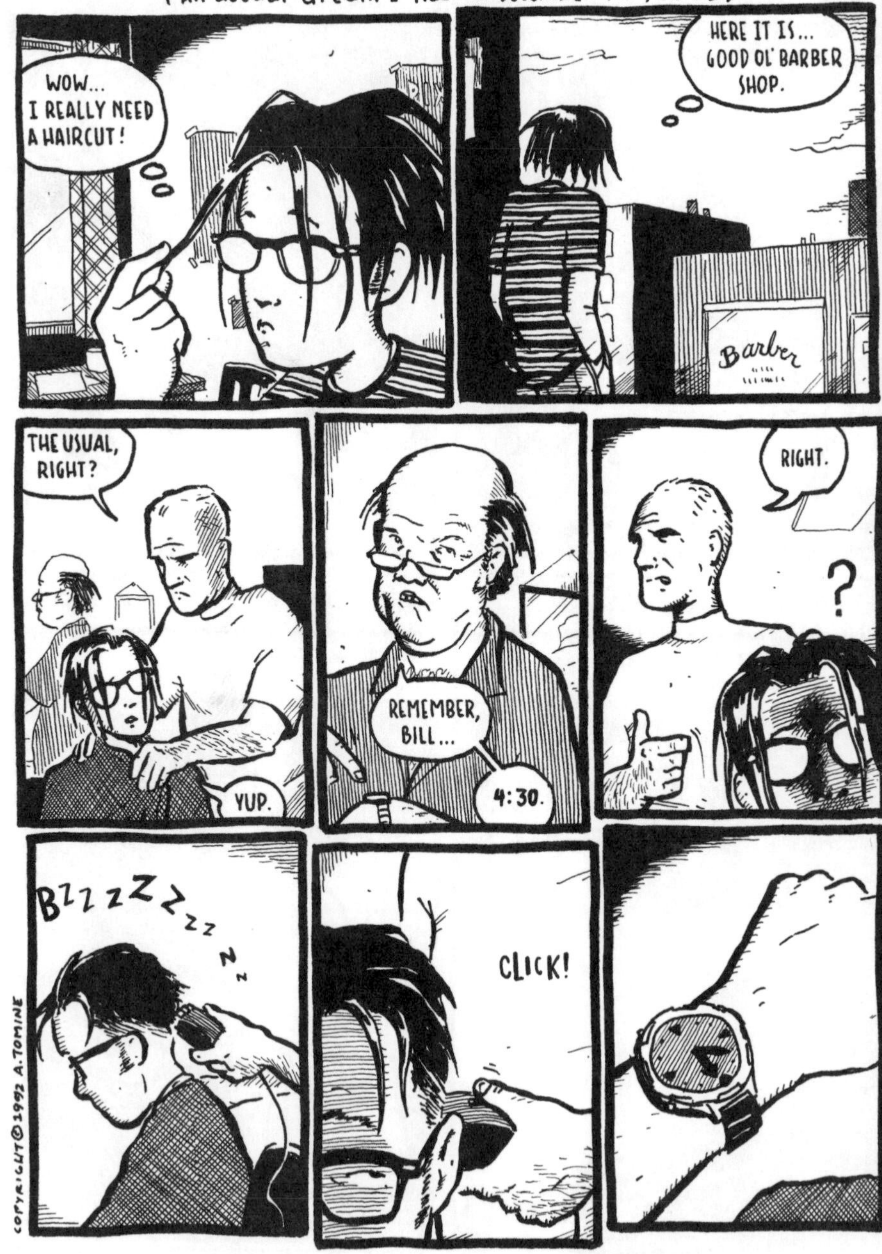
WOW... I REALLY NEED A HAIRCUT!
HERE IT IS... GOOD OL' BARBER SHOP.
Barber
THE USUAL, RIGHT?
YUP.
REMEMBER, BILL...
4:30.
RIGHT.
?
BZZZZZZZZNN
CLICK!
COPYRIGHT © 1992 A. TOMINE

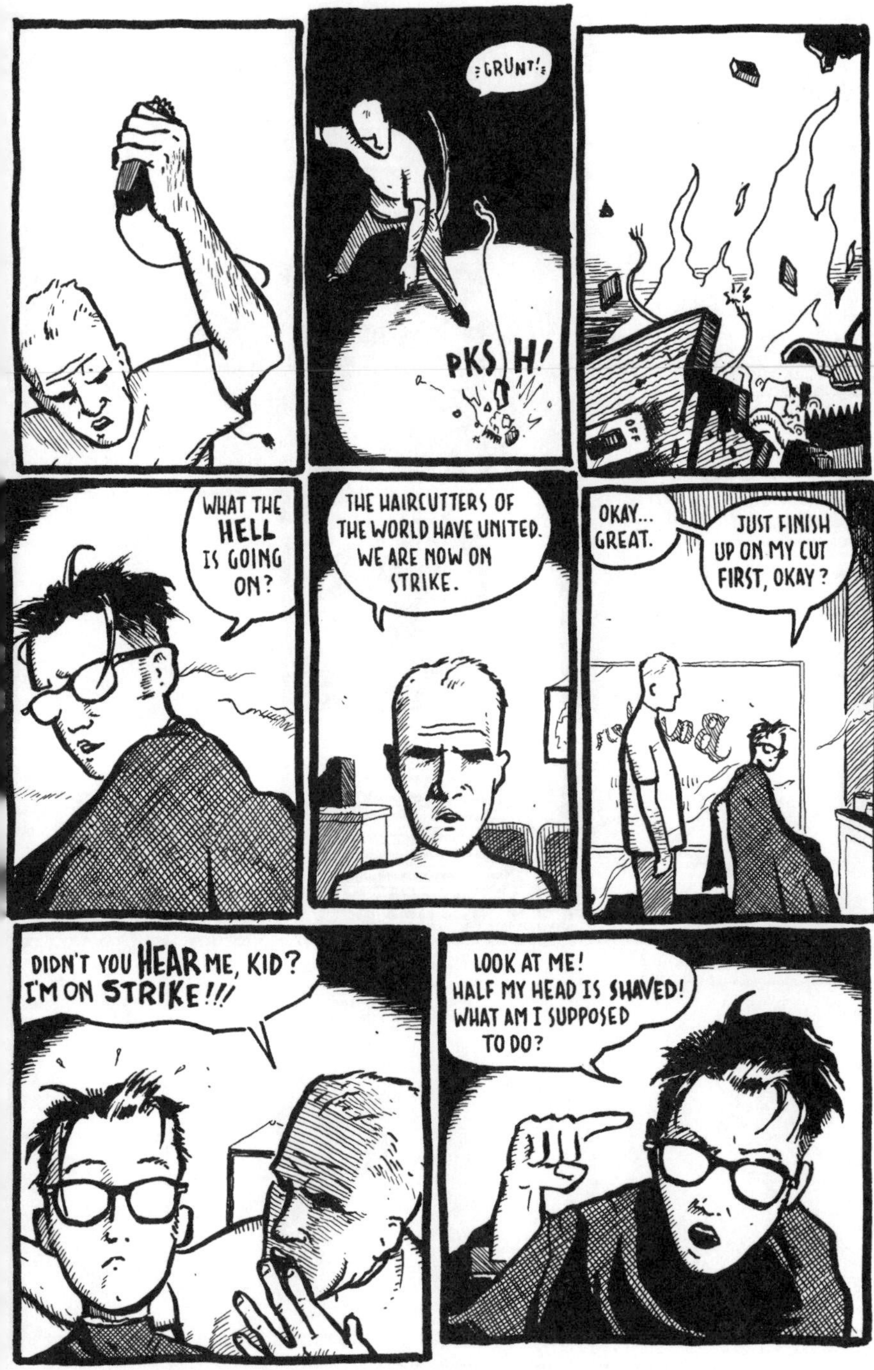
GRUNT!
PKSH!
OFF
WHAT THE HELL IS GOING ON?
THE HAIRCUTTERS OF THE WORLD HAVE UNITED. WE ARE NOW ON STRIKE.
OKAY... GREAT.
JUST FINISH UP ON MY CUT FIRST, OKAY?
DIDN'T YOU HEAR ME, KID? I'M ON STRIKE!!!
LOOK AT ME! HALF MY HEAD IS SHAVED! WHAT AM I SUPPOSED TO DO?

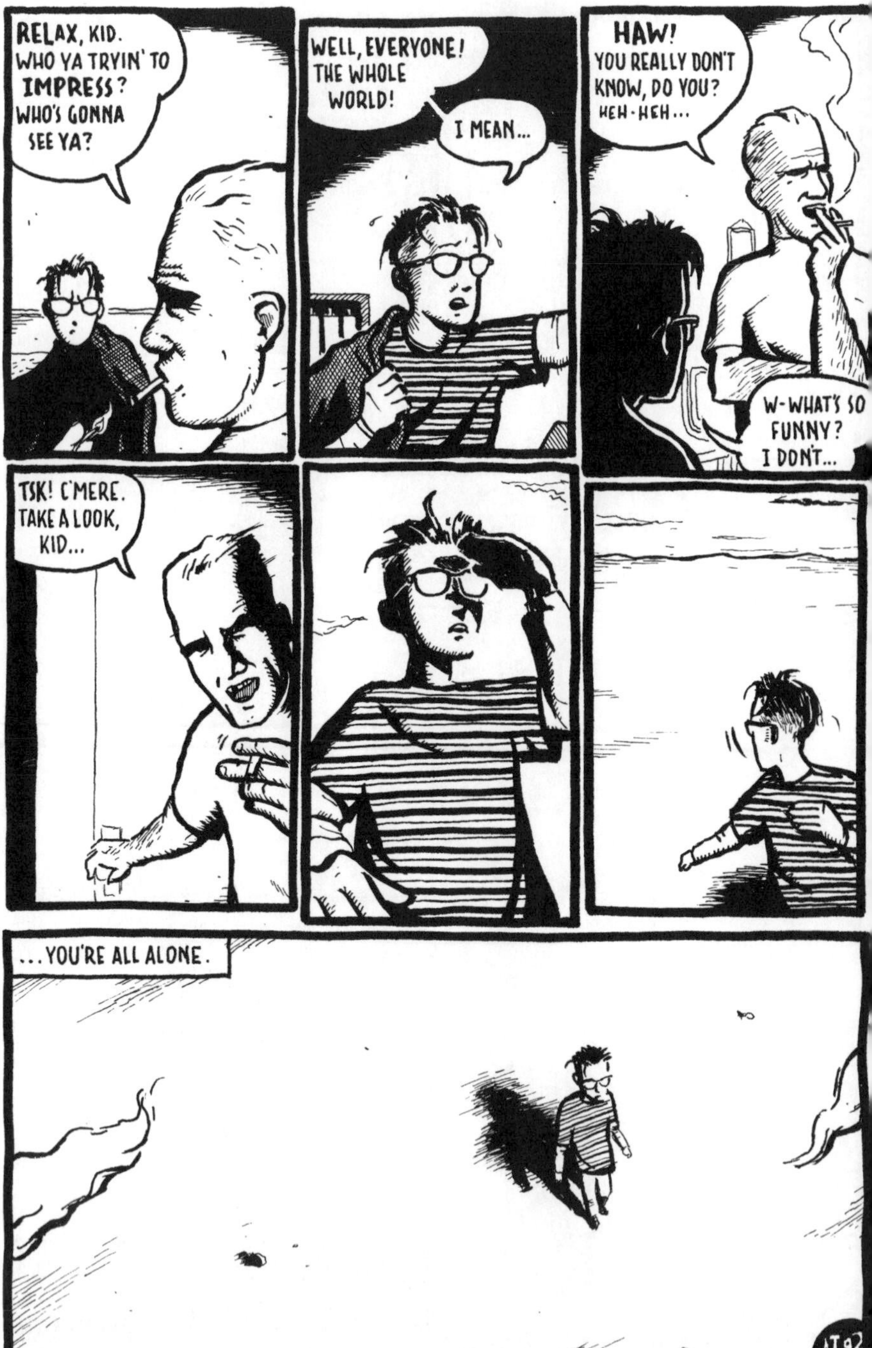
RELAX, KID. WHO YA TRYIN' TO IMPRESS? WHO'S GONNA SEE YA?
WELL, EVERYONE! THE WHOLE WORLD!
I MEAN...
HAW! YOU REALLY DON'T KNOW, DO YOU? HEH-HEH...
W-WHAT'S SO FUNNY? I DON'T...
TSK! C'MERE. TAKE A LOOK, KID...
...YOU'RE ALL ALONE.
AT 92

LIFTER

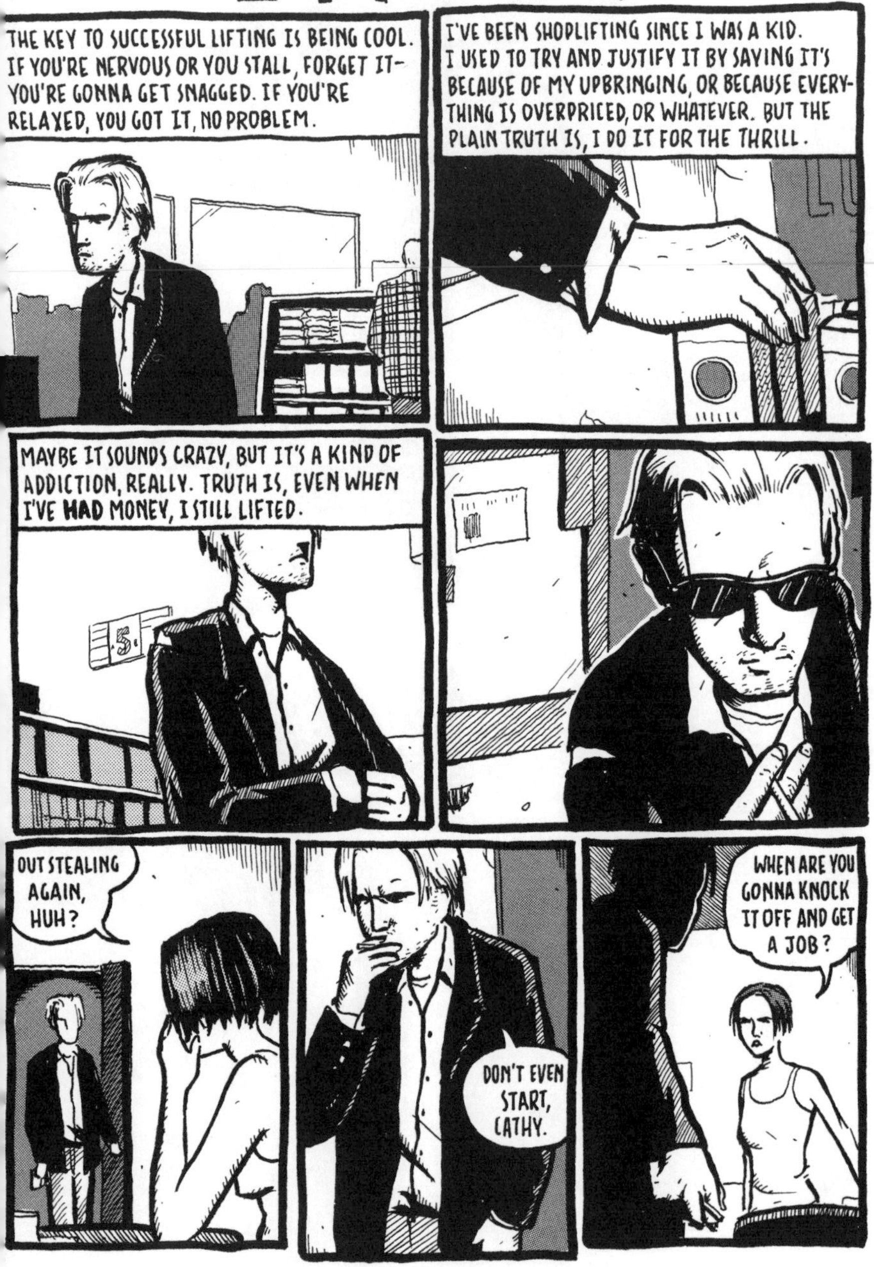
THE KEY TO SUCCESSFUL LIFTING IS BEING COOL. IF YOU'RE NERVOUS OR YOU STALL, FORGET IT- YOU'RE GONNA GET SNAGGED. IF YOU'RE RELAXED, YOU GOT IT, NO PROBLEM.
I'VE BEEN SHOPLIFTING SINCE I WAS A KID. I USED TO TRY AND JUSTIFY IT BY SAYING IT'S BECAUSE OF MY UPBRINGING, OR BECAUSE EVERYTHING IS OVERPRICED, OR WHATEVER. BUT THE PLAIN TRUTH IS, I DO IT FOR THE THRILL.
MAYBE IT SOUNDS CRAZY, BUT IT'S A KIND OF ADDICTION, REALLY. TRUTH IS, EVEN WHEN I'VE **HAD** MONEY, I STILL LIFTED.
OUT STEALING AGAIN, HUH?
DON'T EVEN START, CATHY.
WHEN ARE YOU GONNA KNOCK IT OFF AND GET A JOB?

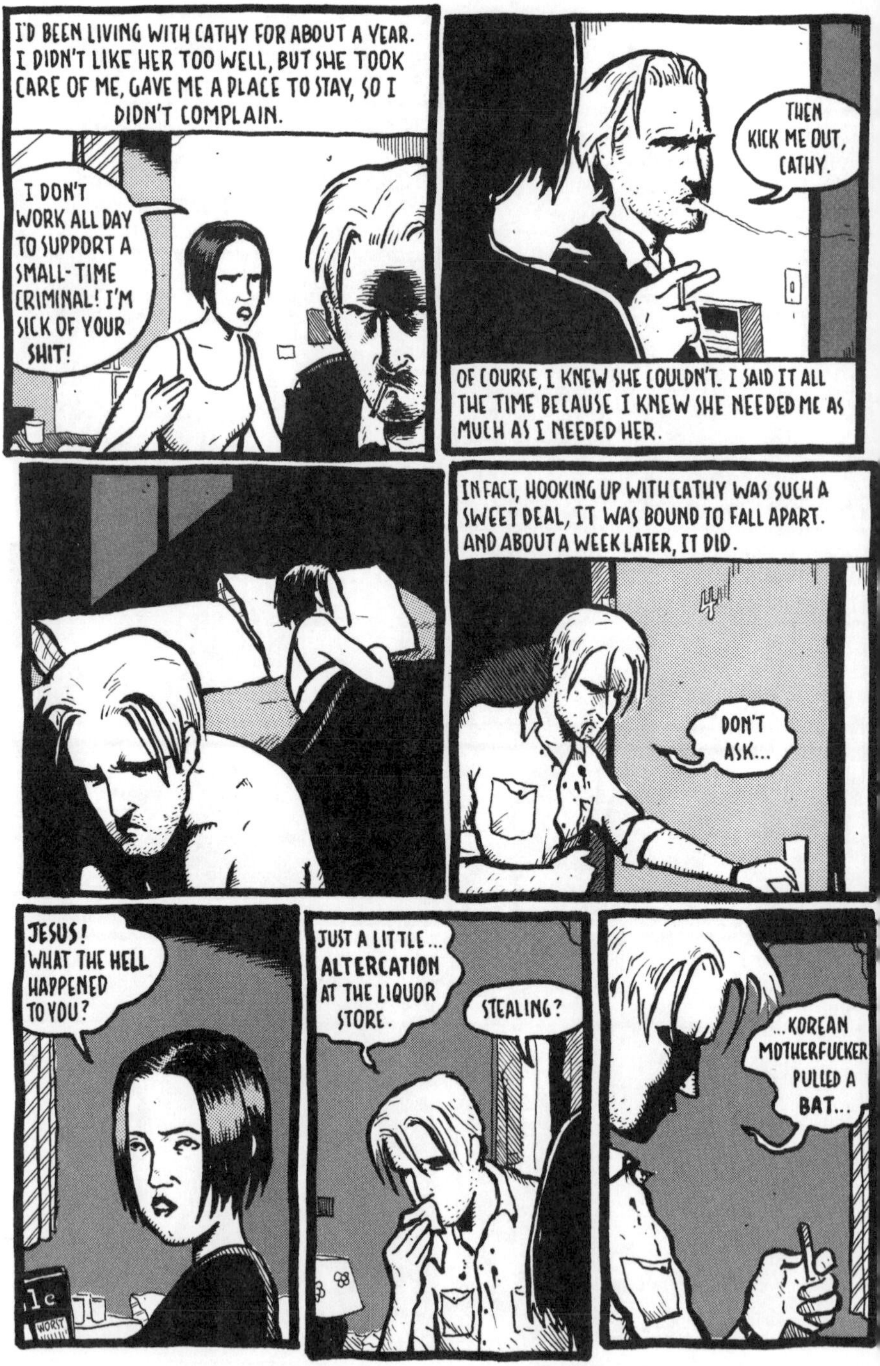
I'D BEEN LIVING WITH CATHY FOR ABOUT A YEAR. I DIDN'T LIKE HER TOO WELL, BUT SHE TOOK CARE OF ME, GAVE ME A PLACE TO STAY, SO I DIDN'T COMPLAIN.
I DON'T WORK ALL DAY TO SUPPORT A SMALL-TIME CRIMINAL! I'M SICK OF YOUR SHIT!
THEN KICK ME OUT, CATHY.
OF COURSE, I KNEW SHE COULDN'T. I SAID IT ALL THE TIME BECAUSE I KNEW SHE NEEDED ME AS MUCH AS I NEEDED HER.
IN FACT, HOOKING UP WITH CATHY WAS SUCH A SWEET DEAL, IT WAS BOUND TO FALL APART. AND ABOUT A WEEK LATER, IT DID.
DON'T ASK...
JESUS! WHAT THE HELL HAPPENED TO YOU?
JUST A LITTLE... ALTERCATION AT THE LIQUOR STORE.
STEALING?
...KOREAN MOTHERFUCKER PULLED A BAT...

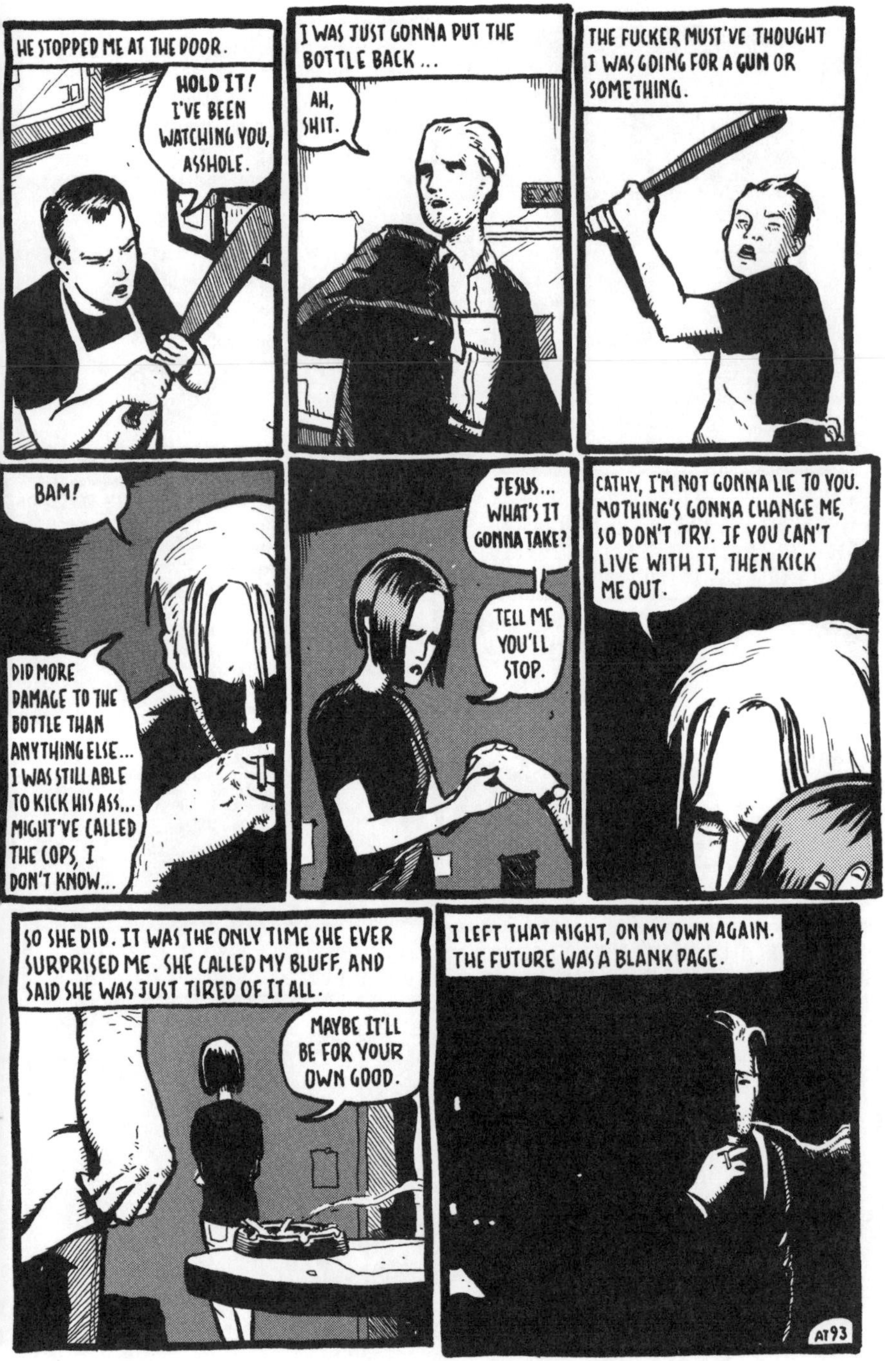

HE STOPPED ME AT THE DOOR.
HOLD IT! I'VE BEEN WATCHING YOU, ASSHOLE.
I WAS JUST GONNA PUT THE BOTTLE BACK...
AH, SHIT.
THE FUCKER MUST'VE THOUGHT I WAS GOING FOR A GUN OR SOMETHING.
BAM!
DID MORE DAMAGE TO THE BOTTLE THAN ANYTHING ELSE... I WAS STILL ABLE TO KICK HIS ASS... MIGHT'VE CALLED THE COPS, I DON'T KNOW...
JESUS... WHAT'S IT GONNA TAKE?
TELL ME YOU'LL STOP.
CATHY, I'M NOT GONNA LIE TO YOU. NOTHING'S GONNA CHANGE ME, SO DON'T TRY. IF YOU CAN'T LIVE WITH IT, THEN KICK ME OUT.
SO SHE DID. IT WAS THE ONLY TIME SHE EVER SURPRISED ME. SHE CALLED MY BLUFF, AND SAID SHE WAS JUST TIRED OF IT ALL.
MAYBE IT'LL BE FOR YOUR OWN GOOD.
I LEFT THAT NIGHT, ON MY OWN AGAIN. THE FUTURE WAS A BLANK PAGE.
AT93

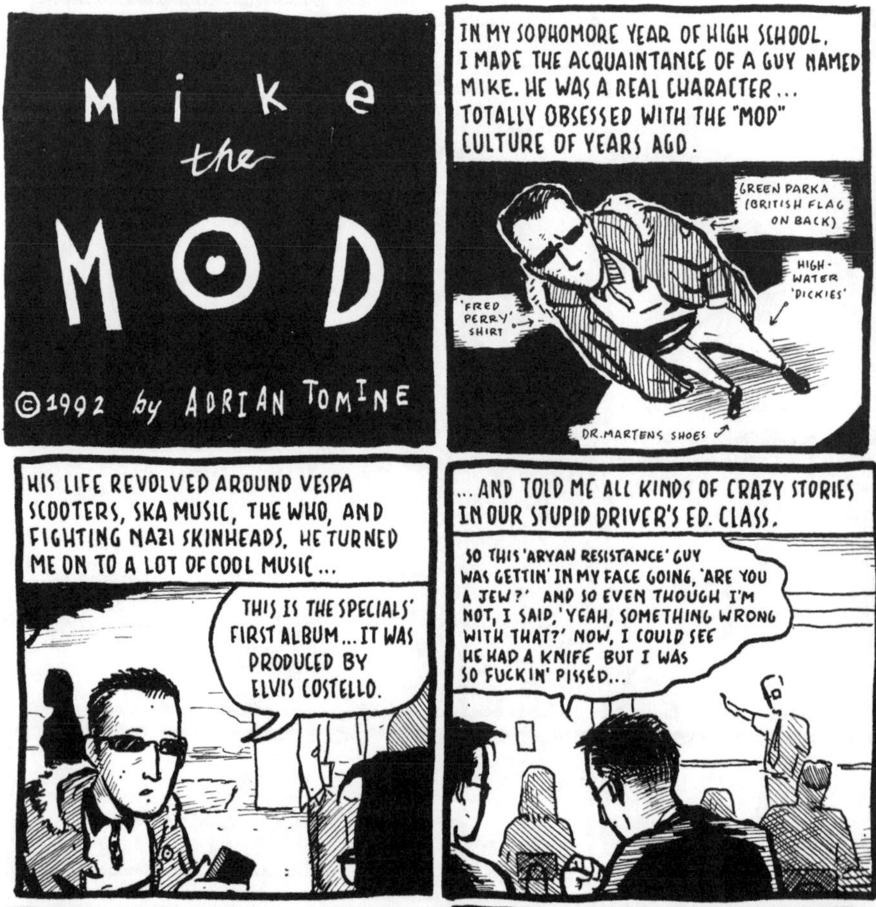
Mike the MOD
©1992 by ADRIAN TOMINE
IN MY SOPHOMORE YEAR OF HIGH SCHOOL, I MADE THE ACQUAINTANCE OF A GUY NAMED MIKE. HE WAS A REAL CHARACTER... TOTALLY OBSESSED WITH THE "MOD" CULTURE OF YEARS AGO.
GREEN PARKA (BRITISH FLAG ON BACK)
HIGH-WATER 'DICKIES'
'FRED PERRY' SHIRT
DR. MARTENS SHOES
HIS LIFE REVOLVED AROUND VESPA SCOOTERS, SKA MUSIC, THE WHO, AND FIGHTING NAZI SKINHEADS. HE TURNED ME ON TO A LOT OF COOL MUSIC...
THIS IS THE SPECIALS' FIRST ALBUM... IT WAS PRODUCED BY ELVIS COSTELLO.
...AND TOLD ME ALL KINDS OF CRAZY STORIES IN OUR STUPID DRIVER'S ED. CLASS.
SO THIS 'ARYAN RESISTANCE' GUY WAS GETTIN' IN MY FACE GOING, 'ARE YOU A JEW?' AND SO EVEN THOUGH I'M NOT, I SAID, 'YEAH, SOMETHING WRONG WITH THAT?' NOW, I COULD SEE HE HAD A KNIFE BUT I WAS SO FUCKIN' PISSED...
HE WAS A REALLY SMART GUY, BUT IT SEEMED LIKE HE SPENT MORE TIME IN THE OFFICE THAN IN CLASS.
THE VICE-PRINCIPAL WOULD LIKE TO SEE YOU, MIKE.
FINE.
THEN ONE DAY, I SAW HIM EMPTYING OUT HIS LOCKER.
WELL, I'M OUTTA HERE, MAN.
HUNH? WHAT DO YOU MEAN?

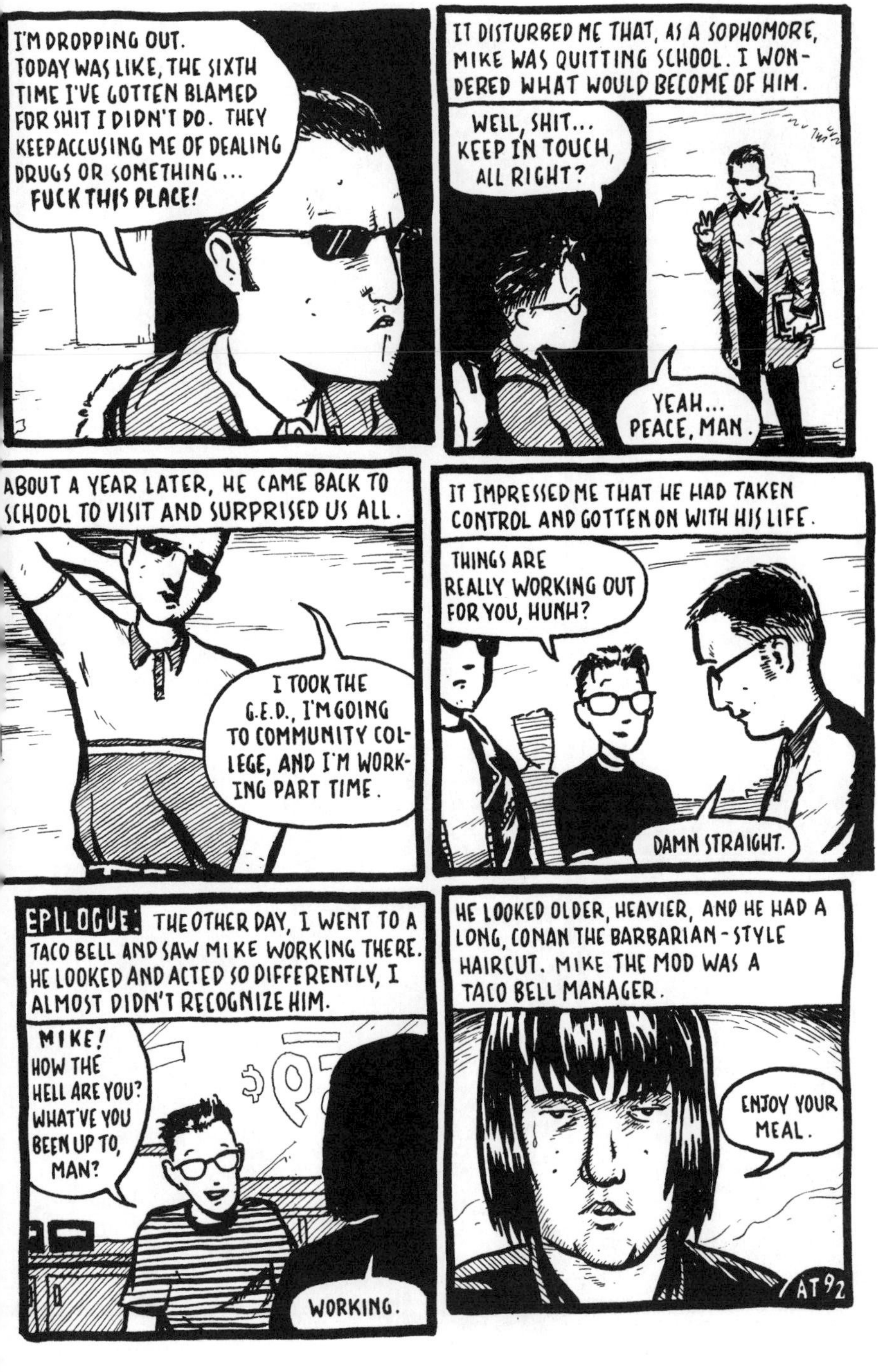
I'M DROPPING OUT. TODAY WAS LIKE, THE SIXTH TIME I'VE GOTTEN BLAMED FOR SHIT I DIDN'T DO. THEY KEEPACCUSING ME OF DEALING DRUGS OR SOMETHING... FUCK THIS PLACE!
IT DISTURBED ME THAT, AS A SOPHOMORE, MIKE WAS QUITTING SCHOOL. I WONDERED WHAT WOULD BECOME OF HIM.
WELL, SHIT... KEEP IN TOUCH, ALL RIGHT?
YEAH... PEACE, MAN.
ABOUT A YEAR LATER, HE CAME BACK TO SCHOOL TO VISIT AND SURPRISED US ALL.
I TOOK THE G.E.D., I'M GOING TO COMMUNITY COLLEGE, AND I'M WORKING PART TIME.
IT IMPRESSED ME THAT HE HAD TAKEN CONTROL AND GOTTEN ON WITH HIS LIFE.
THINGS ARE REALLY WORKING OUT FOR YOU, HUNH?
DAMN STRAIGHT.
EPILOGUE: THE OTHER DAY, I WENT TO A TACO BELL AND SAW MIKE WORKING THERE. HE LOOKED AND ACTED SO DIFFERENTLY, I ALMOST DIDN'T RECOGNIZE HIM.
MIKE! HOW THE HELL ARE YOU? WHAT'VE YOU BEEN UP TO, MAN?
WORKING.
HE LOOKED OLDER, HEAVIER, AND HE HAD A LONG, CONAN THE BARBARIAN-STYLE HAIRCUT. MIKE THE MOD WAS A TACO BELL MANAGER.
ENJOY YOUR MEAL.
AT 92

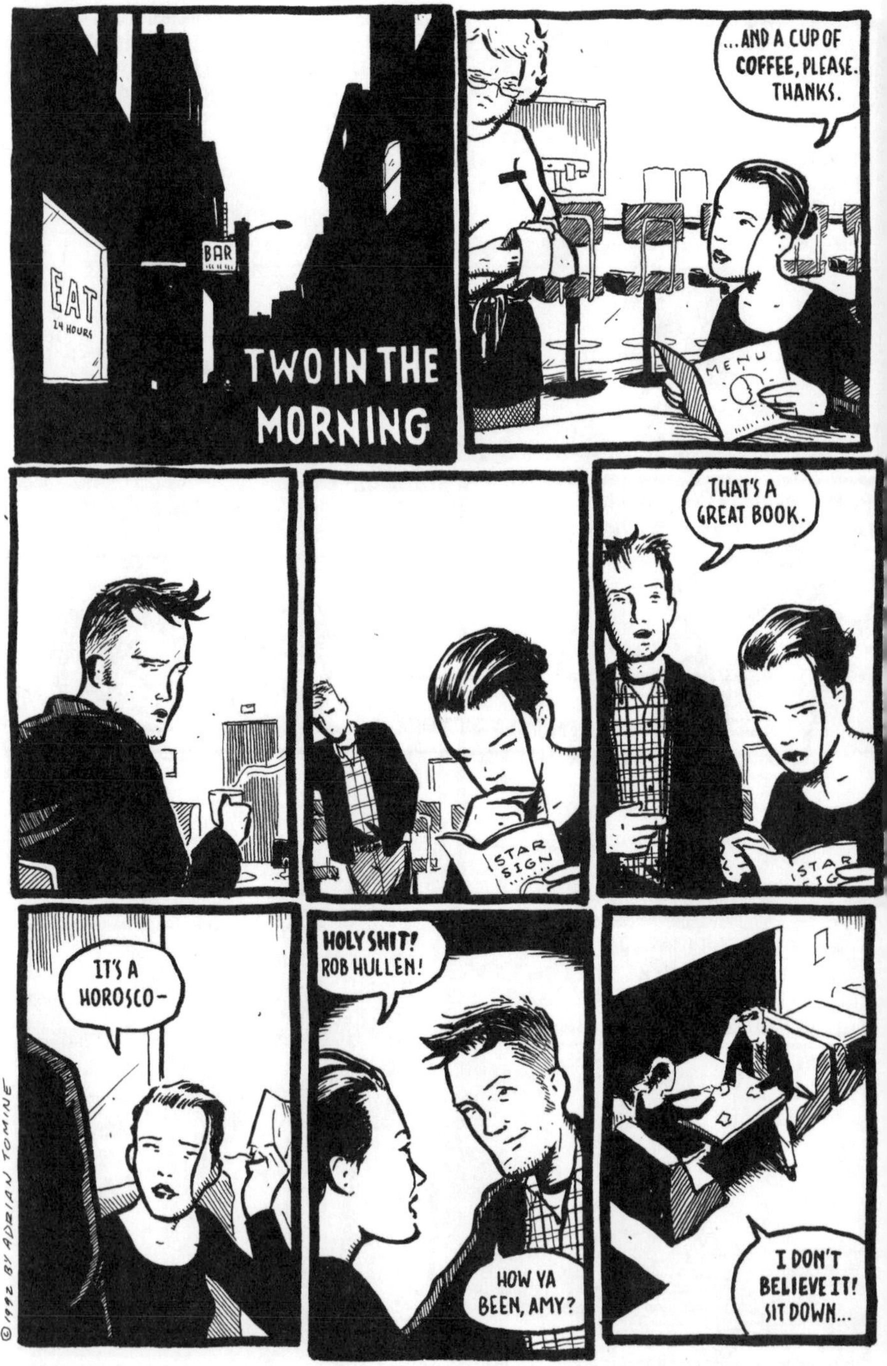
EAT
24 HOURS
BAR
TWO IN THE MORNING
...AND A CUP OF COFFEE, PLEASE. THANKS.
MENU
THAT'S A GREAT BOOK.
STAR SIGN
IT'S A HOROSCO-
HOLY SHIT! ROB HULLEN!
HOW YA BEEN, AMY?
I DON'T BELIEVE IT! SIT DOWN...
©1992 BY ADRIAN TOMINE

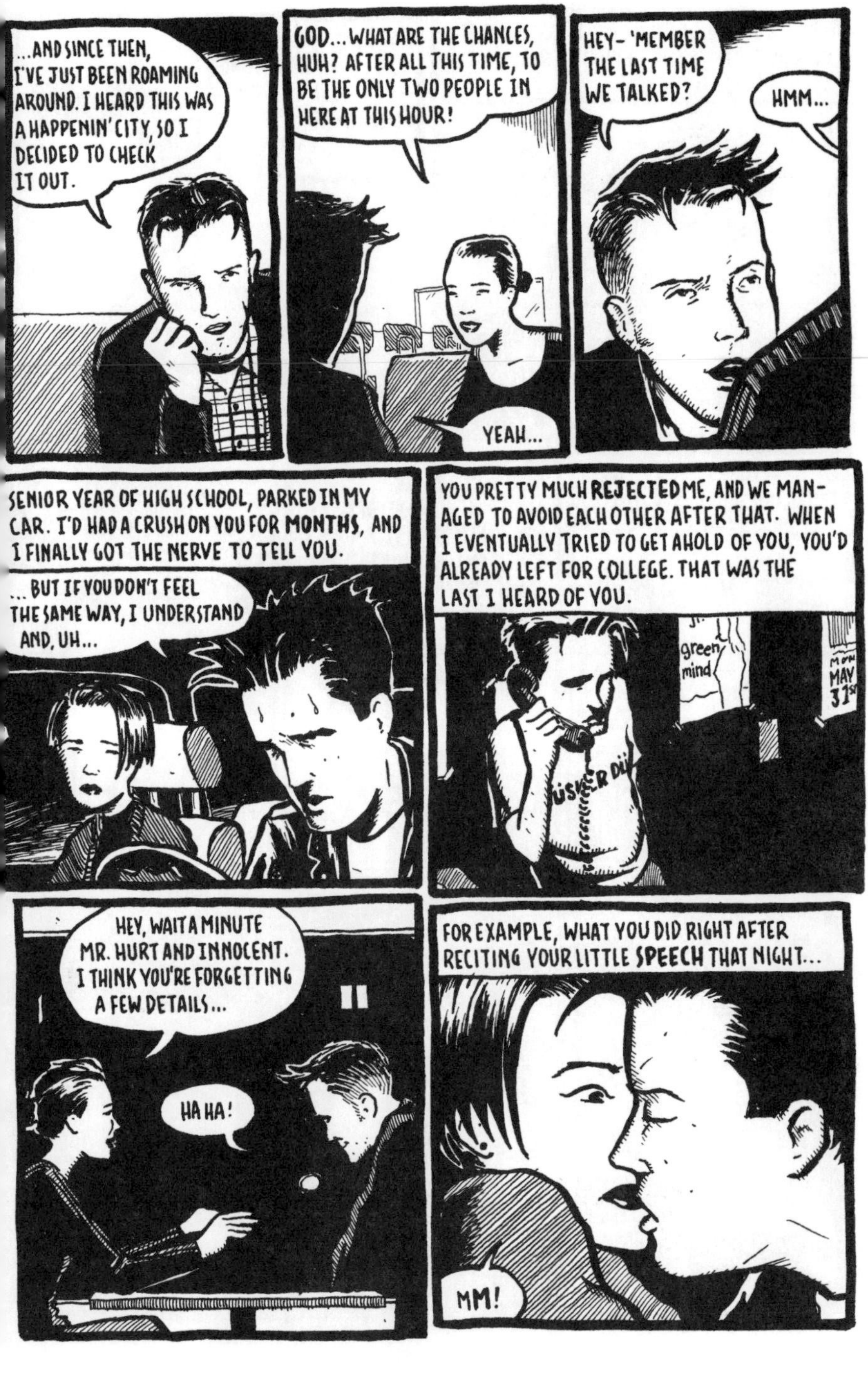
...AND SINCE THEN, I'VE JUST BEEN ROAMING AROUND. I HEARD THIS WAS A HAPPENIN' CITY, SO I DECIDED TO CHECK IT OUT.
GOD... WHAT ARE THE CHANCES, HUH? AFTER ALL THIS TIME, TO BE THE ONLY TWO PEOPLE IN HERE AT THIS HOUR!
YEAH...
HEY- 'MEMBER THE LAST TIME WE TALKED?
HMM...
SENIOR YEAR OF HIGH SCHOOL, PARKED IN MY CAR. I'D HAD A CRUSH ON YOU FOR MONTHS, AND I FINALLY GOT THE NERVE TO TELL YOU.
... BUT IF YOU DON'T FEEL THE SAME WAY, I UNDERSTAND AND, UH...
YOU PRETTY MUCH REJECTED ME, AND WE MANAGED TO AVOID EACH OTHER AFTER THAT. WHEN I EVENTUALLY TRIED TO GET AHOLD OF YOU, YOU'D ALREADY LEFT FOR COLLEGE. THAT WAS THE LAST I HEARD OF YOU.
green mind
MAY 31st
HEY, WAIT A MINUTE MR. HURT AND INNOCENT. I THINK YOU'RE FORGETTING A FEW DETAILS...
HA HA!
FOR EXAMPLE, WHAT YOU DID RIGHT AFTER RECITING YOUR LITTLE SPEECH THAT NIGHT...
MM!

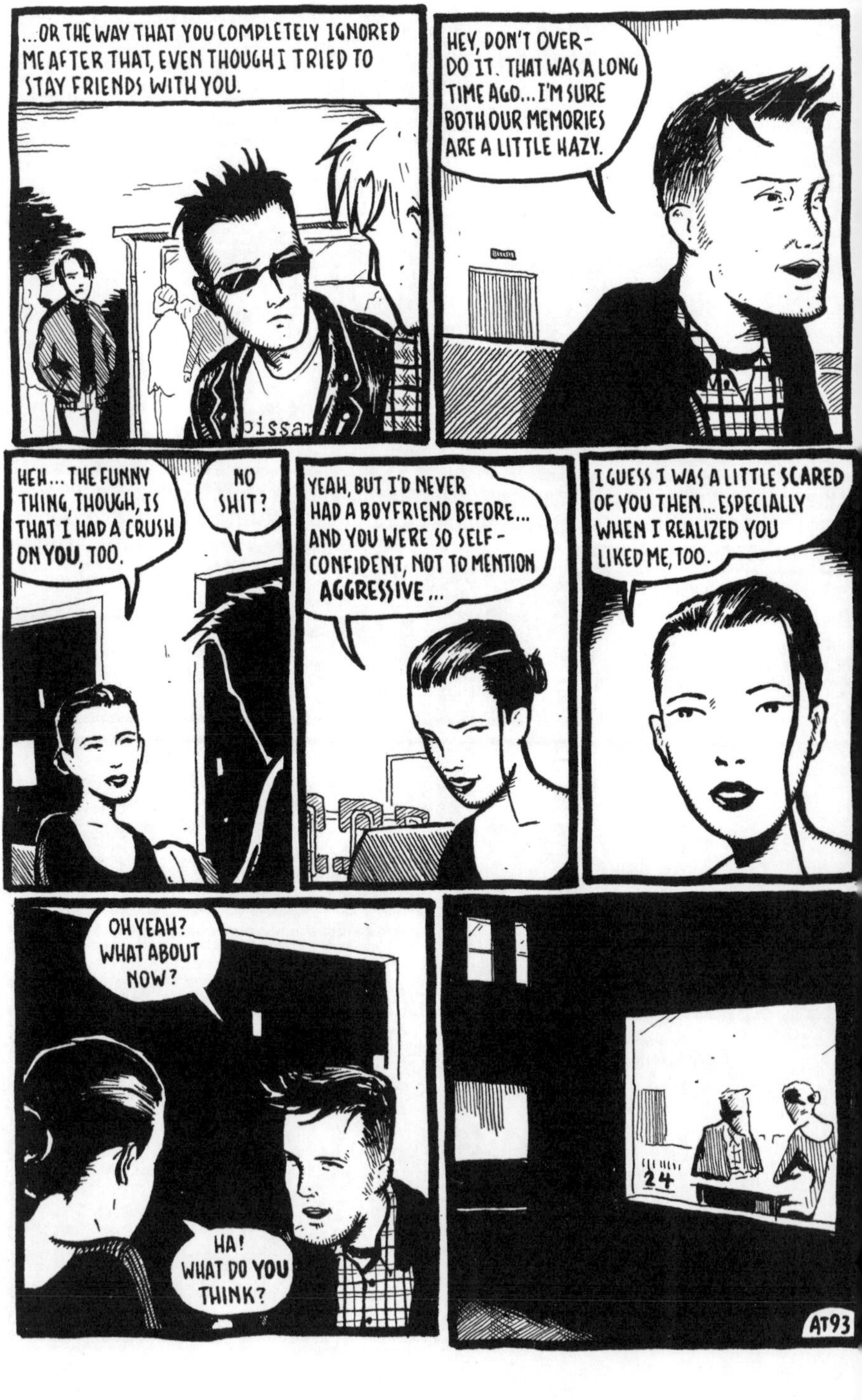
...OR THE WAY THAT YOU COMPLETELY IGNORED ME AFTER THAT, EVEN THOUGH I TRIED TO STAY FRIENDS WITH YOU.
HEY, DON'T OVER-DO IT. THAT WAS A LONG TIME AGO...I'M SURE BOTH OUR MEMORIES ARE A LITTLE HAZY.
HEH... THE FUNNY THING, THOUGH, IS THAT I HAD A CRUSH ON YOU, TOO.
NO SHIT?
YEAH, BUT I'D NEVER HAD A BOYFRIEND BEFORE... AND YOU WERE SO SELF-CONFIDENT, NOT TO MENTION AGGRESSIVE...
I GUESS I WAS A LITTLE SCARED OF YOU THEN... ESPECIALLY WHEN I REALIZED YOU LIKED ME, TOO.
OH YEAH? WHAT ABOUT NOW?
HA! WHAT DO YOU THINK?
24
AT93

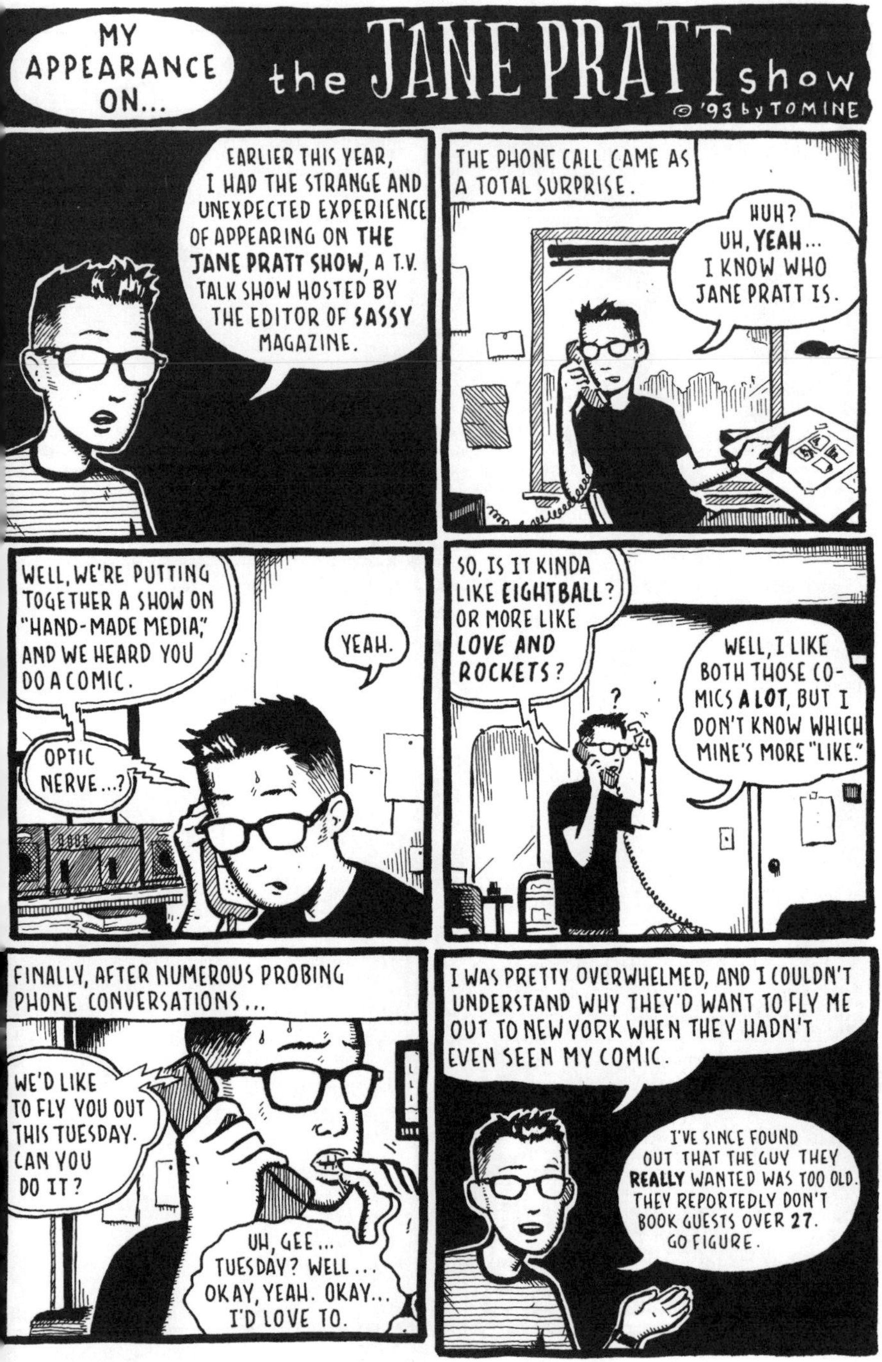
MY APPEARANCE ON...
the JANE PRATT show
© '93 by TOMINE
EARLIER THIS YEAR, I HAD THE STRANGE AND UNEXPECTED EXPERIENCE OF APPEARING ON THE JANE PRATT SHOW, A T.V. TALK SHOW HOSTED BY THE EDITOR OF SASSY MAGAZINE.
THE PHONE CALL CAME AS A TOTAL SURPRISE.
HUH? UH, YEAH... I KNOW WHO JANE PRATT IS.
WELL, WE'RE PUTTING TOGETHER A SHOW ON "HAND-MADE MEDIA," AND WE HEARD YOU DO A COMIC.
YEAH.
OPTIC NERVE...?
SO, IS IT KINDA LIKE EIGHTBALL? OR MORE LIKE LOVE AND ROCKETS?
?
WELL, I LIKE BOTH THOSE COMICS A LOT, BUT I DON'T KNOW WHICH MINE'S MORE "LIKE."
FINALLY, AFTER NUMEROUS PROBING PHONE CONVERSATIONS...
WE'D LIKE TO FLY YOU OUT THIS TUESDAY. CAN YOU DO IT?
UH, GEE... TUESDAY? WELL... OKAY, YEAH. OKAY... I'D LOVE TO.
I WAS PRETTY OVERWHELMED, AND I COULDN'T UNDERSTAND WHY THEY'D WANT TO FLY ME OUT TO NEW YORK WHEN THEY HADN'T EVEN SEEN MY COMIC.
I'VE SINCE FOUND OUT THAT THE GUY THEY REALLY WANTED WAS TOO OLD. THEY REPORTEDLY DON'T BOOK GUESTS OVER 27. GO FIGURE.

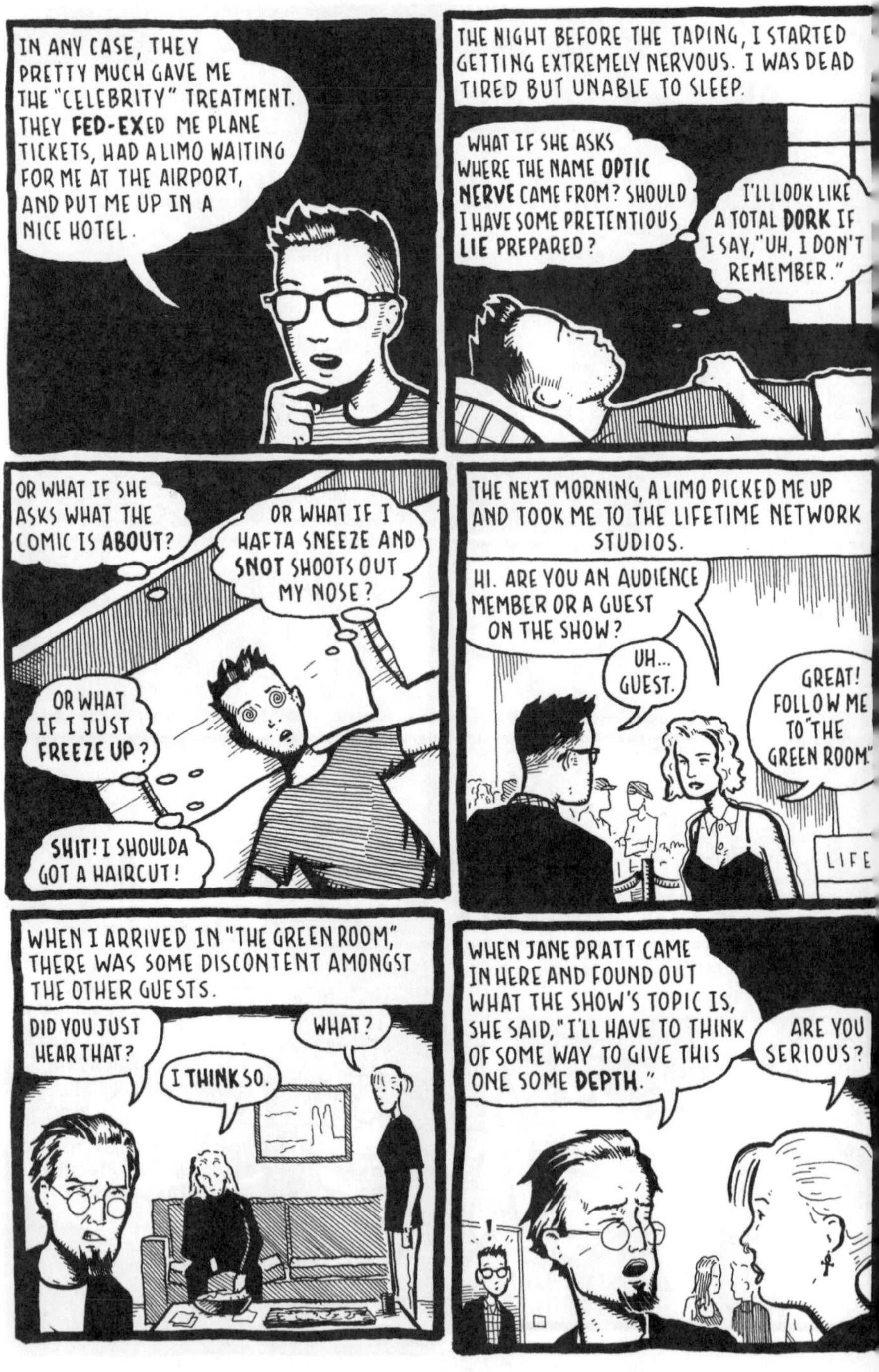
IN ANY CASE, THEY PRETTY MUCH GAVE ME THE "CELEBRITY" TREATMENT. THEY FED-EXED ME PLANE TICKETS, HAD A LIMO WAITING FOR ME AT THE AIRPORT, AND PUT ME UP IN A NICE HOTEL.
THE NIGHT BEFORE THE TAPING, I STARTED GETTING EXTREMELY NERVOUS. I WAS DEAD TIRED BUT UNABLE TO SLEEP.
WHAT IF SHE ASKS WHERE THE NAME OPTIC NERVE CAME FROM? SHOULD I HAVE SOME PRETENTIOUS LIE PREPARED?
I'LL LOOK LIKE A TOTAL DORK IF I SAY, "UH, I DON'T REMEMBER."
OR WHAT IF SHE ASKS WHAT THE COMIC IS ABOUT?
OR WHAT IF I HAFTA SNEEZE AND SNOT SHOOTS OUT MY NOSE?
OR WHAT IF I JUST FREEZE UP?
SHIT! I SHOULDA GOT A HAIRCUT!
THE NEXT MORNING, A LIMO PICKED ME UP AND TOOK ME TO THE LIFETIME NETWORK STUDIOS.
HI. ARE YOU AN AUDIENCE MEMBER OR A GUEST ON THE SHOW?
UH... GUEST.
GREAT! FOLLOW ME TO "THE GREEN ROOM."
LIFE
WHEN I ARRIVED IN "THE GREEN ROOM," THERE WAS SOME DISCONTENT AMONGST THE OTHER GUESTS.
DID YOU JUST HEAR THAT?
WHAT?
I THINK SO.
WHEN JANE PRATT CAME IN HERE AND FOUND OUT WHAT THE SHOW'S TOPIC IS, SHE SAID, "I'LL HAVE TO THINK OF SOME WAY TO GIVE THIS ONE SOME DEPTH."
ARE YOU SERIOUS?
!

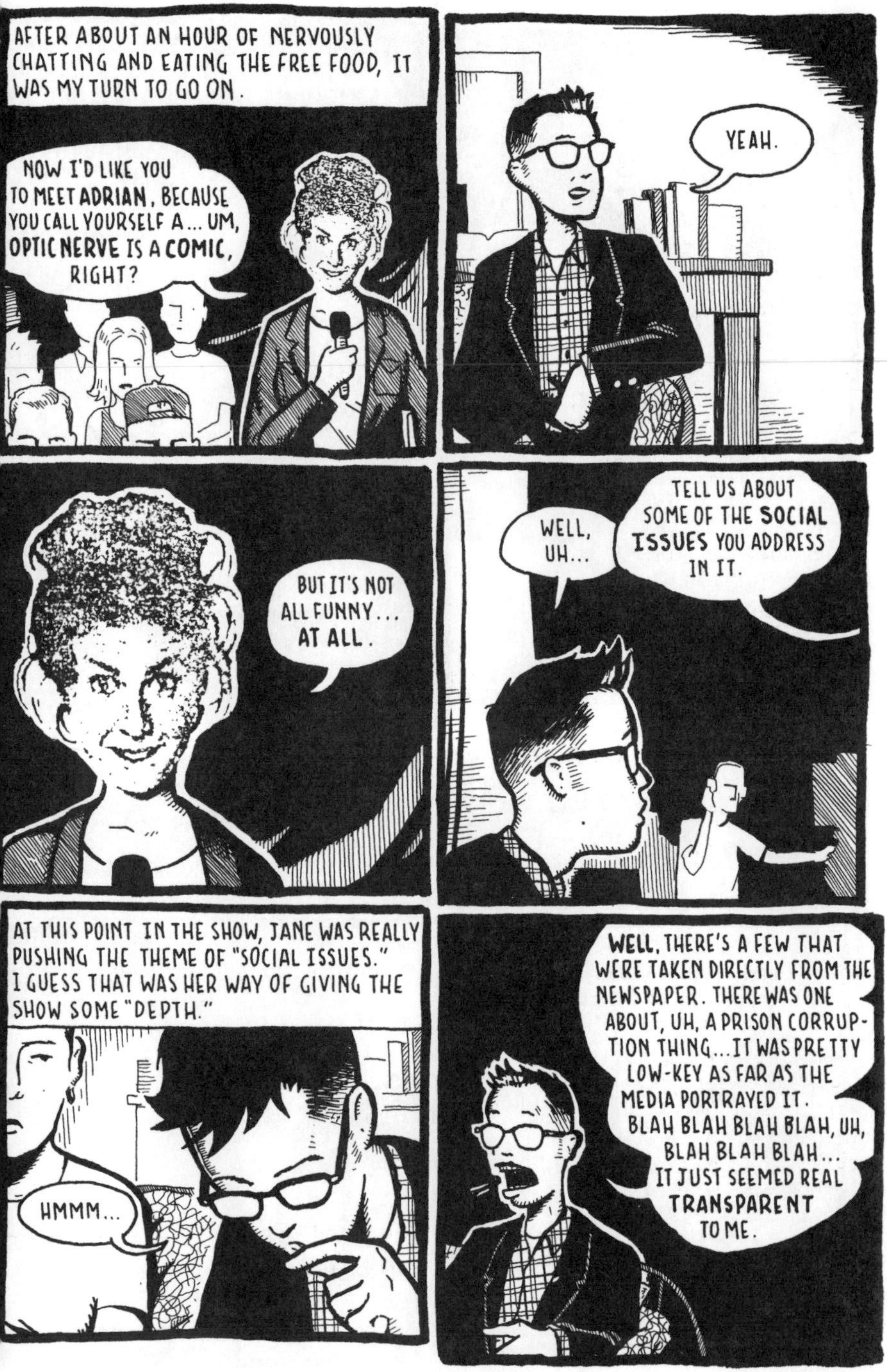

AFTER ABOUT AN HOUR OF NERVOUSLY CHATTING AND EATING THE FREE FOOD, IT WAS MY TURN TO GO ON.
NOW I'D LIKE YOU TO MEET ADRIAN, BECAUSE YOU CALL YOURSELF A... UM, OPTIC NERVE IS A COMIC, RIGHT?
YEAH.
BUT IT'S NOT ALL FUNNY... AT ALL.
TELL US ABOUT SOME OF THE SOCIAL ISSUES YOU ADDRESS IN IT.
WELL, UH...
AT THIS POINT IN THE SHOW, JANE WAS REALLY PUSHING THE THEME OF "SOCIAL ISSUES." I GUESS THAT WAS HER WAY OF GIVING THE SHOW SOME "DEPTH."
HMMM...
WELL, THERE'S A FEW THAT WERE TAKEN DIRECTLY FROM THE NEWSPAPER. THERE WAS ONE ABOUT, UH, A PRISON CORRUPTION THING... IT WAS PRETTY LOW-KEY AS FAR AS THE MEDIA PORTRAYED IT. BLAH BLAH BLAH BLAH, UH, BLAH BLAH BLAH... IT JUST SEEMED REAL TRANSPARENT TO ME.

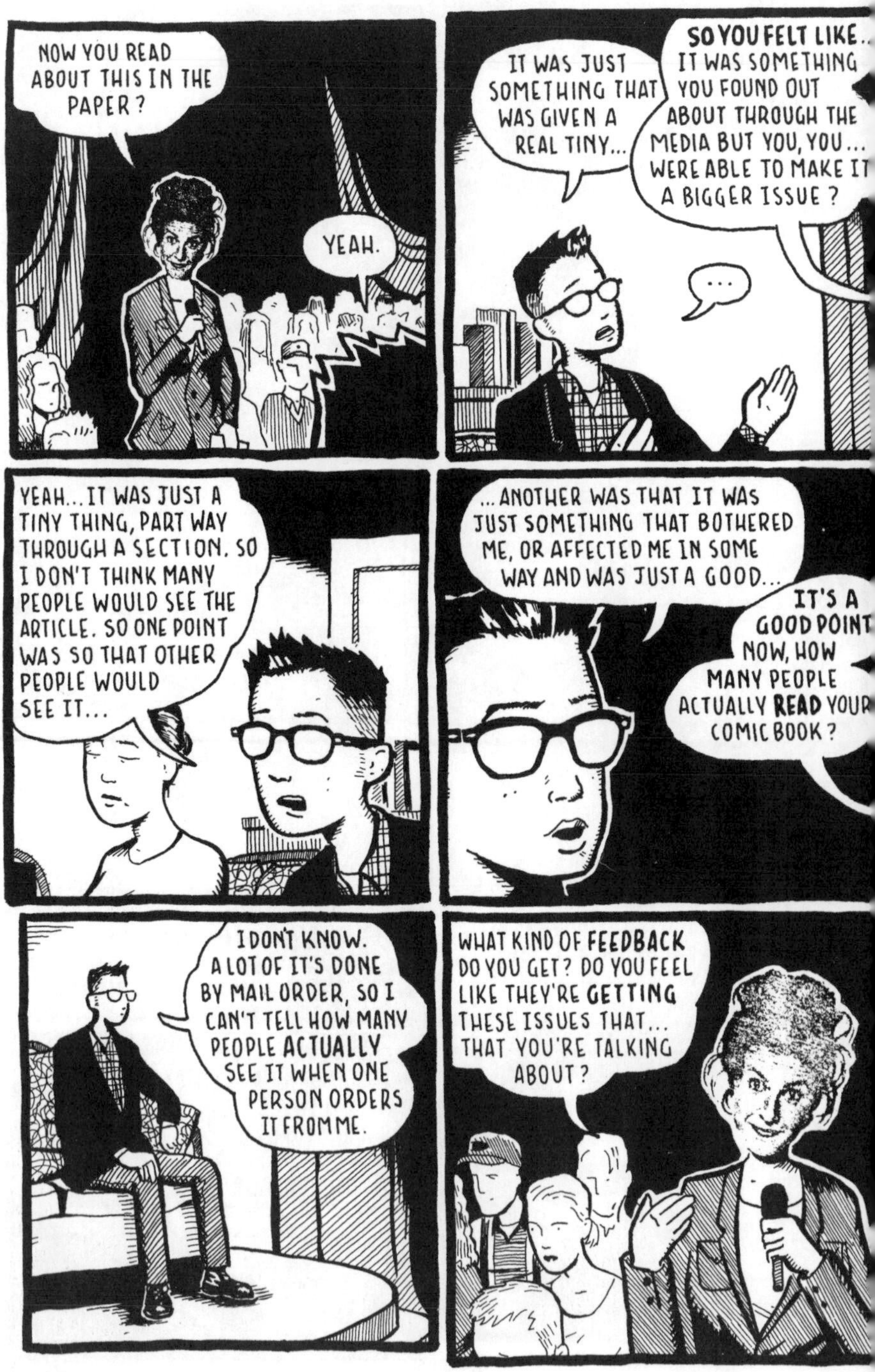
NOW YOU READ ABOUT THIS IN THE PAPER?
YEAH.
IT WAS JUST SOMETHING THAT WAS GIVEN A REAL TINY...
SO YOU FELT LIKE... IT WAS SOMETHING YOU FOUND OUT ABOUT THROUGH THE MEDIA BUT YOU, YOU... WERE ABLE TO MAKE IT A BIGGER ISSUE?
...
YEAH... IT WAS JUST A TINY THING, PART WAY THROUGH A SECTION. SO I DON'T THINK MANY PEOPLE WOULD SEE THE ARTICLE. SO ONE POINT WAS SO THAT OTHER PEOPLE WOULD SEE IT...
...ANOTHER WAS THAT IT WAS JUST SOMETHING THAT BOTHERED ME, OR AFFECTED ME IN SOME WAY AND WAS JUST A GOOD...
IT'S A GOOD POINT NOW, HOW MANY PEOPLE ACTUALLY READ YOUR COMIC BOOK?
I DON'T KNOW. A LOT OF IT'S DONE BY MAIL ORDER, SO I CAN'T TELL HOW MANY PEOPLE ACTUALLY SEE IT WHEN ONE PERSON ORDERS IT FROM ME.
WHAT KIND OF FEEDBACK DO YOU GET? DO YOU FEEL LIKE THEY'RE GETTING THESE ISSUES THAT... THAT YOU'RE TALKING ABOUT?

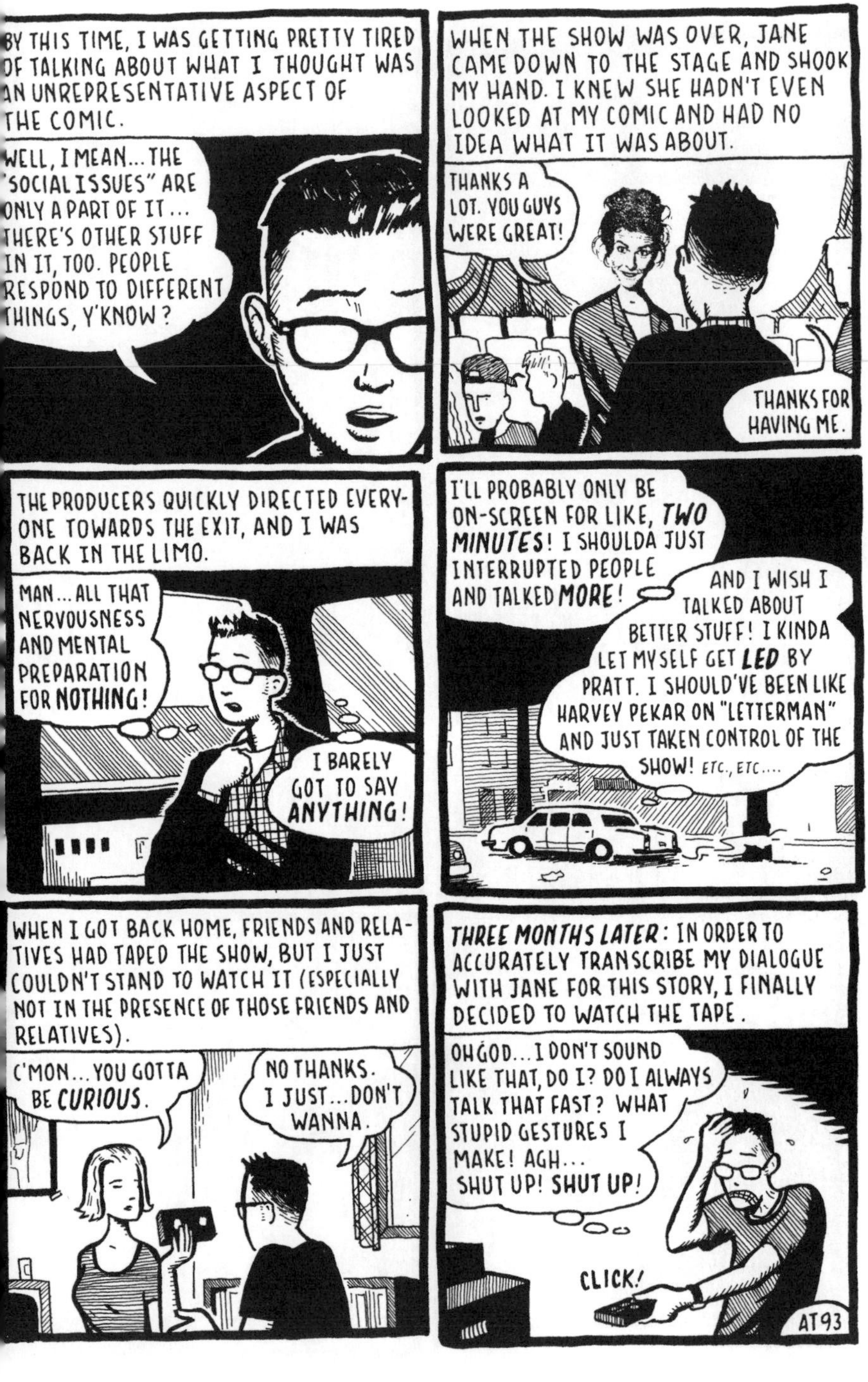
BY THIS TIME, I WAS GETTING PRETTY TIRED OF TALKING ABOUT WHAT I THOUGHT WAS AN UNREPRESENTATIVE ASPECT OF THE COMIC.
WELL, I MEAN... THE "SOCIAL ISSUES" ARE ONLY A PART OF IT... THERE'S OTHER STUFF IN IT, TOO. PEOPLE RESPOND TO DIFFERENT THINGS, Y'KNOW?
WHEN THE SHOW WAS OVER, JANE CAME DOWN TO THE STAGE AND SHOOK MY HAND. I KNEW SHE HADN'T EVEN LOOKED AT MY COMIC AND HAD NO IDEA WHAT IT WAS ABOUT.
THANKS A LOT. YOU GUYS WERE GREAT!
THANKS FOR HAVING ME.
THE PRODUCERS QUICKLY DIRECTED EVERYONE TOWARDS THE EXIT, AND I WAS BACK IN THE LIMO.
MAN... ALL THAT NERVOUSNESS AND MENTAL PREPARATION FOR NOTHING!
I BARELY GOT TO SAY ANYTHING!
I'LL PROBABLY ONLY BE ON-SCREEN FOR LIKE, TWO MINUTES! I SHOULDA JUST INTERRUPTED PEOPLE AND TALKED MORE!
AND I WISH I TALKED ABOUT BETTER STUFF! I KINDA LET MYSELF GET LED BY PRATT. I SHOULD'VE BEEN LIKE HARVEY PEKAR ON "LETTERMAN" AND JUST TAKEN CONTROL OF THE SHOW! ETC., ETC....
WHEN I GOT BACK HOME, FRIENDS AND RELATIVES HAD TAPED THE SHOW, BUT I JUST COULDN'T STAND TO WATCH IT (ESPECIALLY NOT IN THE PRESENCE OF THOSE FRIENDS AND RELATIVES).
C'MON... YOU GOTTA BE CURIOUS.
NO THANKS. I JUST... DON'T WANNA.
THREE MONTHS LATER: IN ORDER TO ACCURATELY TRANSCRIBE MY DIALOGUE WITH JANE FOR THIS STORY, I FINALLY DECIDED TO WATCH THE TAPE.
OH GOD... I DON'T SOUND LIKE THAT, DO I? DO I ALWAYS TALK THAT FAST? WHAT STUPID GESTURES I MAKE! AGH... SHUT UP! SHUT UP!
CLICK!
AT93

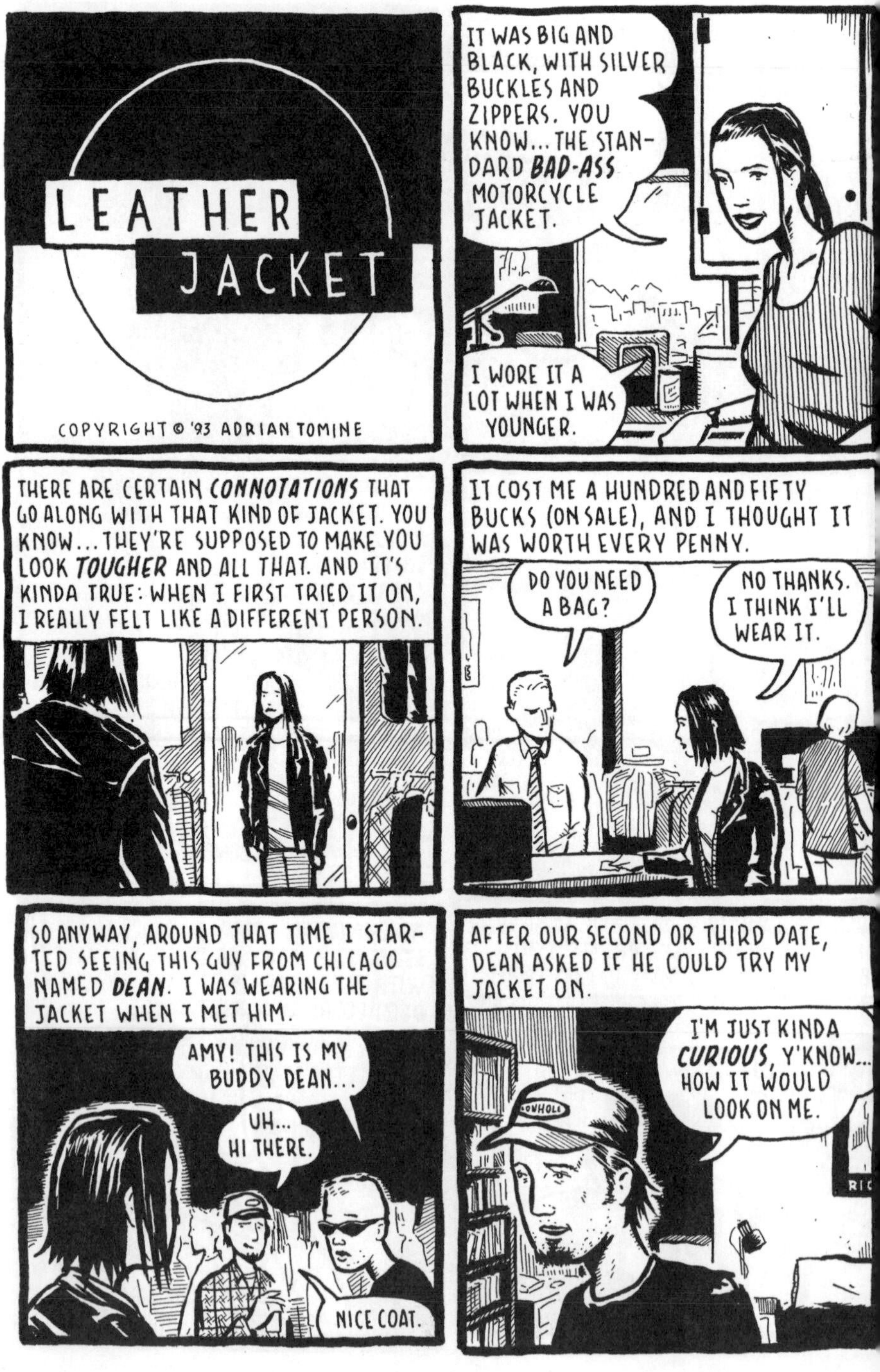
LEATHER JACKET
COPYRIGHT © '93 ADRIAN TOMINE
IT WAS BIG AND BLACK, WITH SILVER BUCKLES AND ZIPPERS. YOU KNOW... THE STANDARD BAD-ASS MOTORCYCLE JACKET.
I WORE IT A LOT WHEN I WAS YOUNGER.
THERE ARE CERTAIN CONNOTATIONS THAT GO ALONG WITH THAT KIND OF JACKET. YOU KNOW... THEY'RE SUPPOSED TO MAKE YOU LOOK TOUGHER AND ALL THAT. AND IT'S KINDA TRUE: WHEN I FIRST TRIED IT ON, I REALLY FELT LIKE A DIFFERENT PERSON.
IT COST ME A HUNDRED AND FIFTY BUCKS (ON SALE), AND I THOUGHT IT WAS WORTH EVERY PENNY.
DO YOU NEED A BAG?
NO THANKS. I THINK I'LL WEAR IT.
SO ANYWAY, AROUND THAT TIME I STARTED SEEING THIS GUY FROM CHICAGO NAMED DEAN. I WAS WEARING THE JACKET WHEN I MET HIM.
AMY! THIS IS MY BUDDY DEAN...
UH... HI THERE.
NICE COAT.
AFTER OUR SECOND OR THIRD DATE, DEAN ASKED IF HE COULD TRY MY JACKET ON.
I'M JUST KINDA CURIOUS, Y'KNOW... HOW IT WOULD LOOK ON ME.

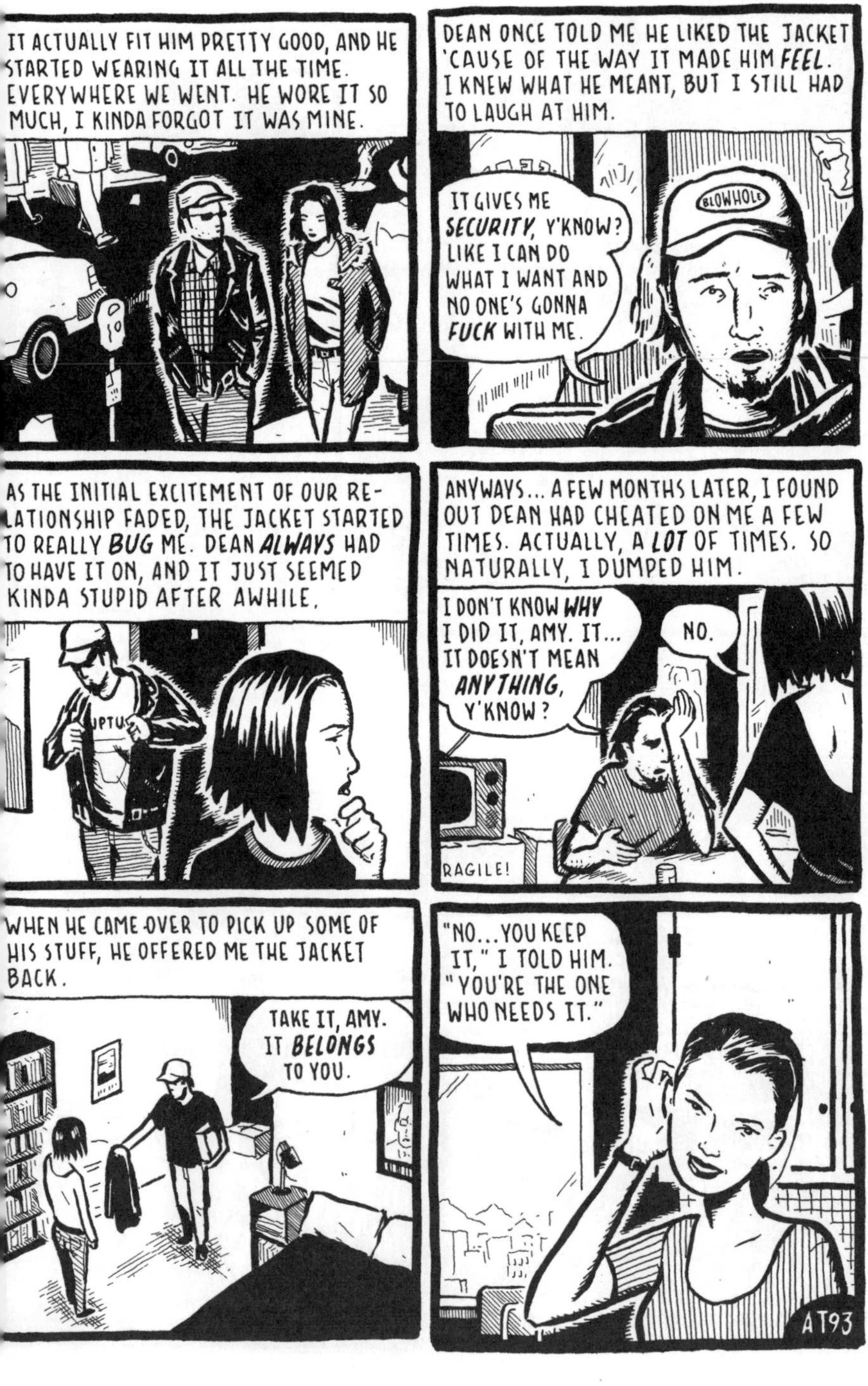
IT ACTUALLY FIT HIM PRETTY GOOD, AND HE STARTED WEARING IT ALL THE TIME. EVERYWHERE WE WENT. HE WORE IT SO MUCH, I KINDA FORGOT IT WAS MINE.
DEAN ONCE TOLD ME HE LIKED THE JACKET 'CAUSE OF THE WAY IT MADE HIM FEEL. I KNEW WHAT HE MEANT, BUT I STILL HAD TO LAUGH AT HIM.
IT GIVES ME SECURITY, Y'KNOW? LIKE I CAN DO WHAT I WANT AND NO ONE'S GONNA FUCK WITH ME.
BLOWHOLE
AS THE INITIAL EXCITEMENT OF OUR RELATIONSHIP FADED, THE JACKET STARTED TO REALLY BUG ME. DEAN ALWAYS HAD TO HAVE IT ON, AND IT JUST SEEMED KINDA STUPID AFTER AWHILE.
ANYWAYS... A FEW MONTHS LATER, I FOUND OUT DEAN HAD CHEATED ON ME A FEW TIMES. ACTUALLY, A LOT OF TIMES. SO NATURALLY, I DUMPED HIM.
I DON'T KNOW WHY I DID IT, AMY. IT... IT DOESN'T MEAN ANYTHING, Y'KNOW?
NO.
RAGILE!
WHEN HE CAME OVER TO PICK UP SOME OF HIS STUFF, HE OFFERED ME THE JACKET BACK.
TAKE IT, AMY. IT BELONGS TO YOU.
"NO... YOU KEEP IT," I TOLD HIM. "YOU'RE THE ONE WHO NEEDS IT."
AT93

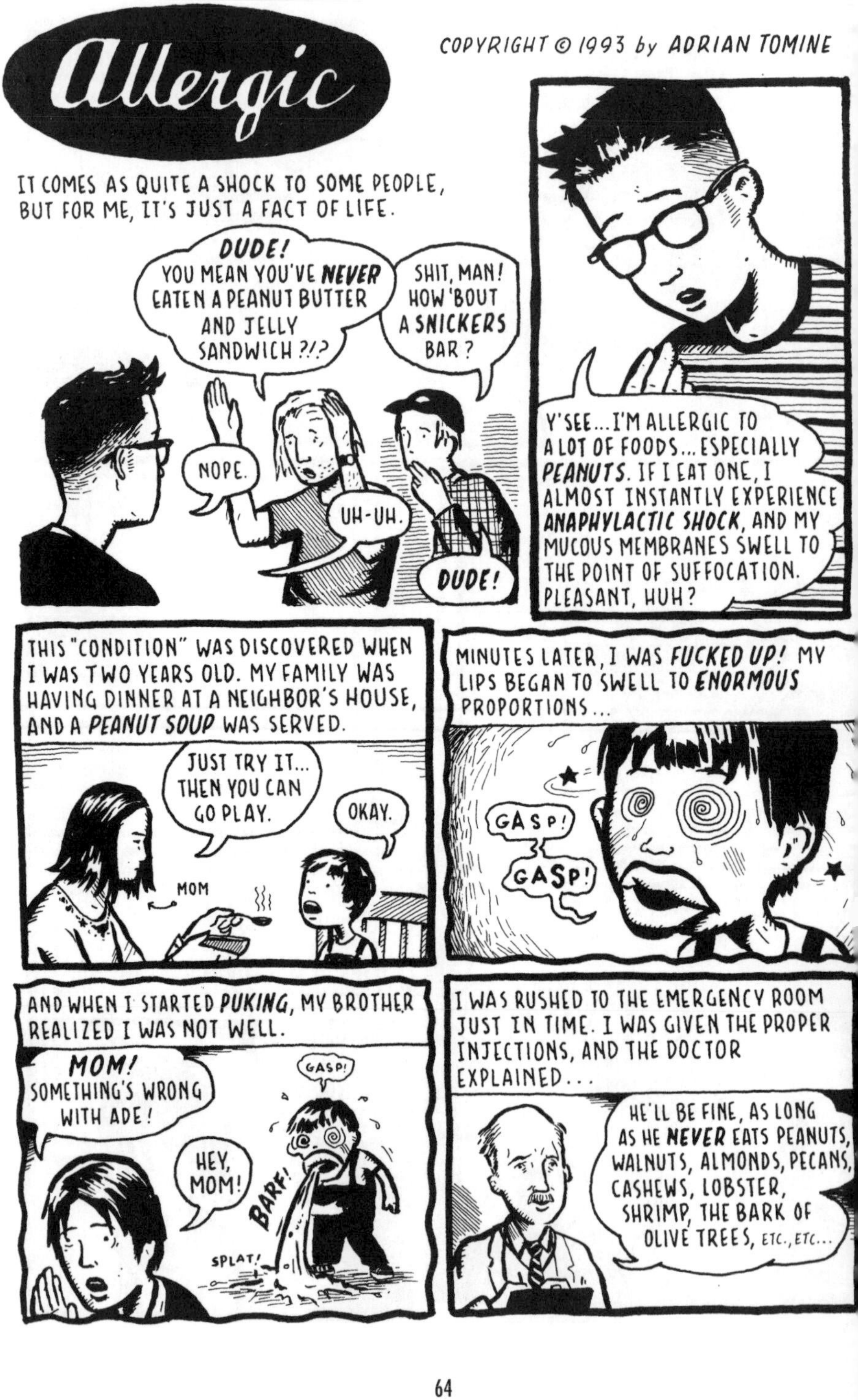
Allergic
COPYRIGHT © 1993 by ADRIAN TOMINE
IT COMES AS QUITE A SHOCK TO SOME PEOPLE, BUT FOR ME, IT'S JUST A FACT OF LIFE.
DUDE! YOU MEAN YOU'VE NEVER EATEN A PEANUT BUTTER AND JELLY SANDWICH ?!?
SHIT, MAN! HOW 'BOUT A SNICKERS BAR ?
NOPE.
UH-UH.
DUDE!
Y'SEE... I'M ALLERGIC TO A LOT OF FOODS... ESPECIALLY PEANUTS. IF I EAT ONE, I ALMOST INSTANTLY EXPERIENCE ANAPHYLACTIC SHOCK, AND MY MUCOUS MEMBRANES SWELL TO THE POINT OF SUFFOCATION. PLEASANT, HUH?
THIS "CONDITION" WAS DISCOVERED WHEN I WAS TWO YEARS OLD. MY FAMILY WAS HAVING DINNER AT A NEIGHBOR'S HOUSE, AND A PEANUT SOUP WAS SERVED.
JUST TRY IT... THEN YOU CAN GO PLAY.
OKAY.
MOM
MINUTES LATER, I WAS FUCKED UP! MY LIPS BEGAN TO SWELL TO ENORMOUS PROPORTIONS...
GASP!
GASP!
AND WHEN I STARTED PUKING, MY BROTHER REALIZED I WAS NOT WELL.
MOM! SOMETHING'S WRONG WITH ADE!
HEY, MOM!
GASP!
BARF!
SPLAT!
I WAS RUSHED TO THE EMERGENCY ROOM JUST IN TIME. I WAS GIVEN THE PROPER INJECTIONS, AND THE DOCTOR EXPLAINED...
HE'LL BE FINE, AS LONG AS HE NEVER EATS PEANUTS, WALNUTS, ALMONDS, PECANS, CASHEWS, LOBSTER, SHRIMP, THE BARK OF OLIVE TREES, ETC., ETC...

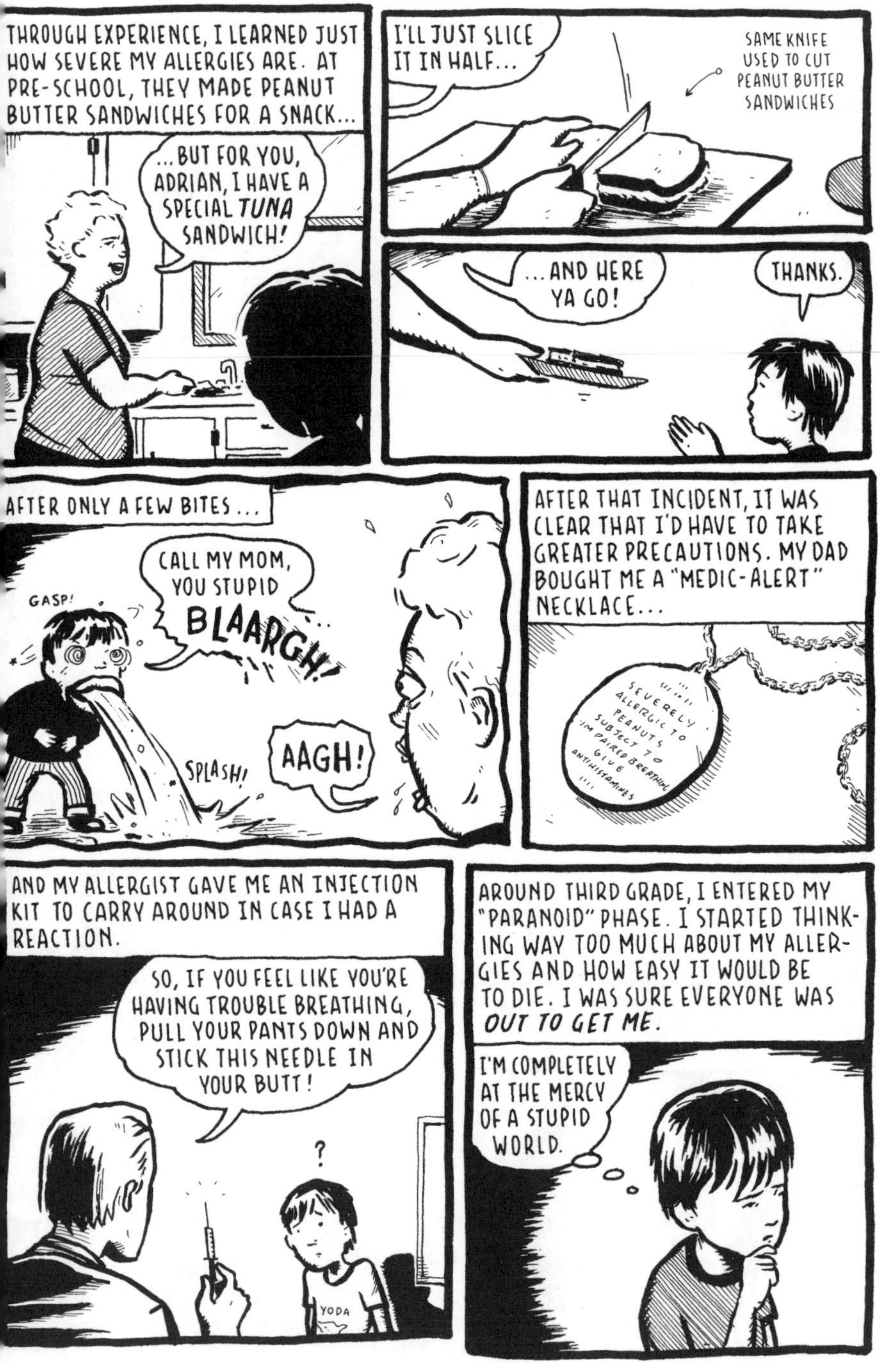
THROUGH EXPERIENCE, I LEARNED JUST HOW SEVERE MY ALLERGIES ARE. AT PRE-SCHOOL, THEY MADE PEANUT BUTTER SANDWICHES FOR A SNACK...
...BUT FOR YOU, ADRIAN, I HAVE A SPECIAL *TUNA* SANDWICH!
I'LL JUST SLICE IT IN HALF...
SAME KNIFE USED TO CUT PEANUT BUTTER SANDWICHES
...AND HERE YA GO!
THANKS.
AFTER ONLY A FEW BITES...
GASP!
CALL MY MOM, YOU STUPID
BLAARGH!
SPLASH!
AAGH!
AFTER THAT INCIDENT, IT WAS CLEAR THAT I'D HAVE TO TAKE GREATER PRECAUTIONS. MY DAD BOUGHT ME A "MEDIC-ALERT" NECKLACE...
SEVERELY ALLERGIC TO PEANUTS SUBJECT TO IMPAIRED BREATHING GIVE ANTIHISTAMINES
AND MY ALLERGIST GAVE ME AN INJECTION KIT TO CARRY AROUND IN CASE I HAD A REACTION.
SO, IF YOU FEEL LIKE YOU'RE HAVING TROUBLE BREATHING, PULL YOUR PANTS DOWN AND STICK THIS NEEDLE IN YOUR BUTT!
?
YODA
AROUND THIRD GRADE, I ENTERED MY "PARANOID" PHASE. I STARTED THINKING WAY TOO MUCH ABOUT MY ALLERGIES AND HOW EASY IT WOULD BE TO DIE. I WAS SURE EVERYONE WAS *OUT TO GET ME*.
I'M COMPLETELY AT THE MERCY OF A STUPID WORLD.

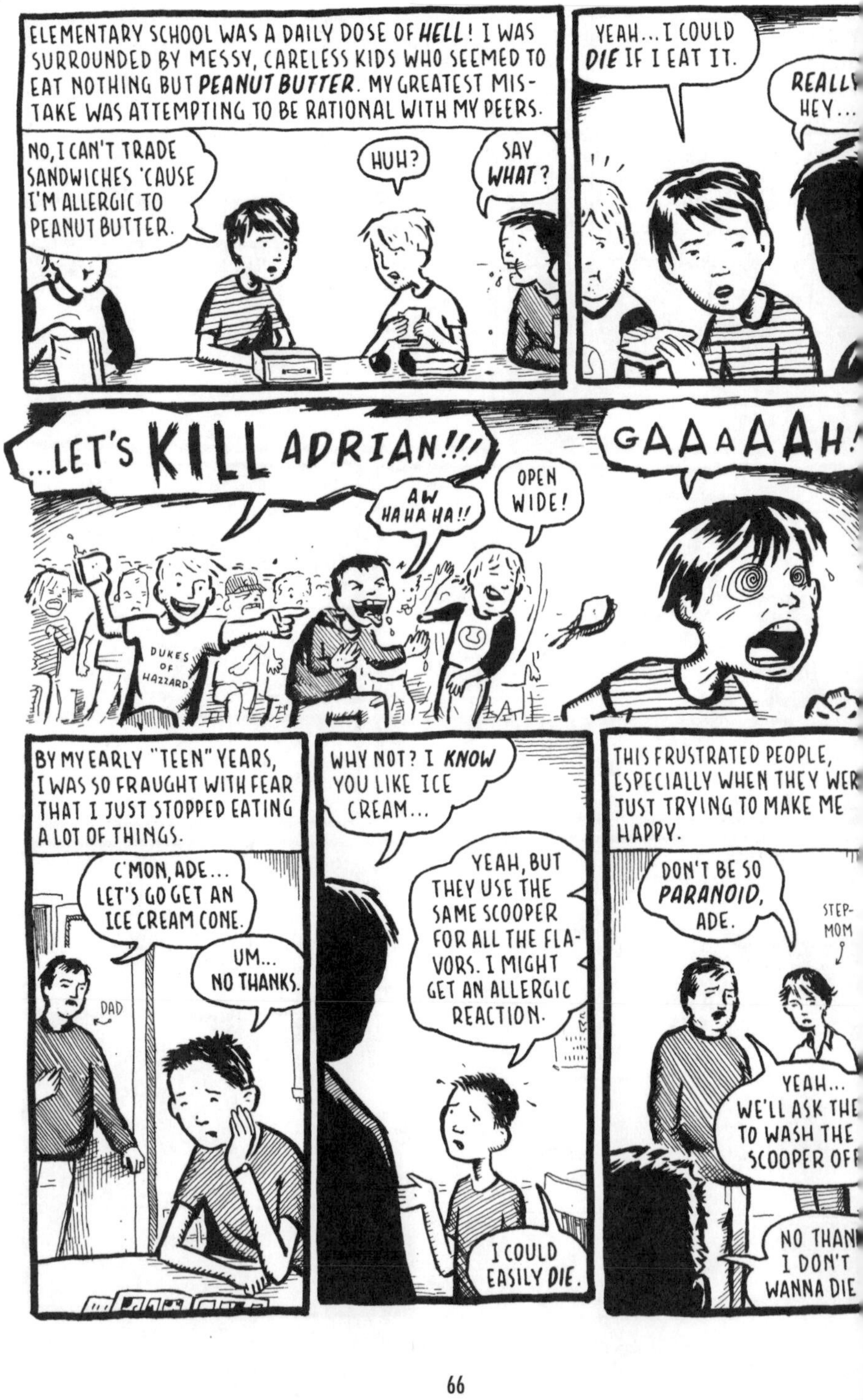
ELEMENTARY SCHOOL WAS A DAILY DOSE OF **HELL**! I WAS SURROUNDED BY MESSY, CARELESS KIDS WHO SEEMED TO EAT NOTHING BUT **PEANUT BUTTER**. MY GREATEST MISTAKE WAS ATTEMPTING TO BE RATIONAL WITH MY PEERS.
NO, I CAN'T TRADE SANDWICHES 'CAUSE I'M ALLERGIC TO PEANUT BUTTER.
HUH?
SAY **WHAT**?
YEAH... I COULD **DIE** IF I EAT IT.
REALL
HEY...
...LET'S KILL ADRIAN!!!
AW HA HA HA!!
OPEN WIDE!
DUKES OF HAZZARD
GAAAAAH!
BY MY EARLY "TEEN" YEARS, I WAS SO FRAUGHT WITH FEAR THAT I JUST STOPPED EATING A LOT OF THINGS.
C'MON, ADE... LET'S GO GET AN ICE CREAM CONE.
DAD
UM... NO THANKS.
WHY NOT? I **KNOW** YOU LIKE ICE CREAM...
YEAH, BUT THEY USE THE SAME SCOOPER FOR ALL THE FLAVORS. I MIGHT GET AN ALLERGIC REACTION.
I COULD EASILY **DIE**.
THIS FRUSTRATED PEOPLE, ESPECIALLY WHEN THEY WER JUST TRYING TO MAKE ME HAPPY.
DON'T BE SO **PARANOID**, ADE.
STEP-MOM
YEAH... WE'LL ASK THE TO WASH THE SCOOPER OF
NO THAN I DON'T WANNA DIE

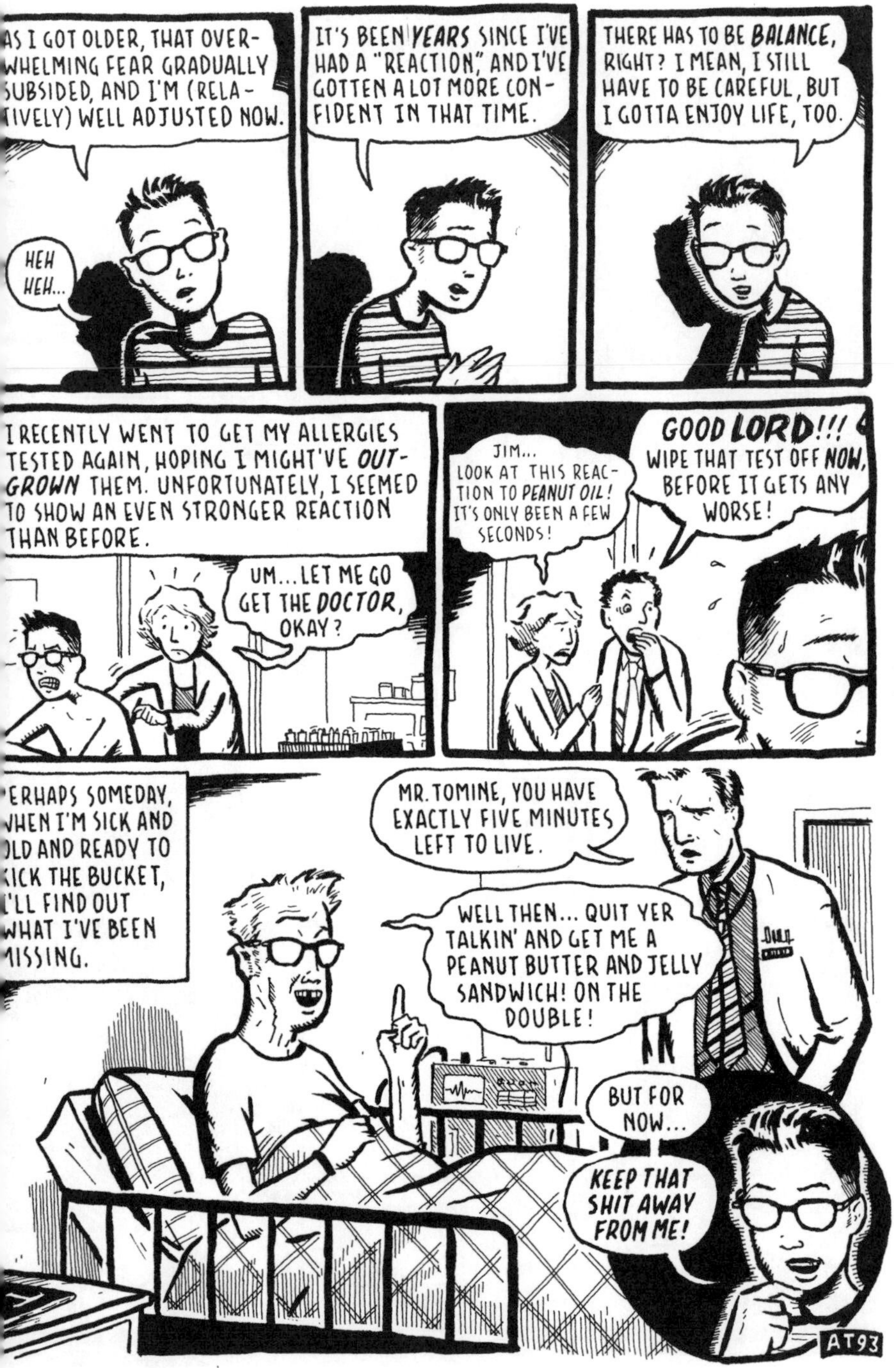
AS I GOT OLDER, THAT OVERWHELMING FEAR GRADUALLY SUBSIDED, AND I'M (RELATIVELY) WELL ADJUSTED NOW.
HEH HEH...
IT'S BEEN YEARS SINCE I'VE HAD A "REACTION," AND I'VE GOTTEN A LOT MORE CONFIDENT IN THAT TIME.
THERE HAS TO BE BALANCE, RIGHT? I MEAN, I STILL HAVE TO BE CAREFUL, BUT I GOTTA ENJOY LIFE, TOO.
I RECENTLY WENT TO GET MY ALLERGIES TESTED AGAIN, HOPING I MIGHT'VE OUTGROWN THEM. UNFORTUNATELY, I SEEMED TO SHOW AN EVEN STRONGER REACTION THAN BEFORE.
UM... LET ME GO GET THE DOCTOR, OKAY?
JIM... LOOK AT THIS REACTION TO PEANUT OIL! IT'S ONLY BEEN A FEW SECONDS!
GOOD LORD!!! WIPE THAT TEST OFF NOW, BEFORE IT GETS ANY WORSE!
ERHAPS SOMEDAY, WHEN I'M SICK AND OLD AND READY TO KICK THE BUCKET, I'LL FIND OUT WHAT I'VE BEEN MISSING.
MR. TOMINE, YOU HAVE EXACTLY FIVE MINUTES LEFT TO LIVE.
WELL THEN... QUIT YER TALKIN' AND GET ME A PEANUT BUTTER AND JELLY SANDWICH! ON THE DOUBLE!
BUT FOR NOW...
KEEP THAT SHIT AWAY FROM ME!
AT93

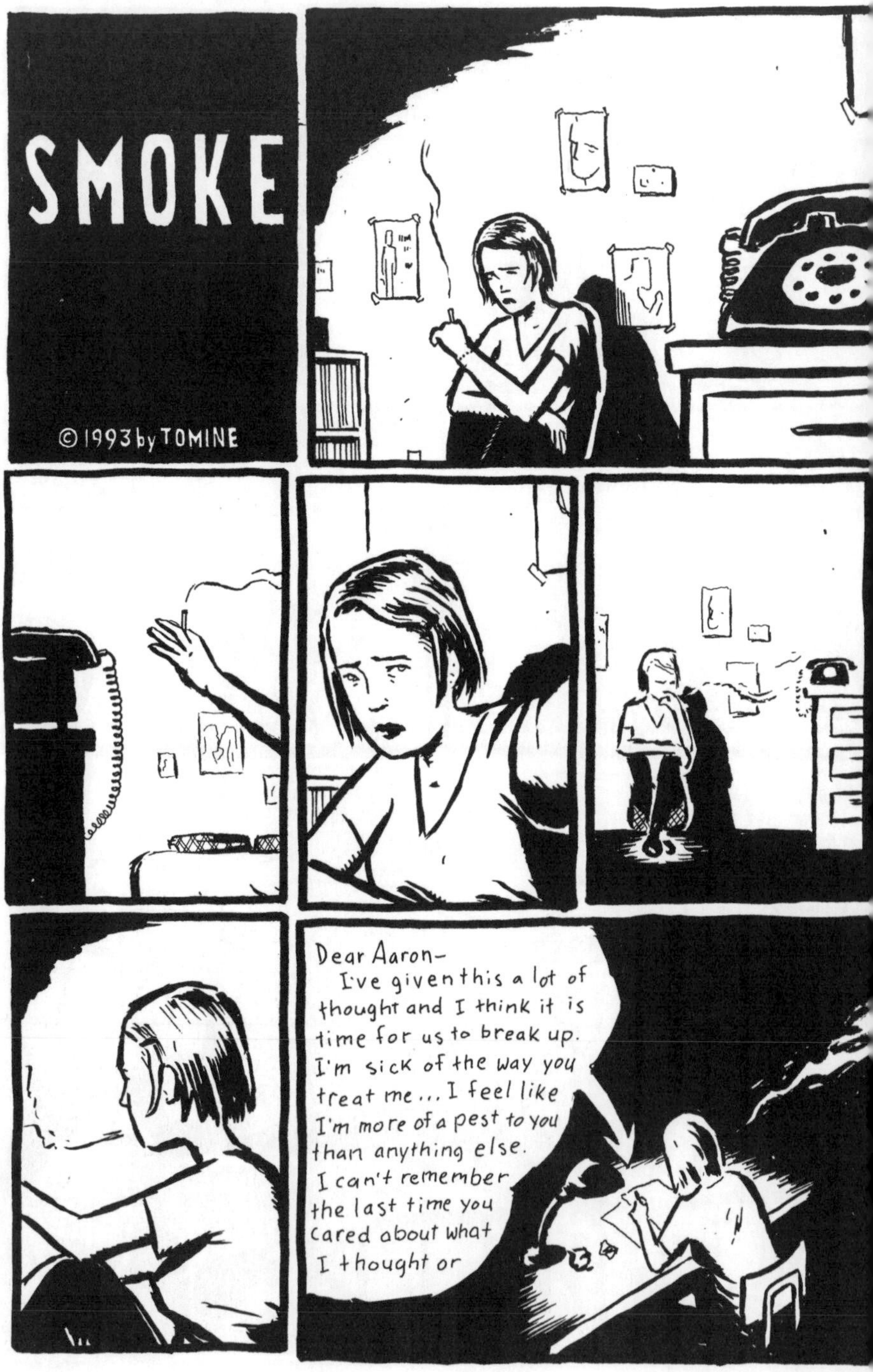
SMOKE
©1993 by TOMINE
Dear Aaron–
I've given this a lot of thought and I think it is time for us to break up. I'm sick of the way you treat me... I feel like I'm more of a pest to you than anything else. I can't remember the last time you cared about what I thought or

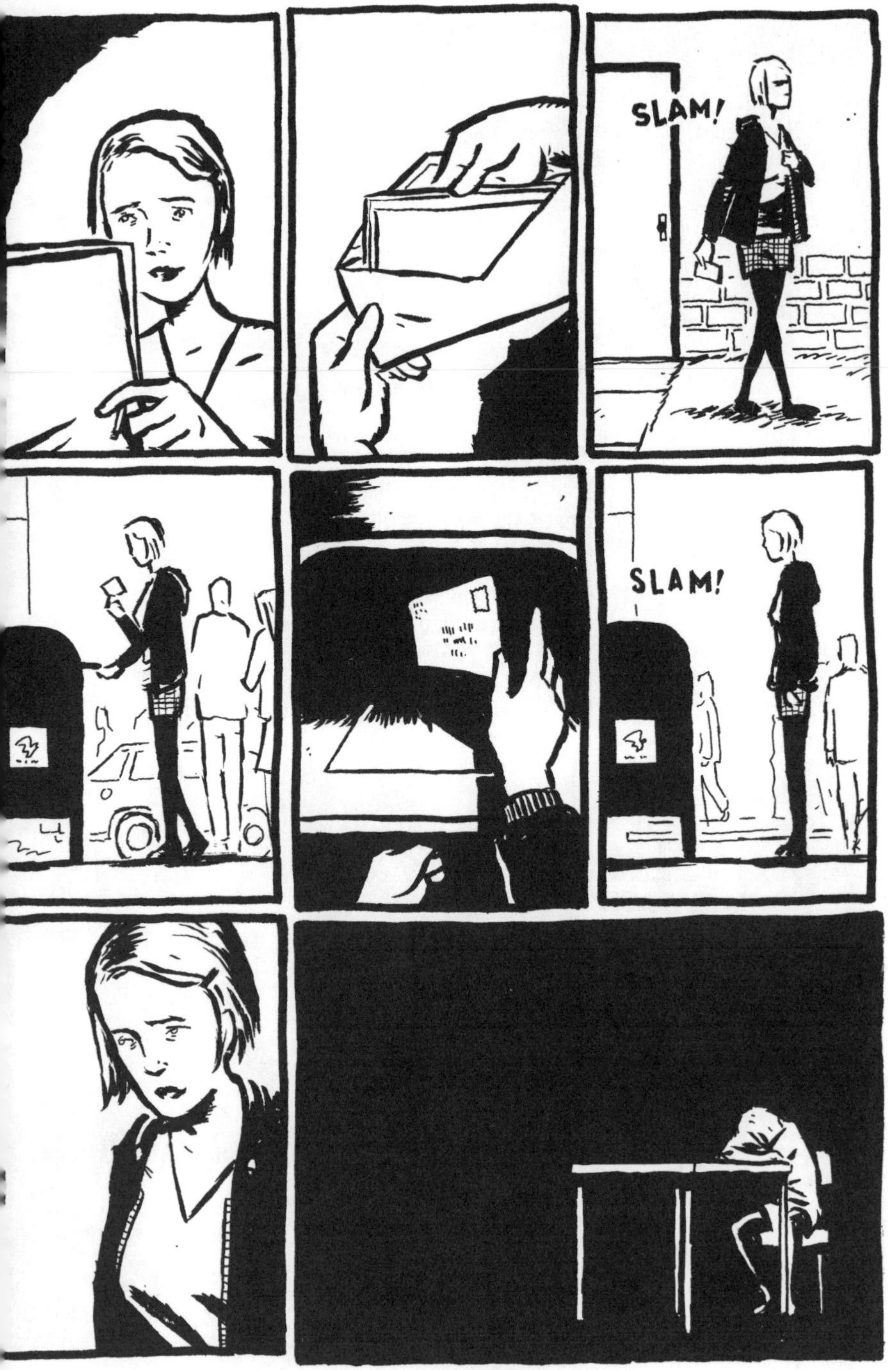
SLAM!
SLAM!

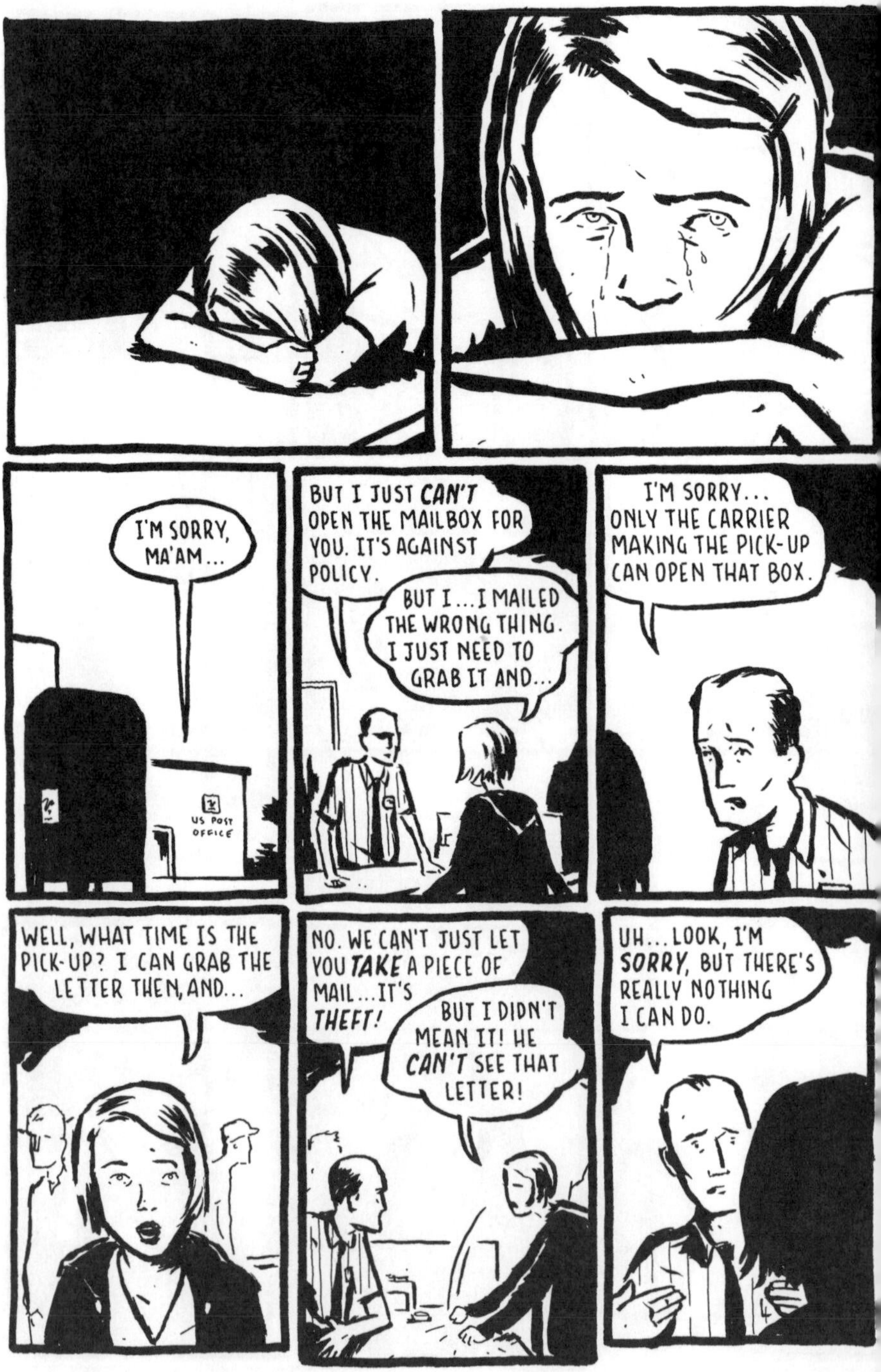
I'M SORRY, MA'AM...
US POST OFFICE
BUT I JUST CAN'T OPEN THE MAILBOX FOR YOU. IT'S AGAINST POLICY.
BUT I... I MAILED THE WRONG THING. I JUST NEED TO GRAB IT AND...
I'M SORRY... ONLY THE CARRIER MAKING THE PICK-UP CAN OPEN THAT BOX.
WELL, WHAT TIME IS THE PICK-UP? I CAN GRAB THE LETTER THEN, AND...
NO. WE CAN'T JUST LET YOU TAKE A PIECE OF MAIL... IT'S THEFT!
BUT I DIDN'T MEAN IT! HE CAN'T SEE THAT LETTER!
UH... LOOK, I'M SORRY, BUT THERE'S REALLY NOTHING I CAN DO.

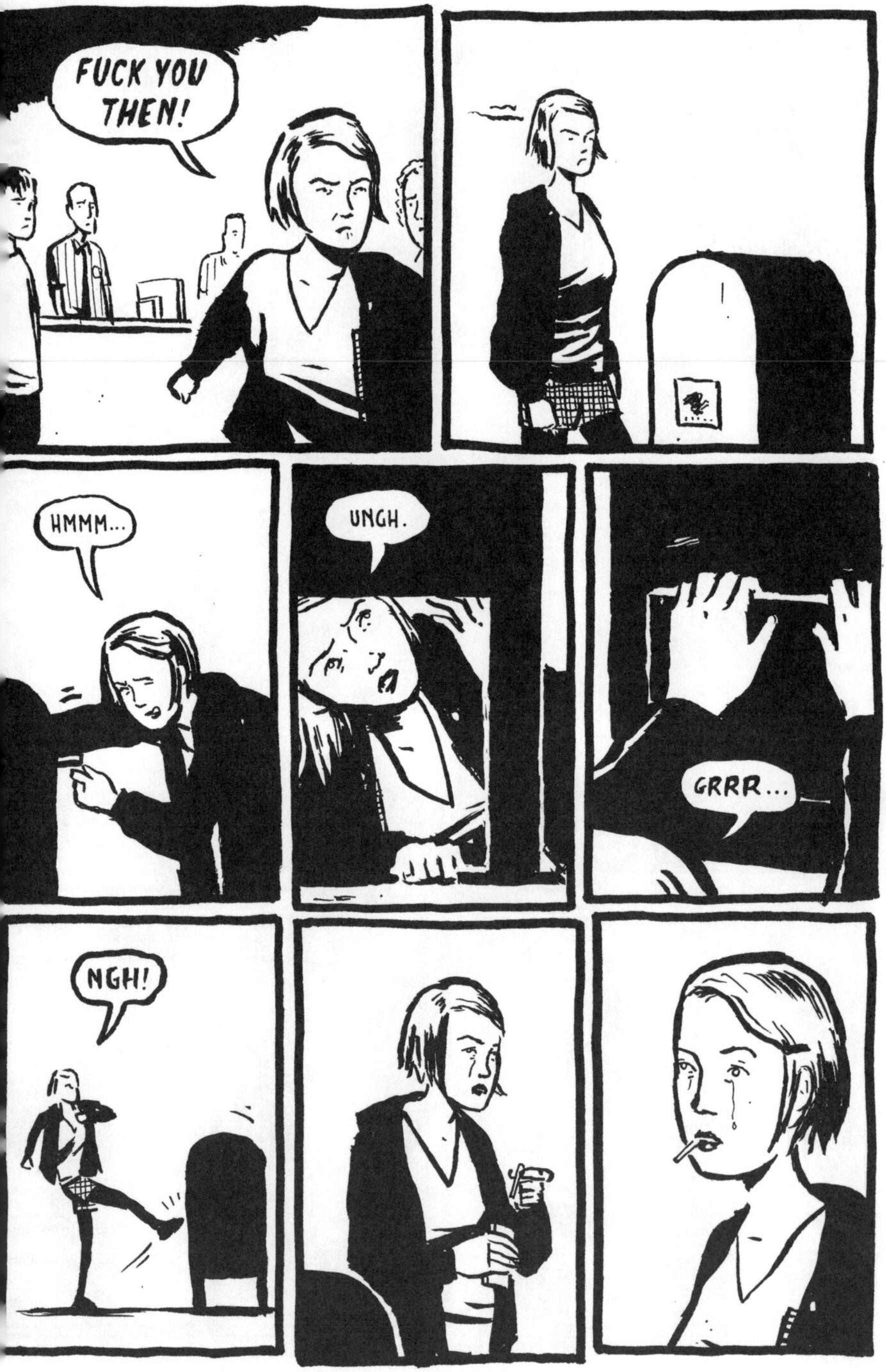
FUCK YOU THEN!
HMMM...
UNGH.
GRRR...
NGH!

SKRIT!

SLAM!

BZZZZT!

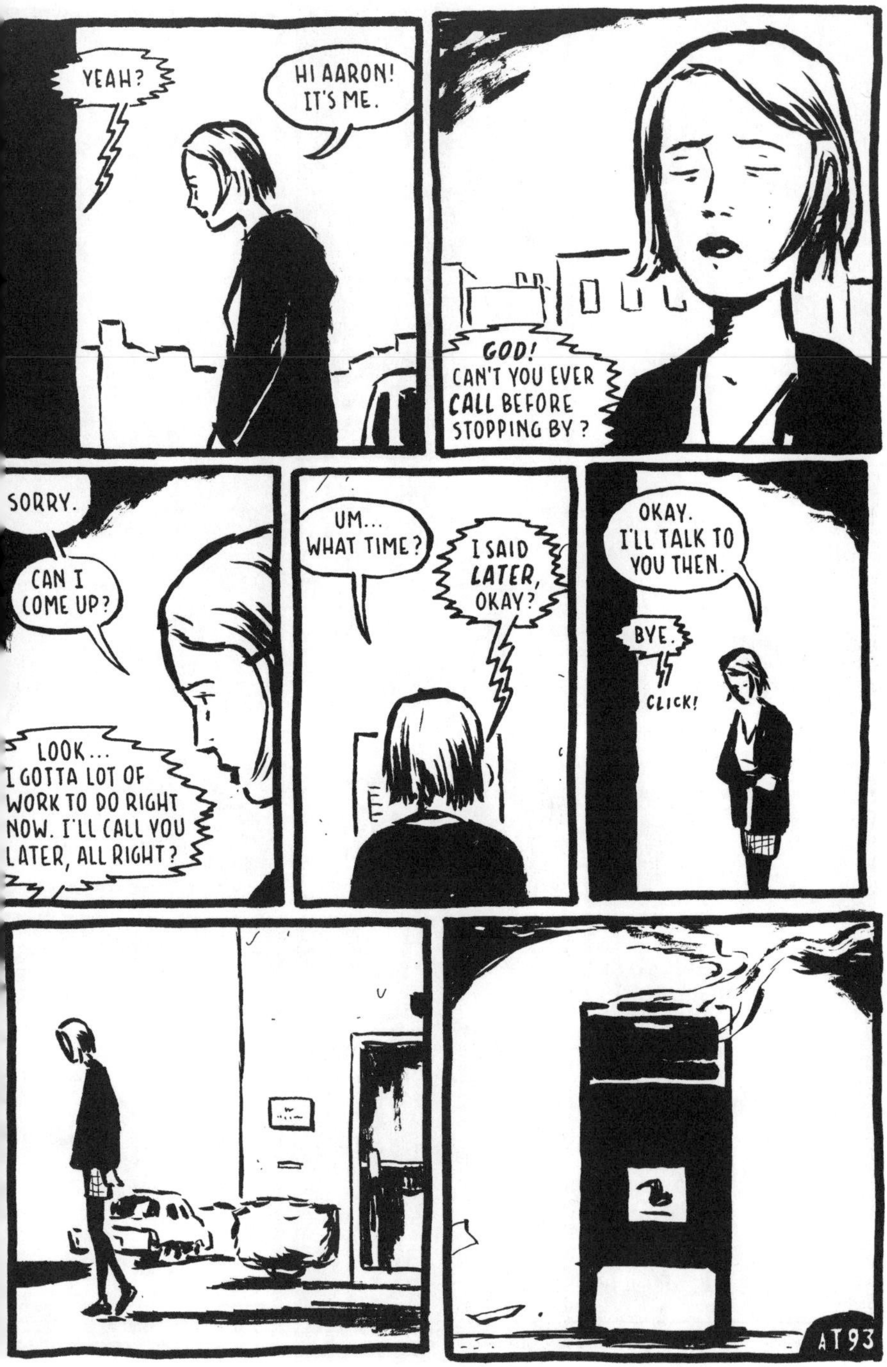
YEAH?
HI AARON! IT'S ME.
GOD! CAN'T YOU EVER CALL BEFORE STOPPING BY?
SORRY.
CAN I COME UP?
LOOK... I GOTTA LOT OF WORK TO DO RIGHT NOW. I'LL CALL YOU LATER, ALL RIGHT?
UM... WHAT TIME?
I SAID LATER, OKAY?
OKAY. I'LL TALK TO YOU THEN.
BYE.
CLICK!
AT93

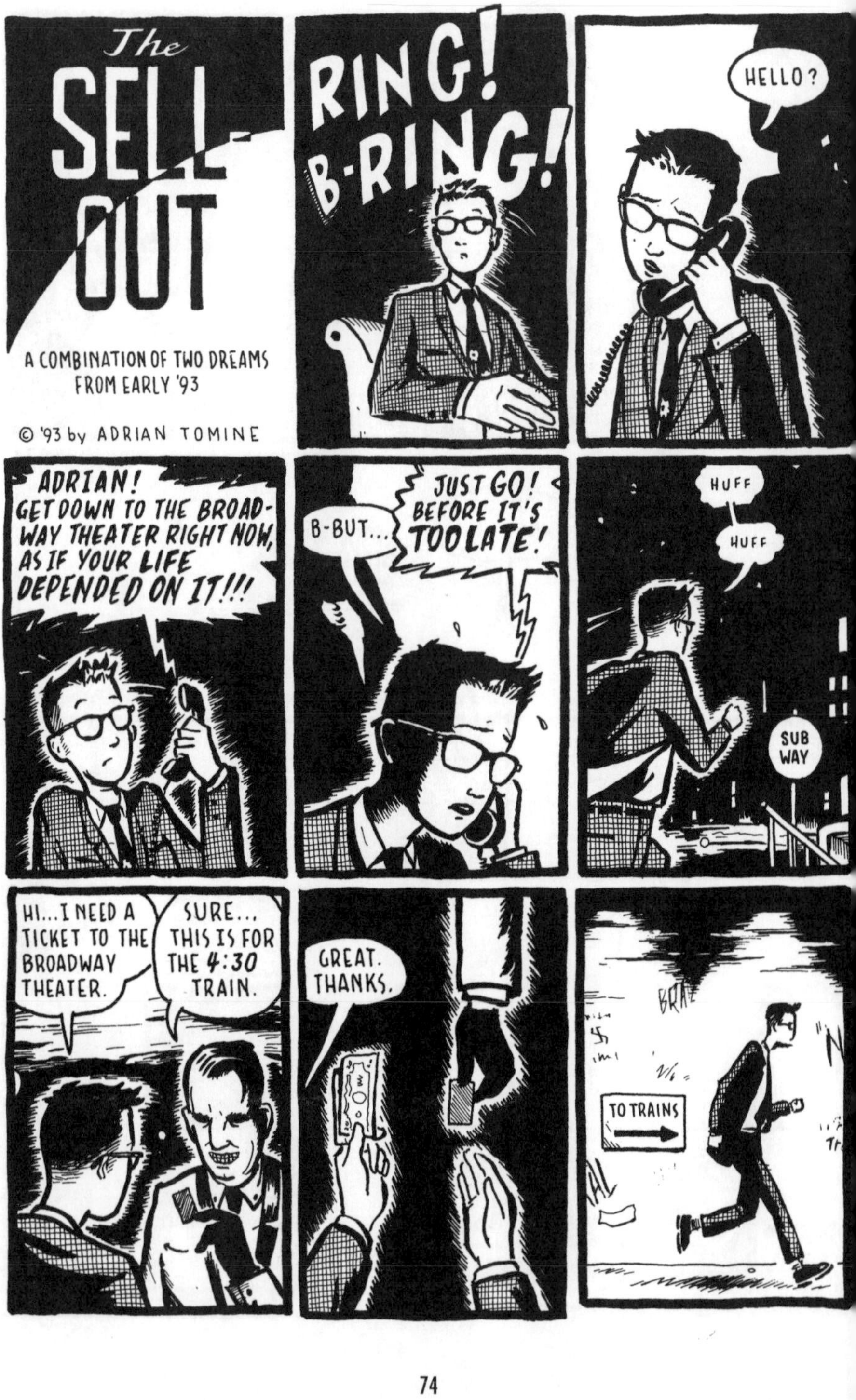
The
SELL-OUT
A COMBINATION OF TWO DREAMS FROM EARLY '93
© '93 by ADRIAN TOMINE
RING! B-RING!
HELLO?
ADRIAN! GET DOWN TO THE BROADWAY THEATER RIGHT NOW, AS IF YOUR LIFE DEPENDED ON IT!!!
B-BUT...
JUST GO! BEFORE IT'S TOO LATE!
HUFF
HUFF
SUB WAY
HI...I NEED A TICKET TO THE BROADWAY THEATER.
SURE... THIS IS FOR THE 4:30 TRAIN.
GREAT. THANKS.
TO TRAINS

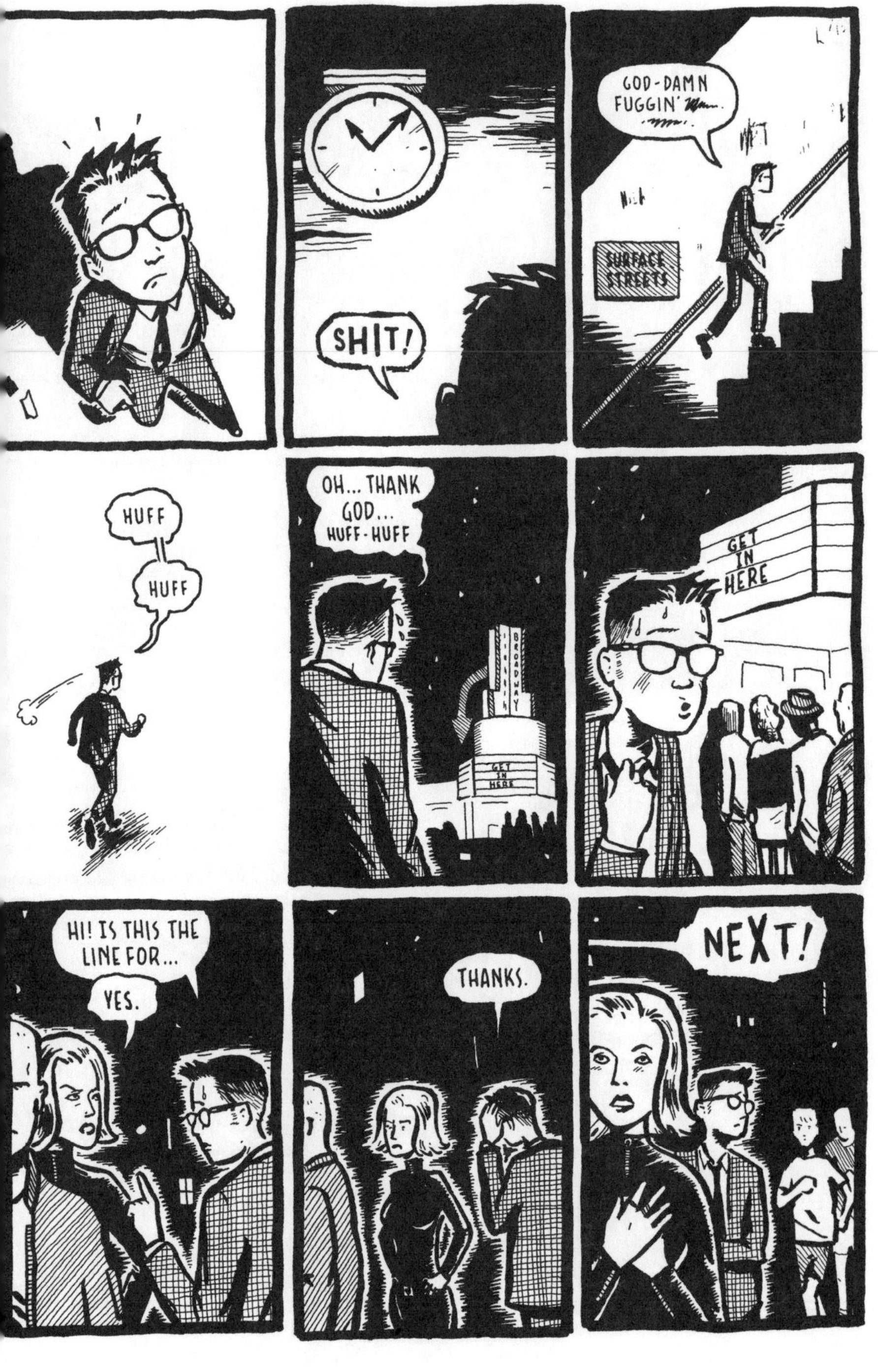
SHIT!
GOD-DAMN FUGGIN'
SURFACE STREETS
HUFF
HUFF
OH... THANK GOD... HUFF-HUFF
BROADWAY
GET IN HERE
GET IN HERE
HI! IS THIS THE LINE FOR...
YES.
THANKS.
NEXT!

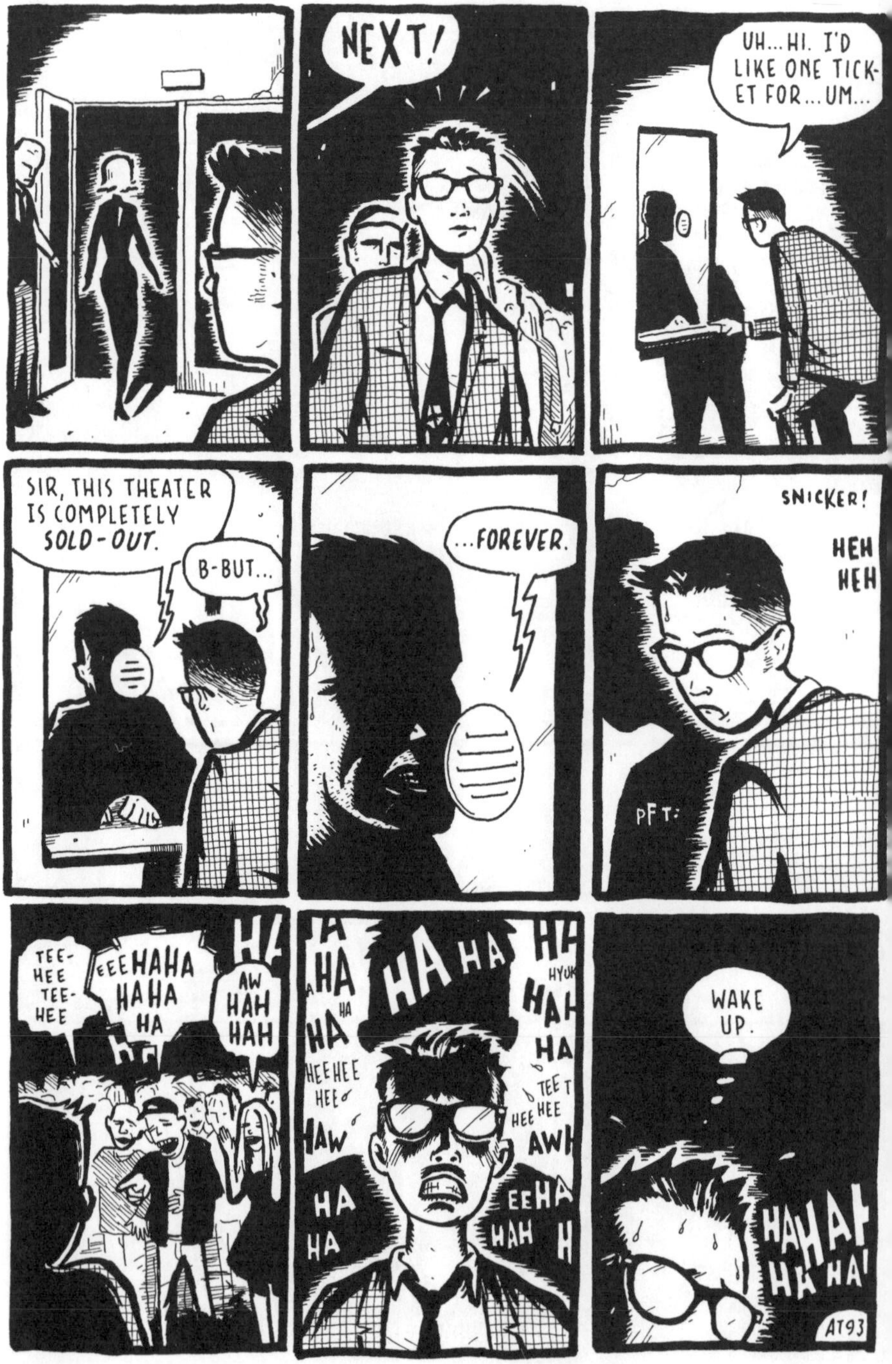
NEXT!
UH... HI. I'D LIKE ONE TICK-ET FOR... UM...
SIR, THIS THEATER IS COMPLETELY SOLD-OUT.
B-BUT...
...FOREVER.
SNICKER!
HEH HEH
PFT:
TEE-HEE TEE-HEE
EEEHAHA HAHA HA
AW HAH HAH
HA HA HA
HA HA HA
HYUK
HEEHEE HEE
HAW
TEE HEE
HEE
AWH
HA HA
EEHA HAH
WAKE UP.
HAHA! HA HA!
AT93

STAMMER

BY ADRIAN TOMINE © 1994

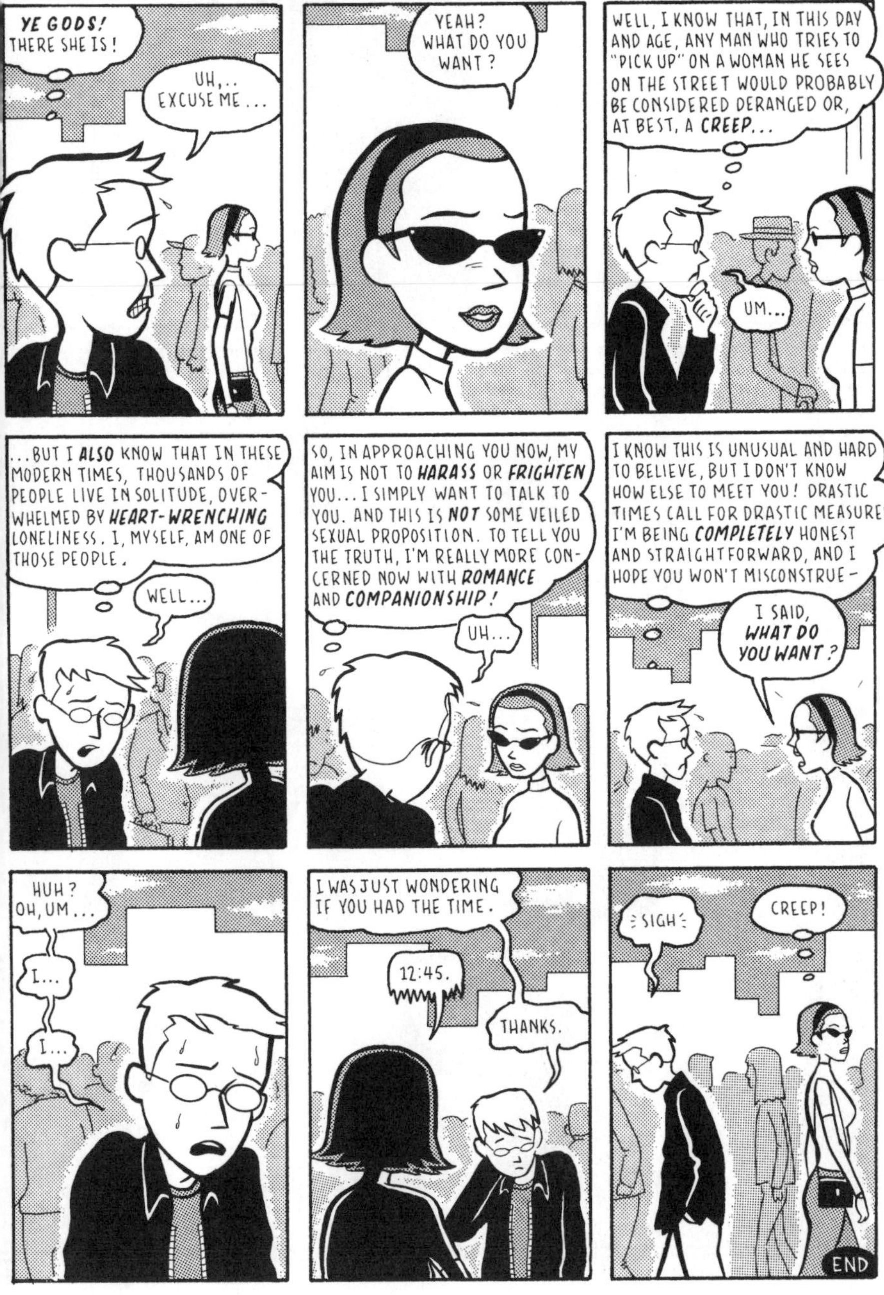
YE GODS! THERE SHE IS!
UH,.. EXCUSE ME...
YEAH? WHAT DO YOU WANT?
WELL, I KNOW THAT, IN THIS DAY AND AGE, ANY MAN WHO TRIES TO "PICK UP" ON A WOMAN HE SEES ON THE STREET WOULD PROBABLY BE CONSIDERED DERANGED OR, AT BEST, A CREEP...
UM...
...BUT I ALSO KNOW THAT IN THESE MODERN TIMES, THOUSANDS OF PEOPLE LIVE IN SOLITUDE, OVER-WHELMED BY HEART-WRENCHING LONELINESS. I, MYSELF, AM ONE OF THOSE PEOPLE.
WELL...
SO, IN APPROACHING YOU NOW, MY AIM IS NOT TO HARASS OR FRIGHTEN YOU... I SIMPLY WANT TO TALK TO YOU. AND THIS IS NOT SOME VEILED SEXUAL PROPOSITION. TO TELL YOU THE TRUTH, I'M REALLY MORE CON-CERNED NOW WITH ROMANCE AND COMPANIONSHIP!
UH...
I KNOW THIS IS UNUSUAL AND HARD TO BELIEVE, BUT I DON'T KNOW HOW ELSE TO MEET YOU! DRASTIC TIMES CALL FOR DRASTIC MEASURES! I'M BEING COMPLETELY HONEST AND STRAIGHTFORWARD, AND I HOPE YOU WON'T MISCONSTRUE-
I SAID, WHAT DO YOU WANT?
HUH? OH, UM...
I...
I...
I WAS JUST WONDERING IF YOU HAD THE TIME.
12:45.
THANKS.
SIGH
CREEP!
END

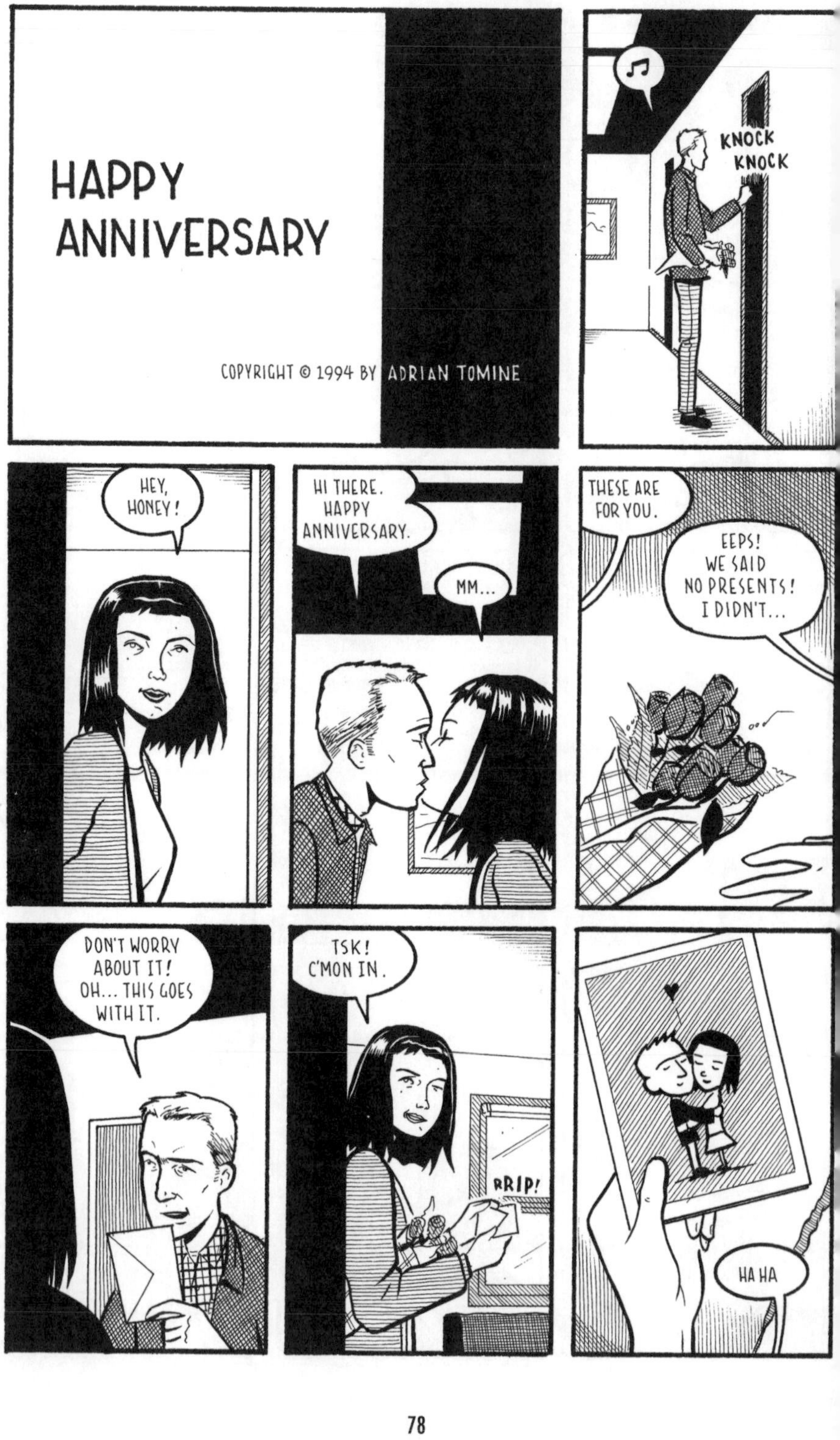
HAPPY ANNIVERSARY
COPYRIGHT © 1994 BY ADRIAN TOMINE
♫
KNOCK KNOCK
HEY, HONEY!
HI THERE. HAPPY ANNIVERSARY.
MM...
THESE ARE FOR YOU.
EEPS! WE SAID NO PRESENTS! I DIDN'T...
DON'T WORRY ABOUT IT! OH... THIS GOES WITH IT.
TSK! C'MON IN.
RRIP!
HA HA

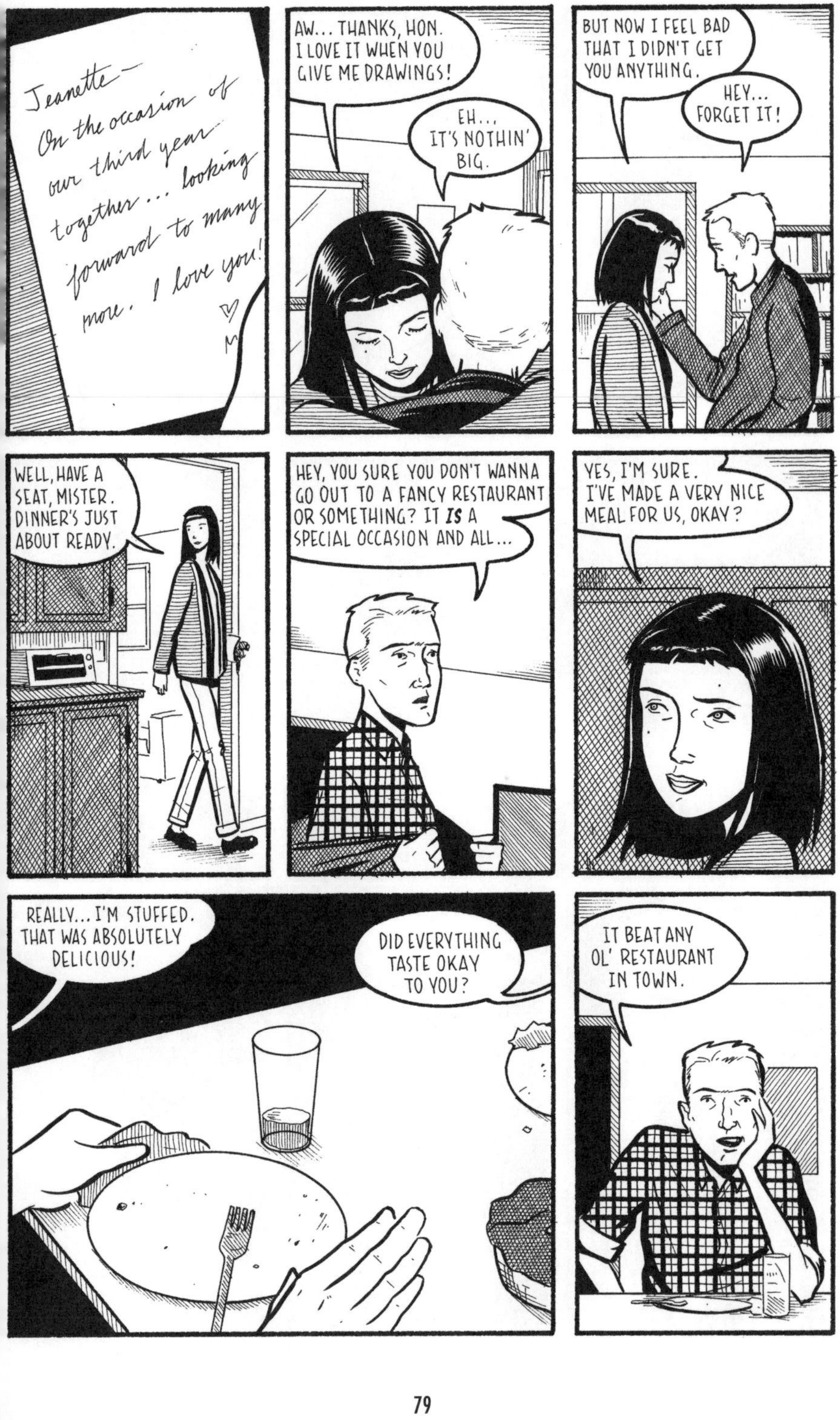
Jeanette— On the occasion of our third year together... looking forward to many more. I love you!
M
AW... THANKS, HON. I LOVE IT WHEN YOU GIVE ME DRAWINGS!
EH... IT'S NOTHIN' BIG.
BUT NOW I FEEL BAD THAT I DIDN'T GET YOU ANYTHING.
HEY... FORGET IT!
WELL, HAVE A SEAT, MISTER. DINNER'S JUST ABOUT READY.
HEY, YOU SURE YOU DON'T WANNA GO OUT TO A FANCY RESTAURANT OR SOMETHING? IT **IS** A SPECIAL OCCASION AND ALL...
YES, I'M SURE. I'VE MADE A VERY NICE MEAL FOR US, OKAY?
REALLY... I'M STUFFED. THAT WAS ABSOLUTELY DELICIOUS!
DID EVERYTHING TASTE OKAY TO YOU?
IT BEAT ANY OL' RESTAURANT IN TOWN.

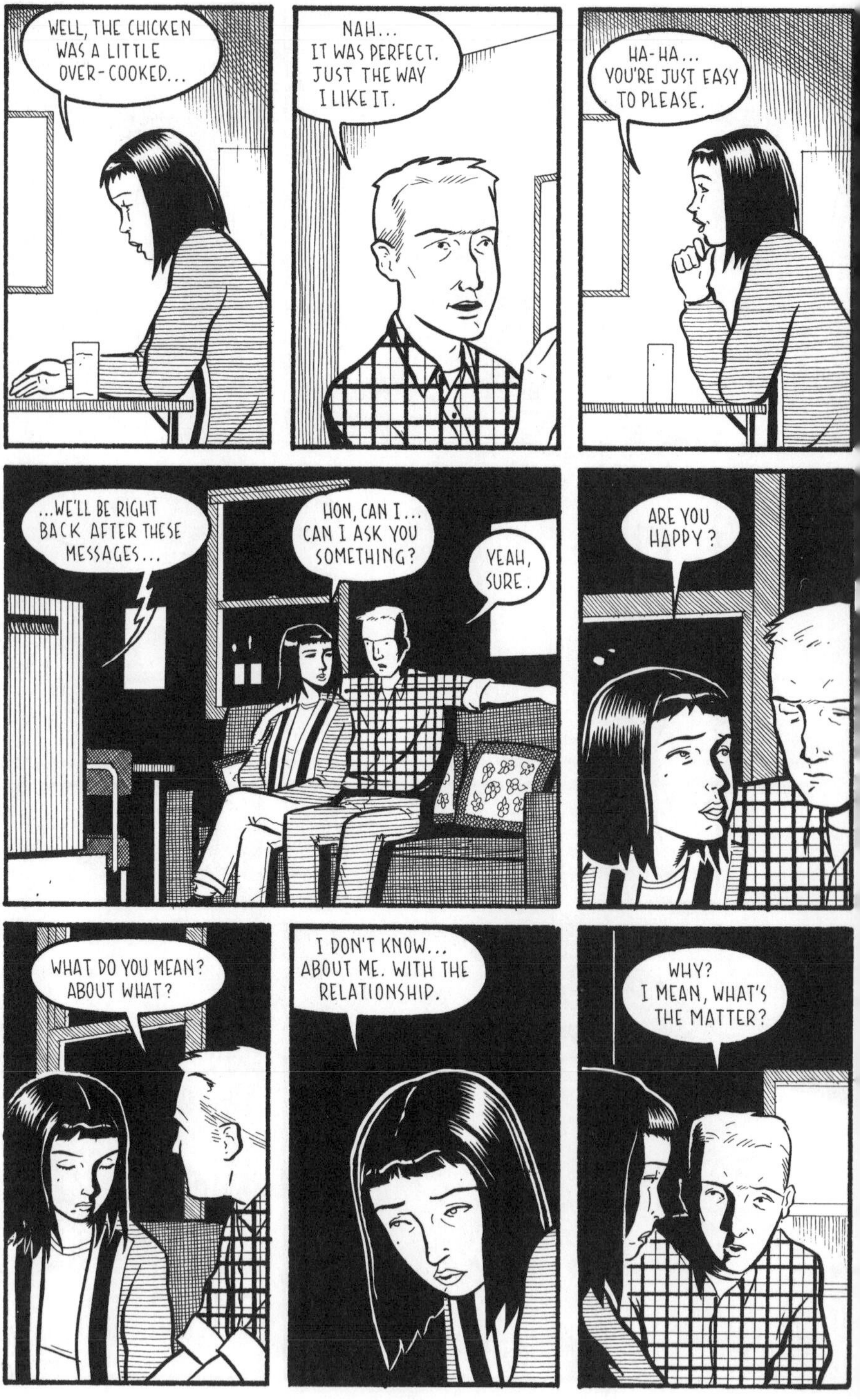

WELL, THE CHICKEN WAS A LITTLE OVER-COOKED...
NAH... IT WAS PERFECT. JUST THE WAY I LIKE IT.
HA-HA... YOU'RE JUST EASY TO PLEASE.
...WE'LL BE RIGHT BACK AFTER THESE MESSAGES...
HON, CAN I... CAN I ASK YOU SOMETHING?
YEAH, SURE.
ARE YOU HAPPY?
WHAT DO YOU MEAN? ABOUT WHAT?
I DON'T KNOW... ABOUT ME. WITH THE RELATIONSHIP.
WHY? I MEAN, WHAT'S THE MATTER?

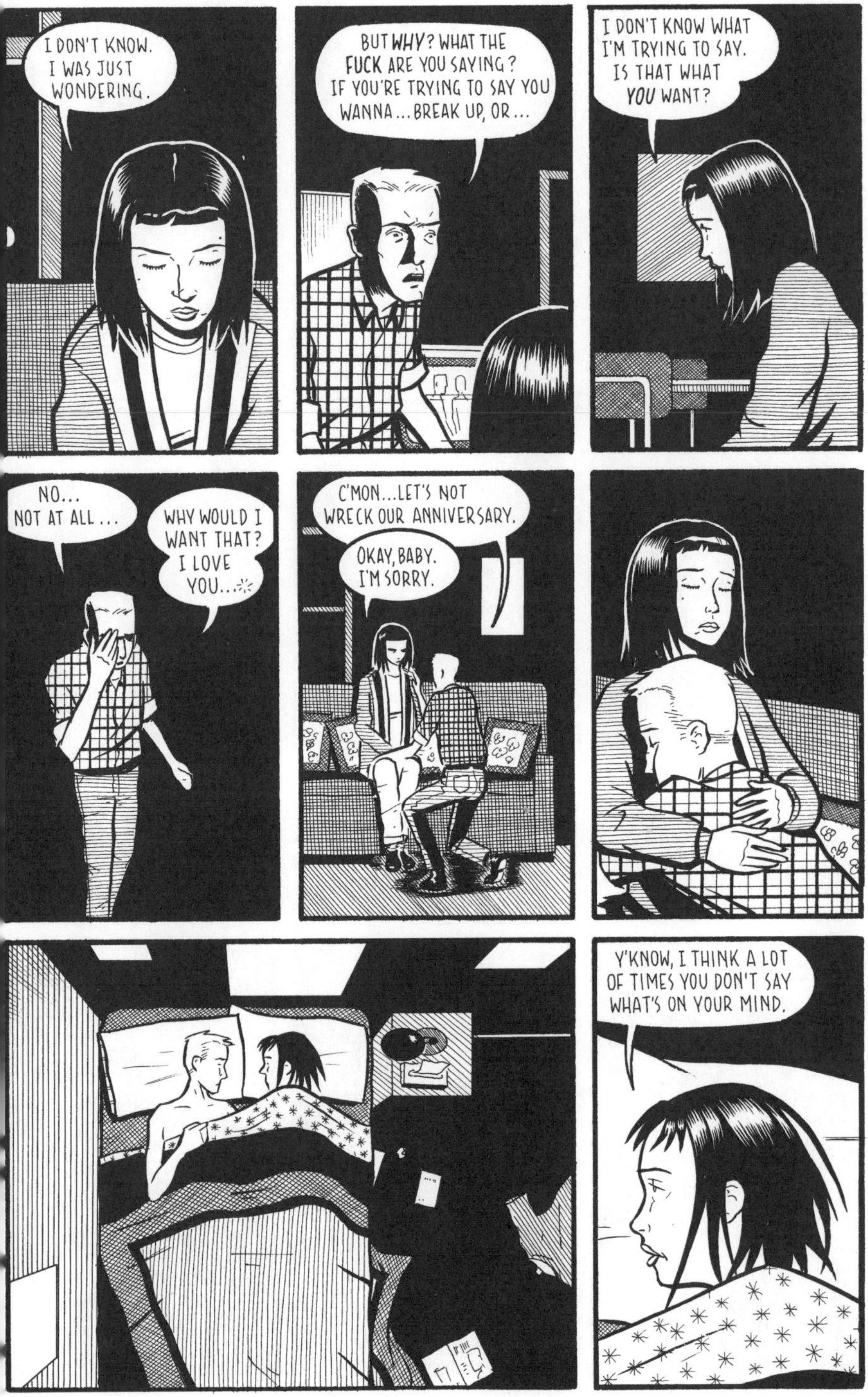
I DON'T KNOW. I WAS JUST WONDERING.
BUT WHY? WHAT THE FUCK ARE YOU SAYING? IF YOU'RE TRYING TO SAY YOU WANNA... BREAK UP, OR...
I DON'T KNOW WHAT I'M TRYING TO SAY. IS THAT WHAT YOU WANT?
NO... NOT AT ALL...
WHY WOULD I WANT THAT? I LOVE YOU...
C'MON... LET'S NOT WRECK OUR ANNIVERSARY.
OKAY, BABY. I'M SORRY.
Y'KNOW, I THINK A LOT OF TIMES YOU DON'T SAY WHAT'S ON YOUR MIND.

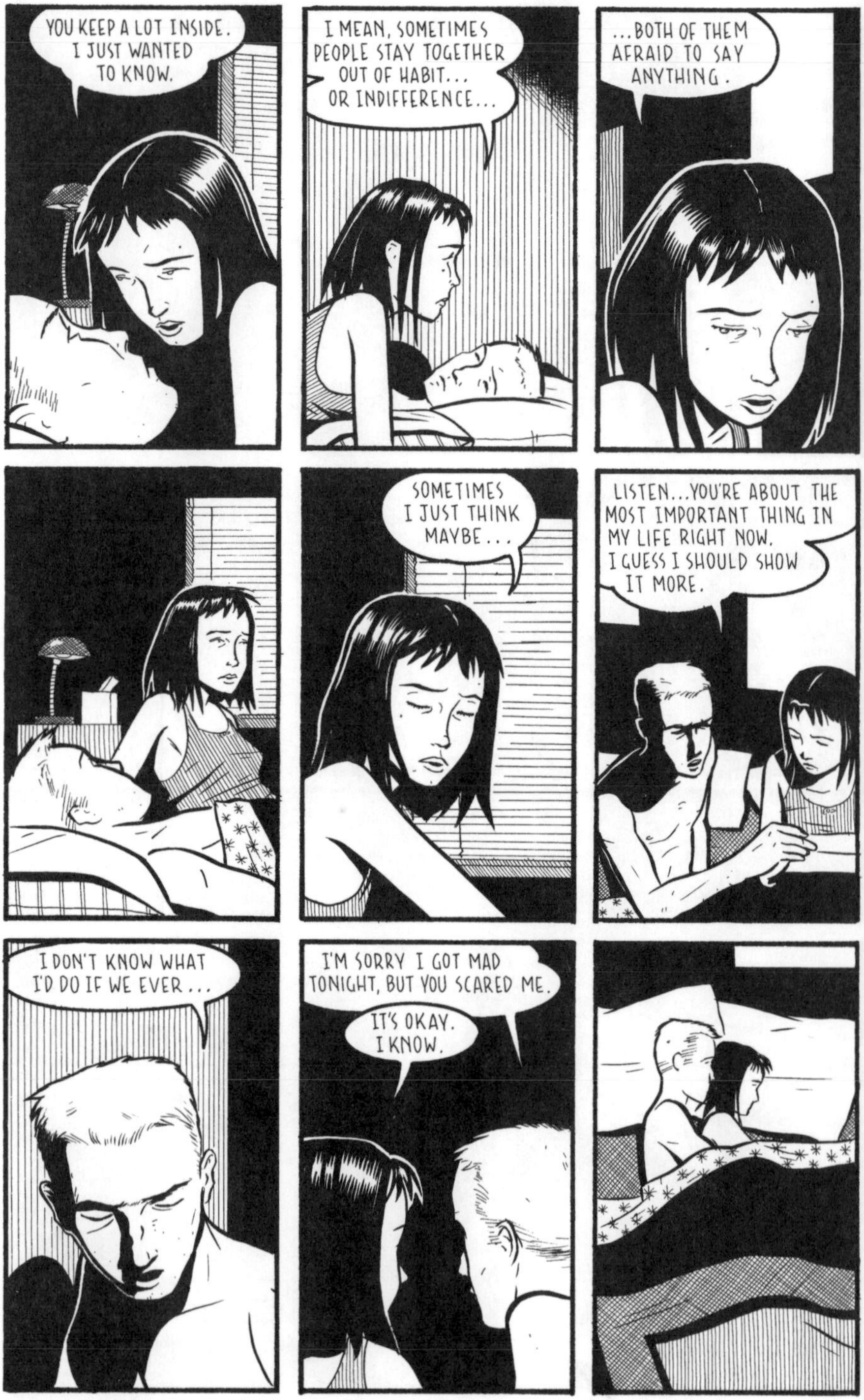
YOU KEEP A LOT INSIDE. I JUST WANTED TO KNOW.
I MEAN, SOMETIMES PEOPLE STAY TOGETHER OUT OF HABIT... OR INDIFFERENCE...
...BOTH OF THEM AFRAID TO SAY ANYTHING.
SOMETIMES I JUST THINK MAYBE...
LISTEN...YOU'RE ABOUT THE MOST IMPORTANT THING IN MY LIFE RIGHT NOW. I GUESS I SHOULD SHOW IT MORE.
I DON'T KNOW WHAT I'D DO IF WE EVER...
I'M SORRY I GOT MAD TONIGHT, BUT YOU SCARED ME.
IT'S OKAY. I KNOW.

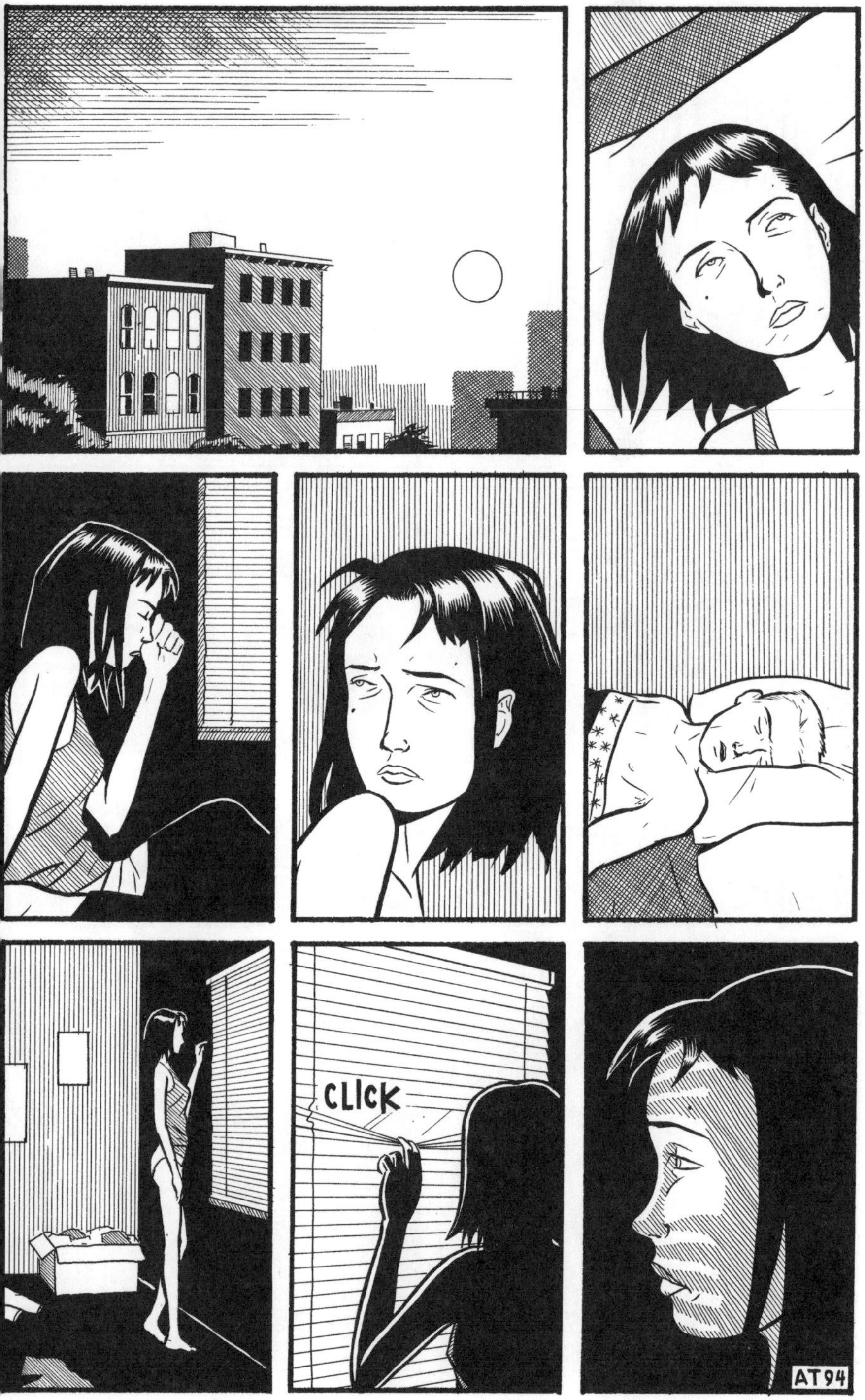
CLICK
AT94

LAUNDRY

BY ADRIAN TOMINE
©1994

NOW, BEFORE YOU GET THE WRONG IDEA, LET ME EXPLAIN IT FROM THE BEGINNING. A COUPLE WEEKS AGO, I WAS AT THE LAUNDROMAT AT 5th AND EL DORADO. AS USUAL, IT WAS PRETTY CROWDED.

MY CLOTHES WERE ALREADY DONE WASHING, SO I'M SITTING THERE, WAITING FOR A DRYER TO OPEN UP, DRINKING 7-11 COFFEE AND READING THE PAPER.

EVENTUALLY, THIS BRUNETTE (A REAL LOOKER, I HAVE TO ADMIT) WALKS OVER TO A MACHINE AND UNLOADS HER WHITES.

SO I GO OVER TO TRANSFER MY WASH INTO THE EMPTY DRYER, AND I SEE SHE'S LEFT SOMETHING BEHIND.

I TRY TO GET HER ATTENTION, BUT SHE'S ALREADY OUT THE DOOR.

I FOLLOW HER INTO THE PARKING LOT, CALLING OUT TO HER, BUT SHE CAN'T HEAR ME.

BY THE TIME I CATCH UP WITH HER, SHE'S ALREADY IN HER CAR, DRIVING AWAY. I GUESS SHE DIDN'T SEE ME.

HI THERE.

SLAM!

BITCH...

SO ANYWAY, THAT'S WHY I HAVE THESE. I KEEP THEM WITH ME.

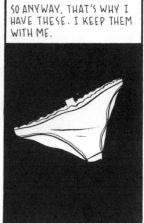

I MEAN, SHE PROBABLY LIVES AROUND HERE...I'M BOUND TO BUMP INTO HER AGAIN SOON ENOUGH. AND WHEN I DO, I'LL HAND THEM TO HER AND SAY...

EXCUSE ME... I BELIEVE THESE ARE YOURS.

SHE'LL THANK ME FOR THAT.

END

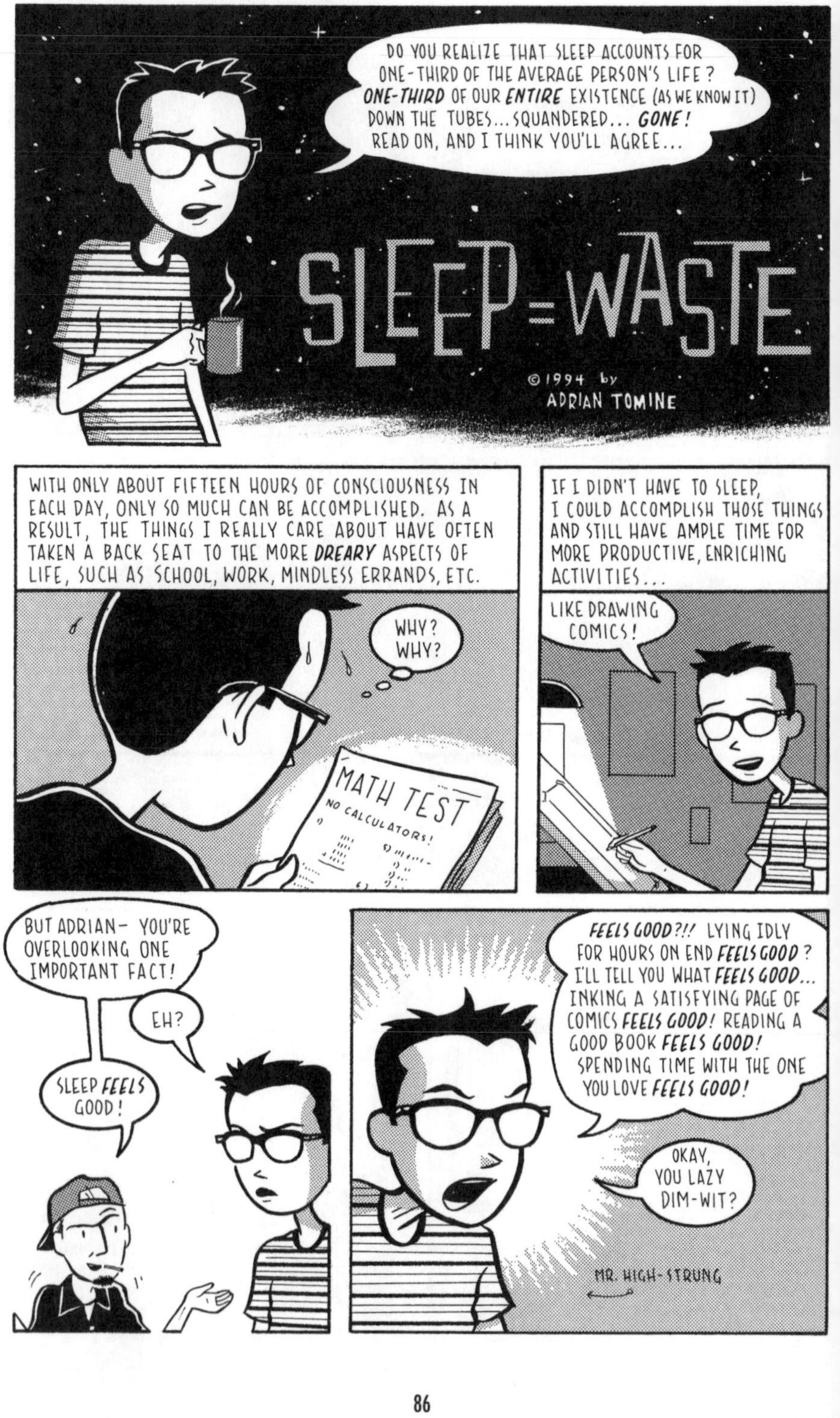
DO YOU REALIZE THAT SLEEP ACCOUNTS FOR ONE-THIRD OF THE AVERAGE PERSON'S LIFE? ONE-THIRD OF OUR ENTIRE EXISTENCE (AS WE KNOW IT) DOWN THE TUBES... SQUANDERED... GONE! READ ON, AND I THINK YOU'LL AGREE...
SLEEP = WASTE
©1994 by ADRIAN TOMINE
WITH ONLY ABOUT FIFTEEN HOURS OF CONSCIOUSNESS IN EACH DAY, ONLY SO MUCH CAN BE ACCOMPLISHED. AS A RESULT, THE THINGS I REALLY CARE ABOUT HAVE OFTEN TAKEN A BACK SEAT TO THE MORE DREARY ASPECTS OF LIFE, SUCH AS SCHOOL, WORK, MINDLESS ERRANDS, ETC.
WHY? WHY?
MATH TEST
NO CALCULATORS!
IF I DIDN'T HAVE TO SLEEP, I COULD ACCOMPLISH THOSE THINGS AND STILL HAVE AMPLE TIME FOR MORE PRODUCTIVE, ENRICHING ACTIVITIES...
LIKE DRAWING COMICS!
BUT ADRIAN– YOU'RE OVERLOOKING ONE IMPORTANT FACT!
EH?
SLEEP FEELS GOOD!
FEELS GOOD?!! LYING IDLY FOR HOURS ON END FEELS GOOD? I'LL TELL YOU WHAT FEELS GOOD... INKING A SATISFYING PAGE OF COMICS FEELS GOOD! READING A GOOD BOOK FEELS GOOD! SPENDING TIME WITH THE ONE YOU LOVE FEELS GOOD!
OKAY, YOU LAZY DIM-WIT?
MR. HIGH-STRUNG

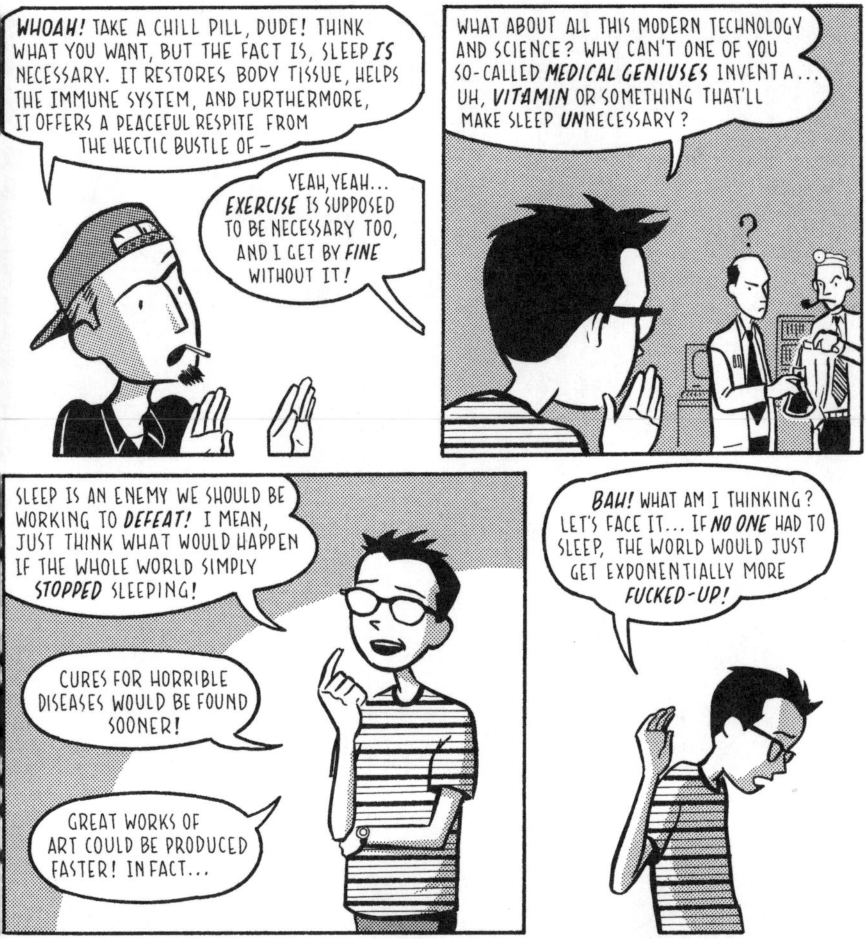
WHOAH! TAKE A CHILL PILL, DUDE! THINK WHAT YOU WANT, BUT THE FACT IS, SLEEP IS NECESSARY. IT RESTORES BODY TISSUE, HELPS THE IMMUNE SYSTEM, AND FURTHERMORE, IT OFFERS A PEACEFUL RESPITE FROM THE HECTIC BUSTLE OF –
YEAH, YEAH... EXERCISE IS SUPPOSED TO BE NECESSARY TOO, AND I GET BY FINE WITHOUT IT!
WHAT ABOUT ALL THIS MODERN TECHNOLOGY AND SCIENCE? WHY CAN'T ONE OF YOU SO-CALLED MEDICAL GENIUSES INVENT A... UH, VITAMIN OR SOMETHING THAT'LL MAKE SLEEP UNNECESSARY?
?
SLEEP IS AN ENEMY WE SHOULD BE WORKING TO DEFEAT! I MEAN, JUST THINK WHAT WOULD HAPPEN IF THE WHOLE WORLD SIMPLY STOPPED SLEEPING!
CURES FOR HORRIBLE DISEASES WOULD BE FOUND SOONER!
GREAT WORKS OF ART COULD BE PRODUCED FASTER! IN FACT...
BAH! WHAT AM I THINKING? LET'S FACE IT... IF NO ONE HAD TO SLEEP, THE WORLD WOULD JUST GET EXPONENTIALLY MORE FUCKED-UP!

SINCE IT SEEMS THAT MANY CONFLICTS ARISE SIMPLY FROM PEOPLE'S CONSTANT INTERACTION AND CONTACT WITH EACH OTHER, VIOLENCE AND UNHAPPINESS WOULD ABOUND!

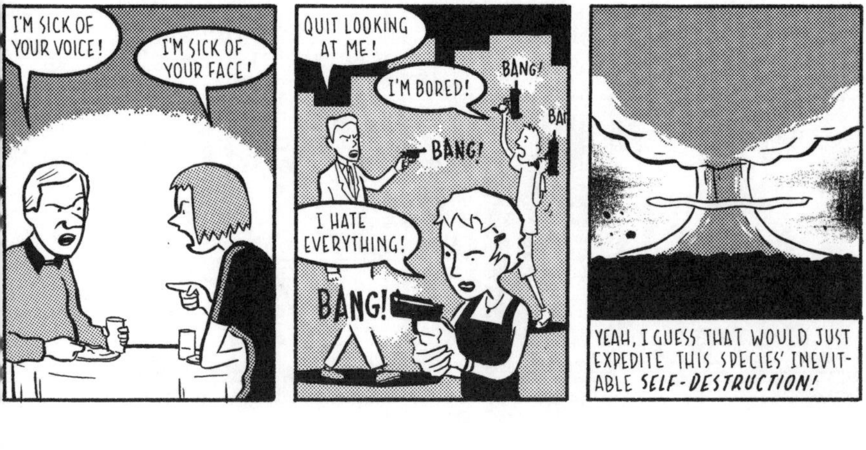
I'M SICK OF YOUR VOICE!
I'M SICK OF YOUR FACE!
QUIT LOOKING AT ME!
I'M BORED!
BANG!
BANG!
I HATE EVERYTHING!
BANG!
YEAH, I GUESS THAT WOULD JUST EXPEDITE THIS SPECIES' INEVITABLE SELF-DESTRUCTION!

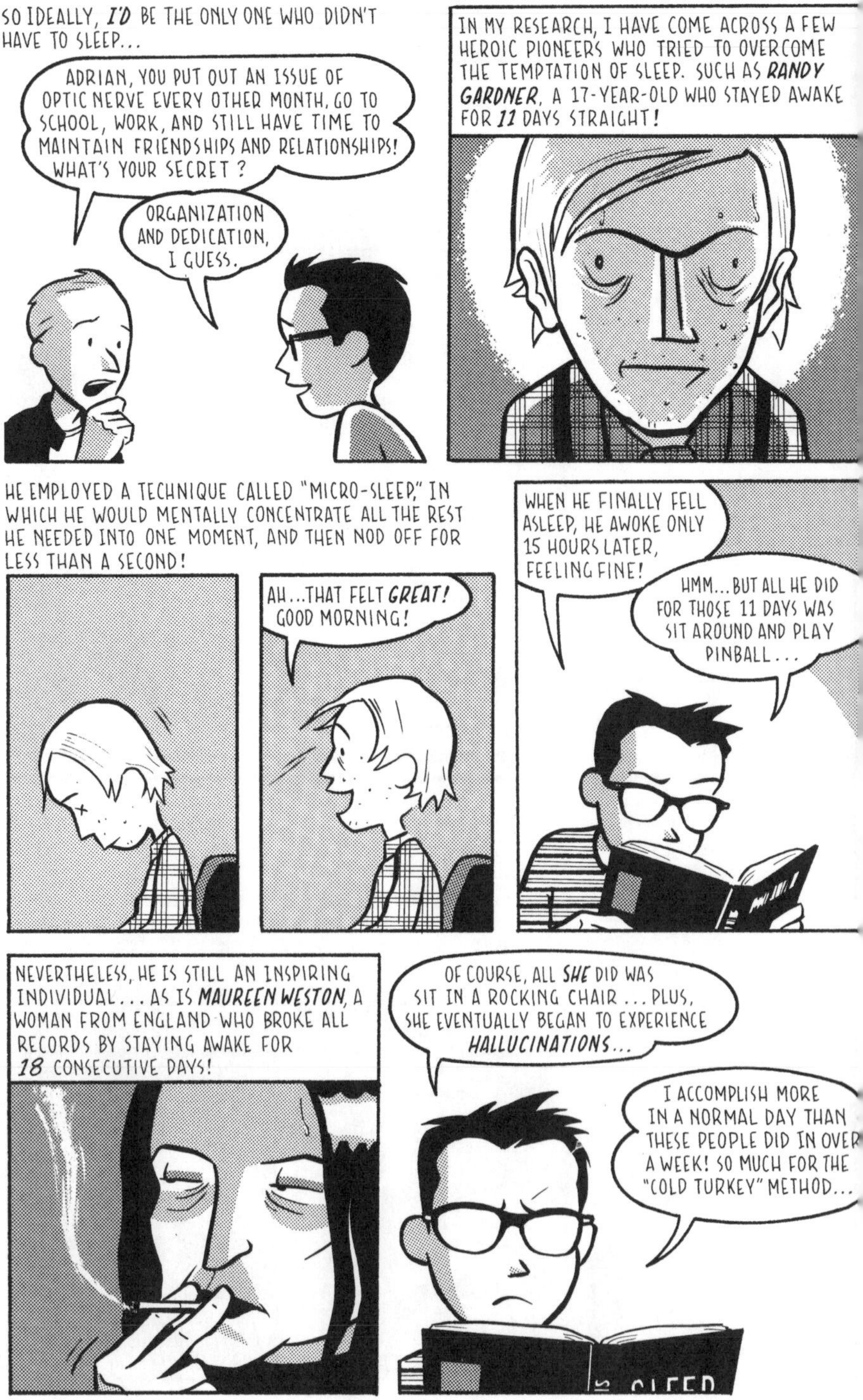

SO IDEALLY, *I'D* BE THE ONLY ONE WHO DIDN'T HAVE TO SLEEP...
ADRIAN, YOU PUT OUT AN ISSUE OF OPTIC NERVE EVERY OTHER MONTH, GO TO SCHOOL, WORK, AND STILL HAVE TIME TO MAINTAIN FRIENDSHIPS AND RELATIONSHIPS! WHAT'S YOUR SECRET?
ORGANIZATION AND DEDICATION, I GUESS.
IN MY RESEARCH, I HAVE COME ACROSS A FEW HEROIC PIONEERS WHO TRIED TO OVERCOME THE TEMPTATION OF SLEEP. SUCH AS **RANDY GARDNER**, A 17-YEAR-OLD WHO STAYED AWAKE FOR **11** DAYS STRAIGHT!
HE EMPLOYED A TECHNIQUE CALLED "MICRO-SLEEP," IN WHICH HE WOULD MENTALLY CONCENTRATE ALL THE REST HE NEEDED INTO ONE MOMENT, AND THEN NOD OFF FOR LESS THAN A SECOND!
AH...THAT FELT **GREAT!** GOOD MORNING!
WHEN HE FINALLY FELL ASLEEP, HE AWOKE ONLY 15 HOURS LATER, FEELING FINE!
HMM...BUT ALL HE DID FOR THOSE 11 DAYS WAS SIT AROUND AND PLAY PINBALL...
NEVERTHELESS, HE IS STILL AN INSPIRING INDIVIDUAL... AS IS **MAUREEN WESTON**, A WOMAN FROM ENGLAND WHO BROKE ALL RECORDS BY STAYING AWAKE FOR *18* CONSECUTIVE DAYS!
OF COURSE, ALL **SHE** DID WAS SIT IN A ROCKING CHAIR ... PLUS, SHE EVENTUALLY BEGAN TO EXPERIENCE **HALLUCINATIONS**...
I ACCOMPLISH MORE IN A NORMAL DAY THAN THESE PEOPLE DID IN OVER A WEEK! SO MUCH FOR THE "COLD TURKEY" METHOD...

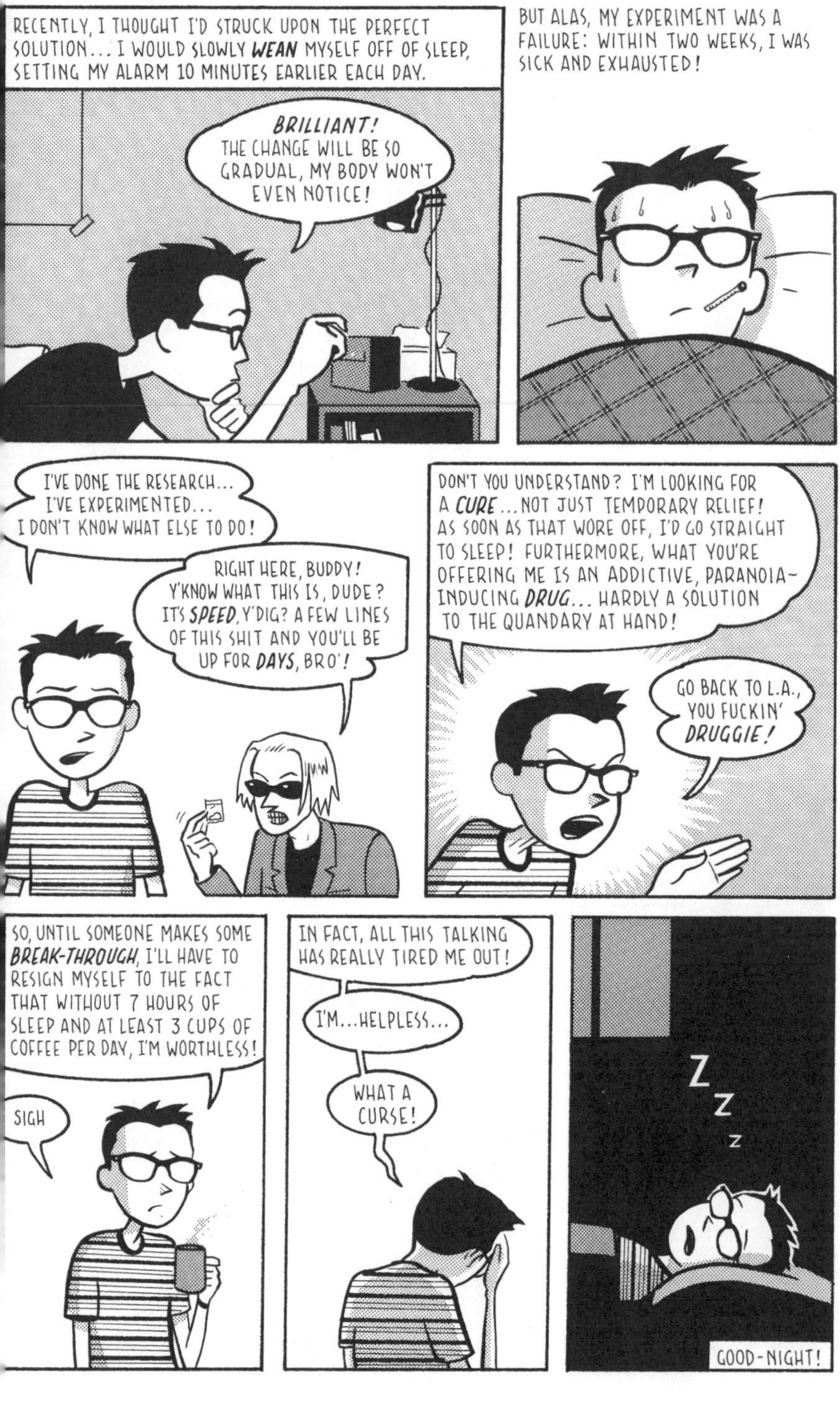
RECENTLY, I THOUGHT I'D STRUCK UPON THE PERFECT SOLUTION... I WOULD SLOWLY WEAN MYSELF OFF OF SLEEP, SETTING MY ALARM 10 MINUTES EARLIER EACH DAY.
BRILLIANT! THE CHANGE WILL BE SO GRADUAL, MY BODY WON'T EVEN NOTICE!
BUT ALAS, MY EXPERIMENT WAS A FAILURE: WITHIN TWO WEEKS, I WAS SICK AND EXHAUSTED!
I'VE DONE THE RESEARCH... I'VE EXPERIMENTED... I DON'T KNOW WHAT ELSE TO DO!
RIGHT HERE, BUDDY! Y'KNOW WHAT THIS IS, DUDE? IT'S SPEED, Y'DIG? A FEW LINES OF THIS SHIT AND YOU'LL BE UP FOR DAYS, BRO'!
DON'T YOU UNDERSTAND? I'M LOOKING FOR A CURE... NOT JUST TEMPORARY RELIEF! AS SOON AS THAT WORE OFF, I'D GO STRAIGHT TO SLEEP! FURTHERMORE, WHAT YOU'RE OFFERING ME IS AN ADDICTIVE, PARANOIA-INDUCING DRUG... HARDLY A SOLUTION TO THE QUANDARY AT HAND!
GO BACK TO L.A., YOU FUCKIN' DRUGGIE!
SO, UNTIL SOMEONE MAKES SOME BREAK-THROUGH, I'LL HAVE TO RESIGN MYSELF TO THE FACT THAT WITHOUT 7 HOURS OF SLEEP AND AT LEAST 3 CUPS OF COFFEE PER DAY, I'M WORTHLESS!
SIGH
IN FACT, ALL THIS TALKING HAS REALLY TIRED ME OUT!
I'M...HELPLESS...
WHAT A CURSE!
Z Z Z
GOOD-NIGHT!

DINE *and* DASH

by ADRIAN TOMINE

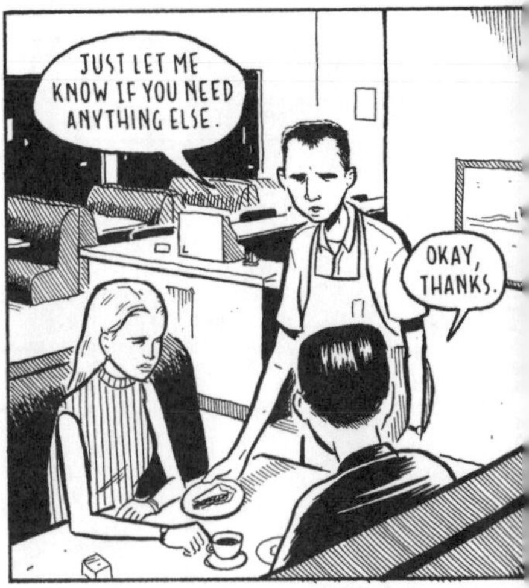
JUST LET ME KNOW IF YOU NEED ANYTHING ELSE.
OKAY, THANKS.

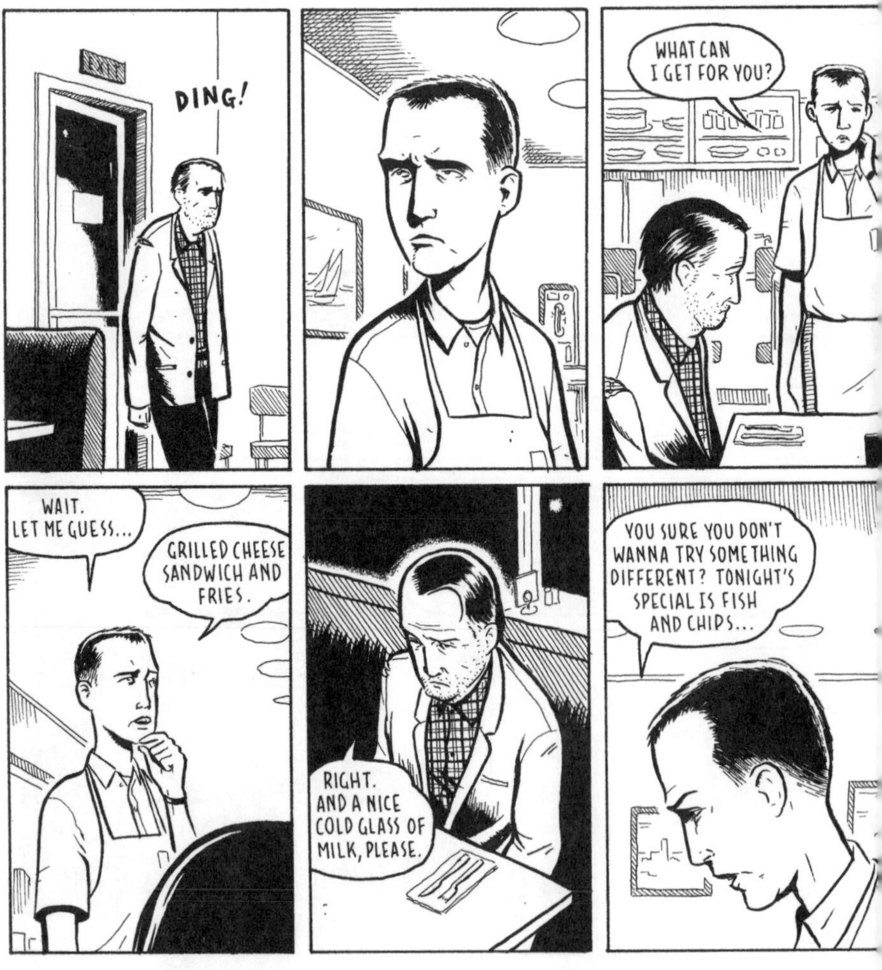
DING!
WHAT CAN I GET FOR YOU?
WAIT. LET ME GUESS...
GRILLED CHEESE SANDWICH AND FRIES.
RIGHT. AND A NICE COLD GLASS OF MILK, PLEASE.
YOU SURE YOU DON'T WANNA TRY SOMETHING DIFFERENT? TONIGHT'S SPECIAL IS FISH AND CHIPS...

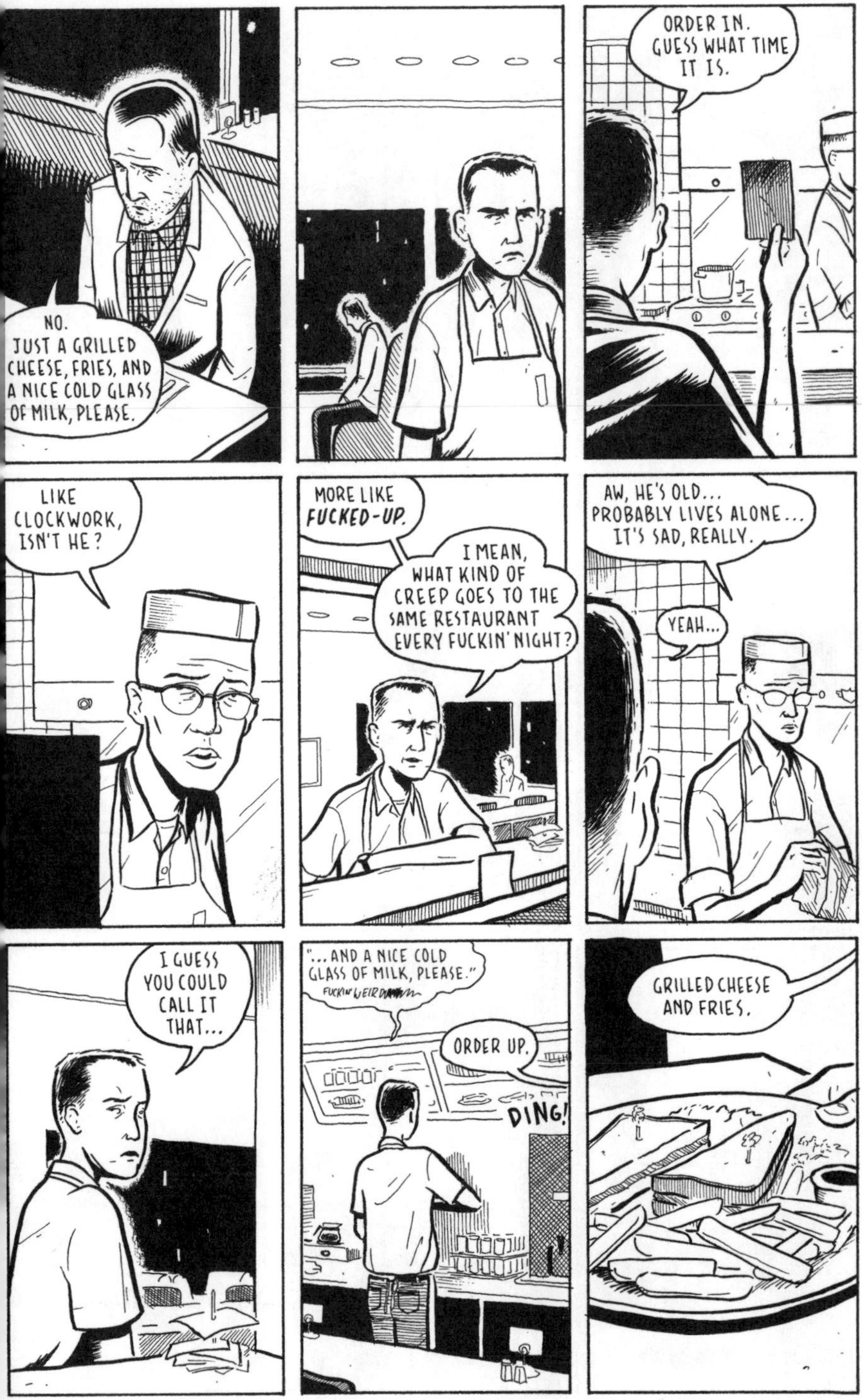
NO. JUST A GRILLED CHEESE, FRIES, AND A NICE COLD GLASS OF MILK, PLEASE.
ORDER IN. GUESS WHAT TIME IT IS.
LIKE CLOCKWORK, ISN'T HE?
MORE LIKE **FUCKED-UP.**
I MEAN, WHAT KIND OF CREEP GOES TO THE SAME RESTAURANT EVERY FUCKIN' NIGHT?
AW, HE'S OLD... PROBABLY LIVES ALONE... IT'S SAD, REALLY.
YEAH...
I GUESS YOU COULD CALL IT THAT...
"...AND A NICE COLD GLASS OF MILK, PLEASE."
FUCKIN' WEIRD
ORDER UP.
DING!
GRILLED CHEESE AND FRIES.

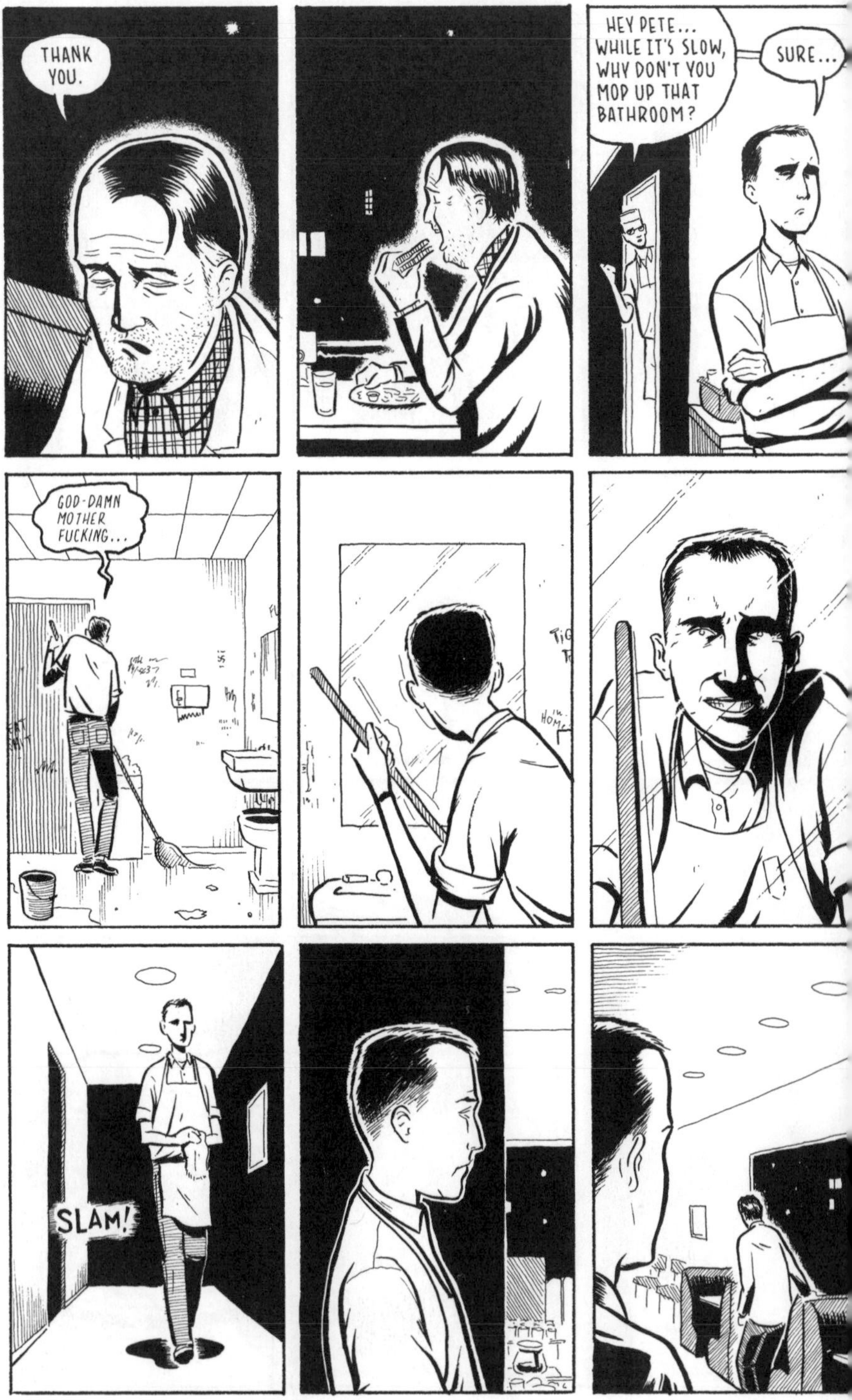
THANK YOU.
HEY PETE... WHILE IT'S SLOW, WHY DON'T YOU MOP UP THAT BATHROOM?
SURE...
GOD-DAMN MOTHER FUCKING...
SLAM!

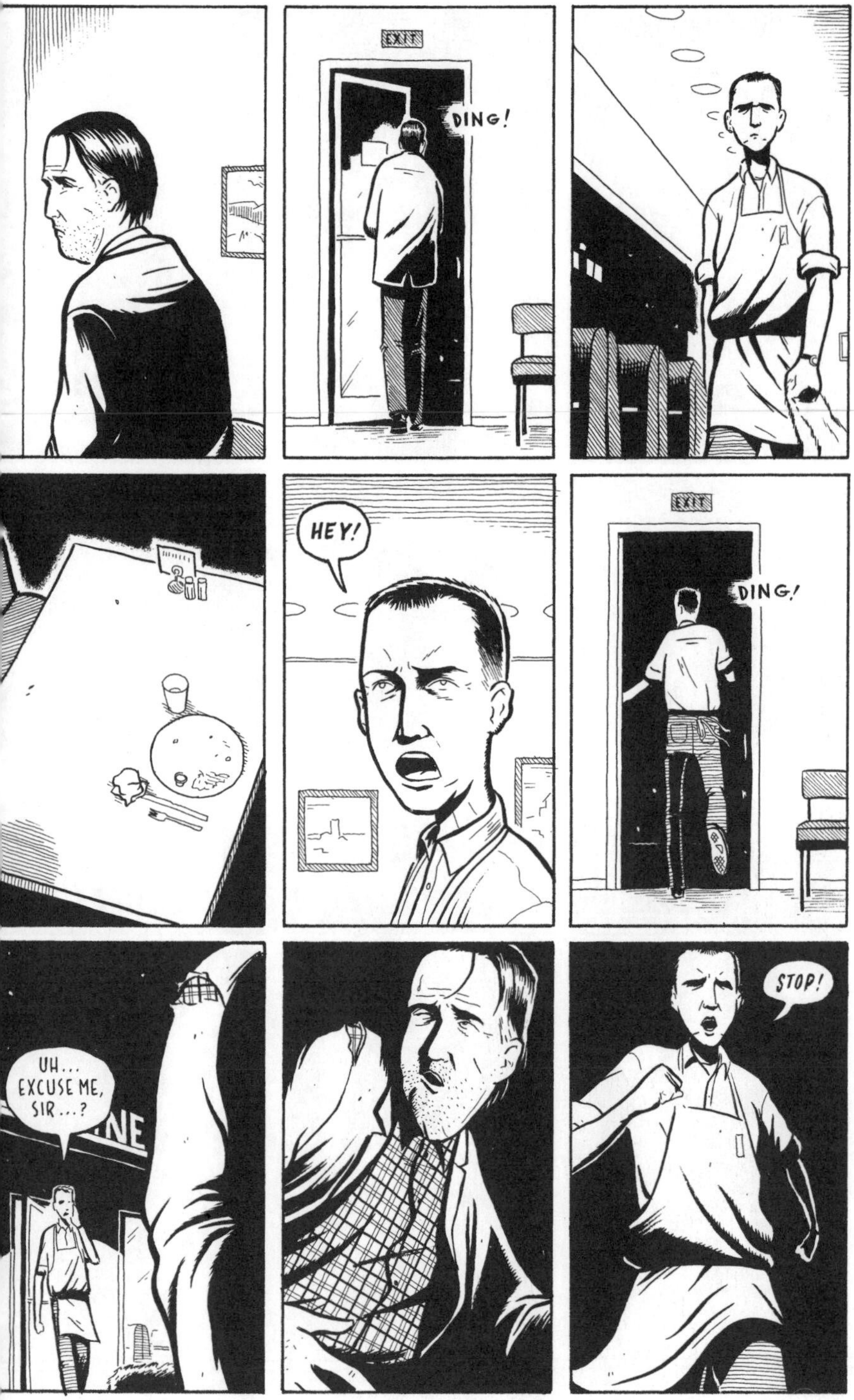
DING!
HEY!
DING!
UH... EXCUSE ME, SIR...?
STOP!

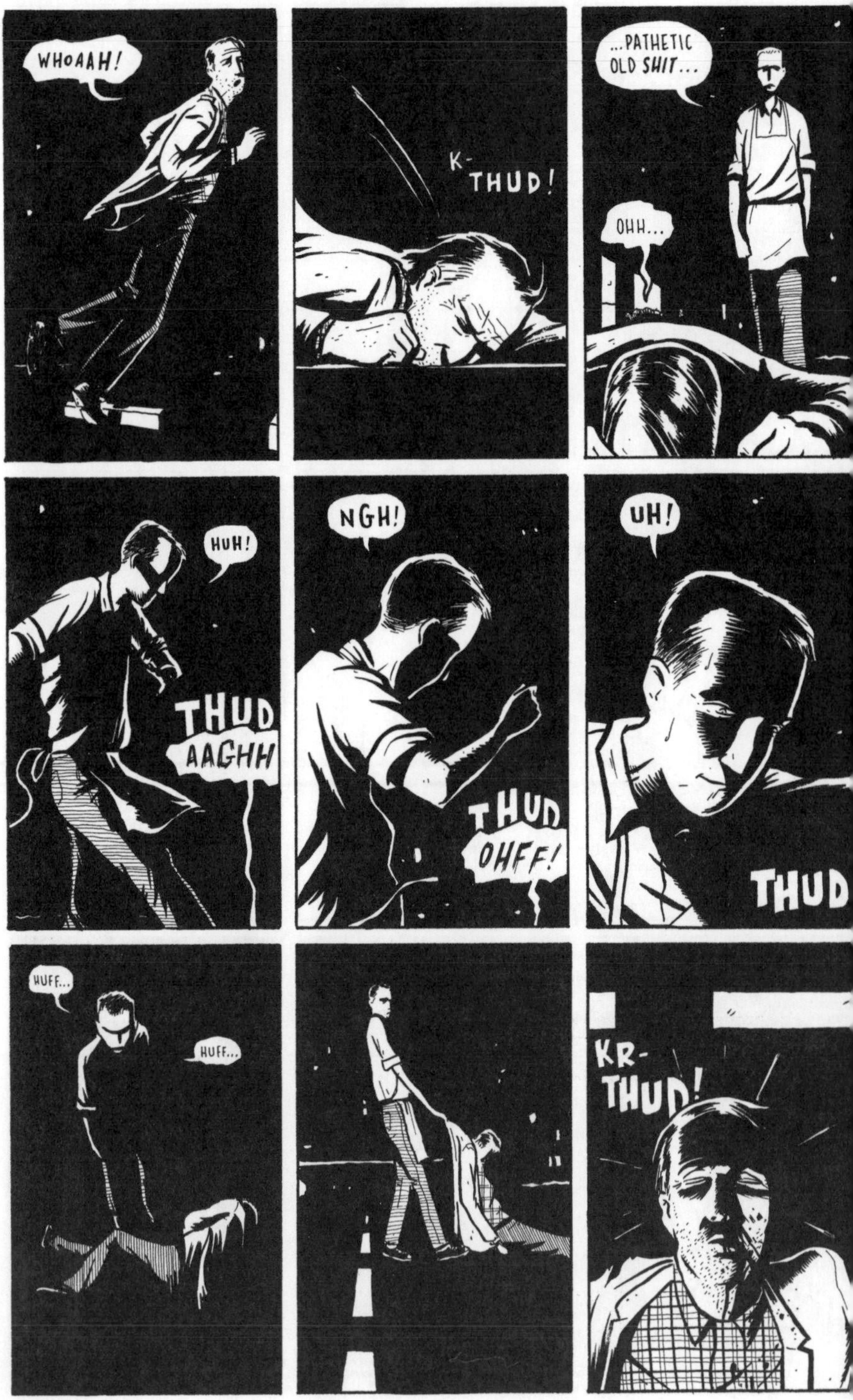
WHOAAH!
K-THUD!
...PATHETIC OLD SHIT...
OHH...
HUH!
THUD
AAGHH
NGH!
THUD
OHFF!
UH!
THUD
HUFF...
HUFF...
KR-THUD!

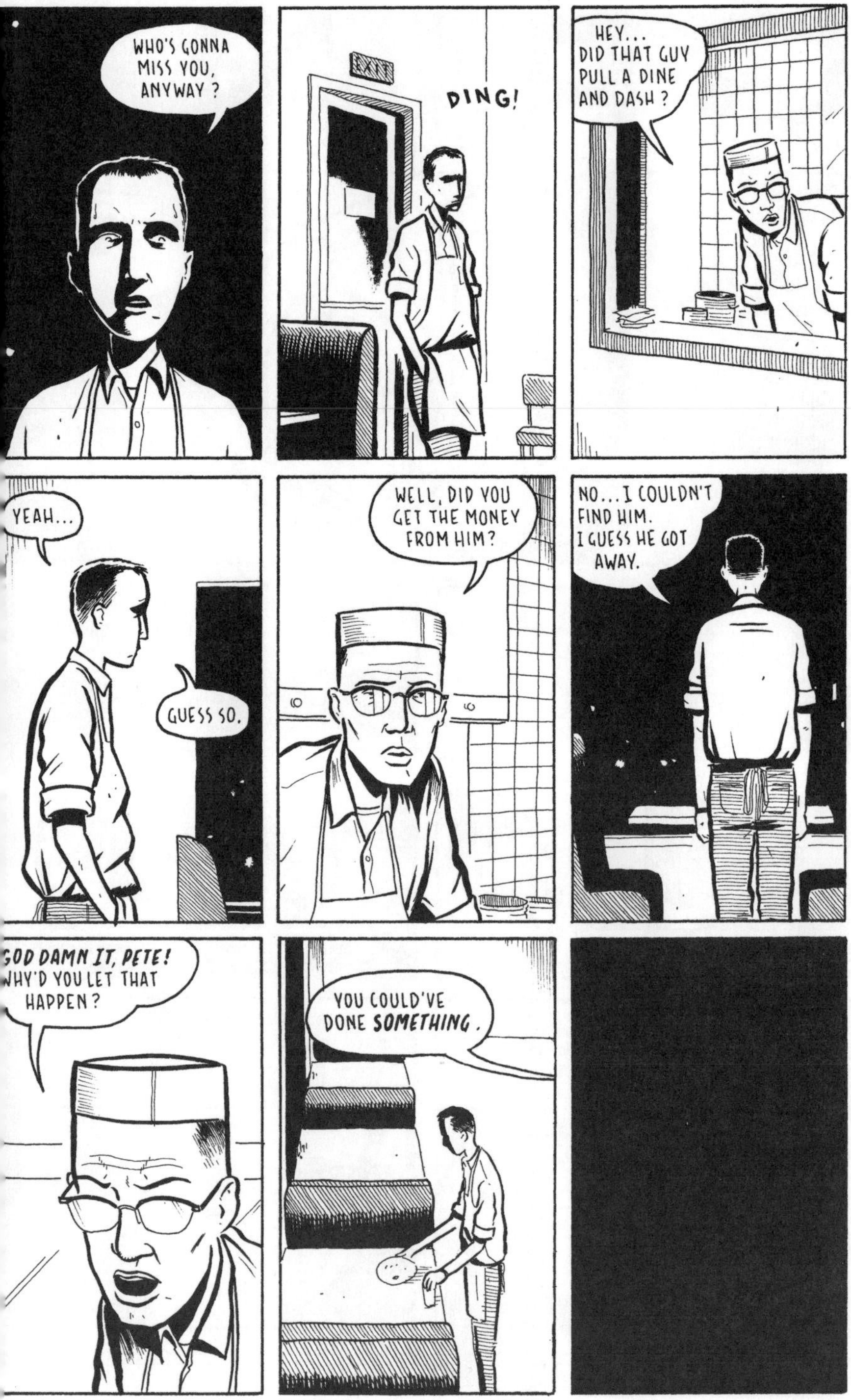
WHO'S GONNA MISS YOU, ANYWAY ?
EXIT
DING!
HEY... DID THAT GUY PULL A DINE AND DASH ?
YEAH...
GUESS SO.
WELL, DID YOU GET THE MONEY FROM HIM?
NO... I COULDN'T FIND HIM. I GUESS HE GOT AWAY.
GOD DAMN IT, PETE! WHY'D YOU LET THAT HAPPEN ?
YOU COULD'VE DONE SOMETHING.

GRIND

BY ADRIAN TOMINE © 1994

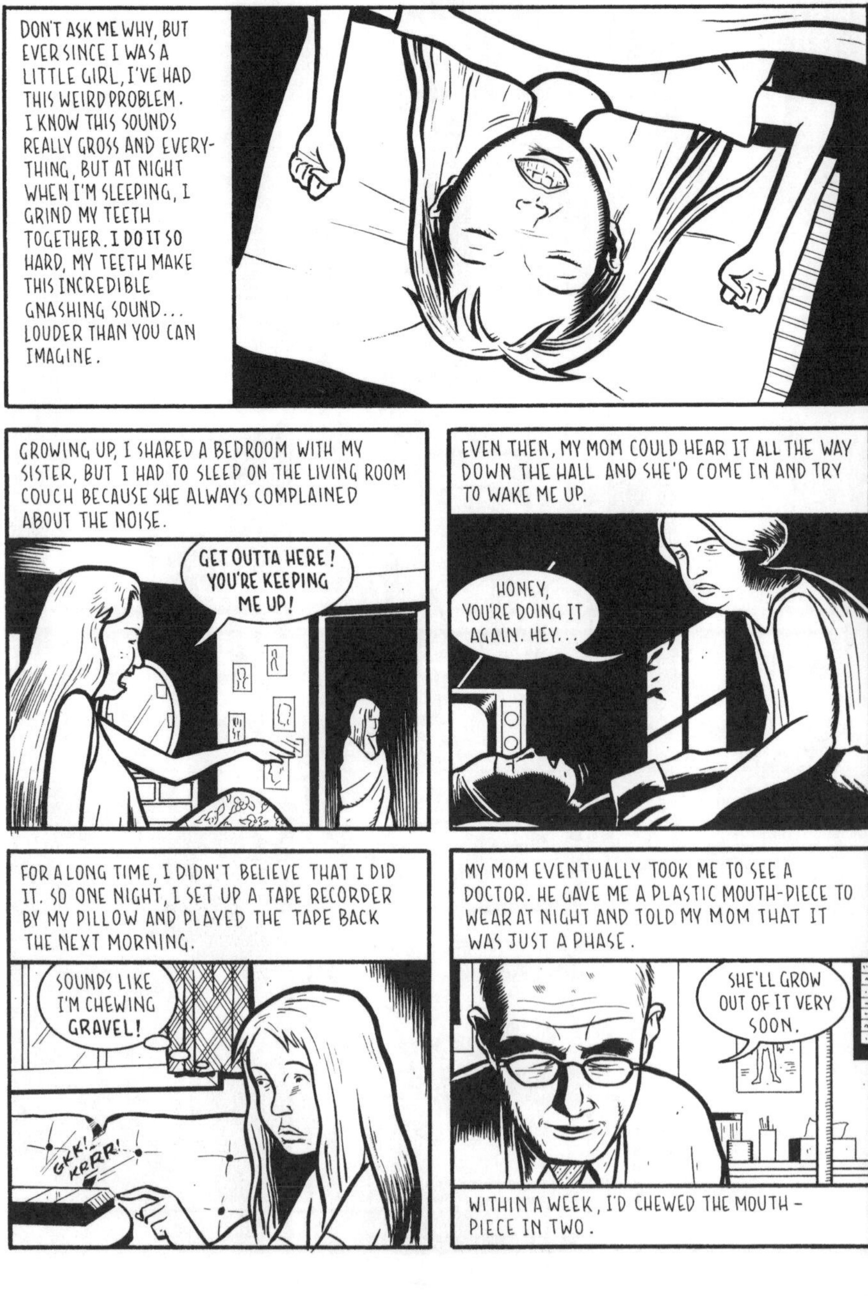
DON'T ASK ME WHY, BUT EVER SINCE I WAS A LITTLE GIRL, I'VE HAD THIS WEIRD PROBLEM. I KNOW THIS SOUNDS REALLY GROSS AND EVERY-THING, BUT AT NIGHT WHEN I'M SLEEPING, I GRIND MY TEETH TOGETHER. I DO IT SO HARD, MY TEETH MAKE THIS INCREDIBLE GNASHING SOUND... LOUDER THAN YOU CAN IMAGINE.
GROWING UP, I SHARED A BEDROOM WITH MY SISTER, BUT I HAD TO SLEEP ON THE LIVING ROOM COUCH BECAUSE SHE ALWAYS COMPLAINED ABOUT THE NOISE.
GET OUTTA HERE! YOU'RE KEEPING ME UP!
EVEN THEN, MY MOM COULD HEAR IT ALL THE WAY DOWN THE HALL AND SHE'D COME IN AND TRY TO WAKE ME UP.
HONEY, YOU'RE DOING IT AGAIN. HEY...
FOR A LONG TIME, I DIDN'T BELIEVE THAT I DID IT. SO ONE NIGHT, I SET UP A TAPE RECORDER BY MY PILLOW AND PLAYED THE TAPE BACK THE NEXT MORNING.
SOUNDS LIKE I'M CHEWING GRAVEL!
GKK! KRRR!
MY MOM EVENTUALLY TOOK ME TO SEE A DOCTOR. HE GAVE ME A PLASTIC MOUTH-PIECE TO WEAR AT NIGHT AND TOLD MY MOM THAT IT WAS JUST A PHASE.
SHE'LL GROW OUT OF IT VERY SOON.
WITHIN A WEEK, I'D CHEWED THE MOUTH-PIECE IN TWO.

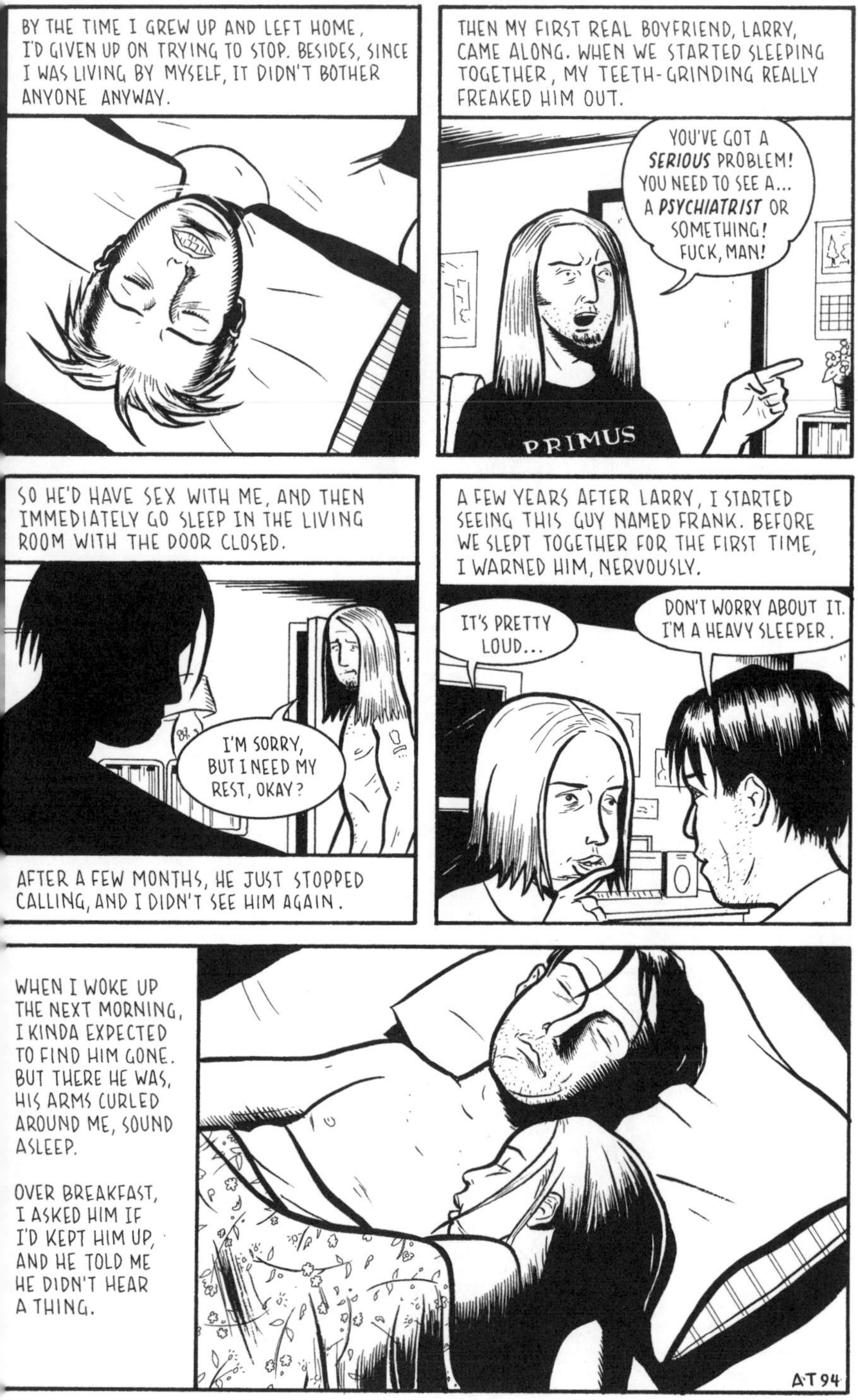
BY THE TIME I GREW UP AND LEFT HOME, I'D GIVEN UP ON TRYING TO STOP. BESIDES, SINCE I WAS LIVING BY MYSELF, IT DIDN'T BOTHER ANYONE ANYWAY.
THEN MY FIRST REAL BOYFRIEND, LARRY, CAME ALONG. WHEN WE STARTED SLEEPING TOGETHER, MY TEETH-GRINDING REALLY FREAKED HIM OUT.
YOU'VE GOT A SERIOUS PROBLEM! YOU NEED TO SEE A... A PSYCHIATRIST OR SOMETHING! FUCK, MAN!
PRIMUS
SO HE'D HAVE SEX WITH ME, AND THEN IMMEDIATELY GO SLEEP IN THE LIVING ROOM WITH THE DOOR CLOSED.
I'M SORRY, BUT I NEED MY REST, OKAY?
AFTER A FEW MONTHS, HE JUST STOPPED CALLING, AND I DIDN'T SEE HIM AGAIN.
A FEW YEARS AFTER LARRY, I STARTED SEEING THIS GUY NAMED FRANK. BEFORE WE SLEPT TOGETHER FOR THE FIRST TIME, I WARNED HIM, NERVOUSLY.
IT'S PRETTY LOUD...
DON'T WORRY ABOUT IT. I'M A HEAVY SLEEPER.
WHEN I WOKE UP THE NEXT MORNING, I KINDA EXPECTED TO FIND HIM GONE. BUT THERE HE WAS, HIS ARMS CURLED AROUND ME, SOUND ASLEEP.
OVER BREAKFAST, I ASKED HIM IF I'D KEPT HIM UP, AND HE TOLD ME HE DIDN'T HEAR A THING.
AT 94

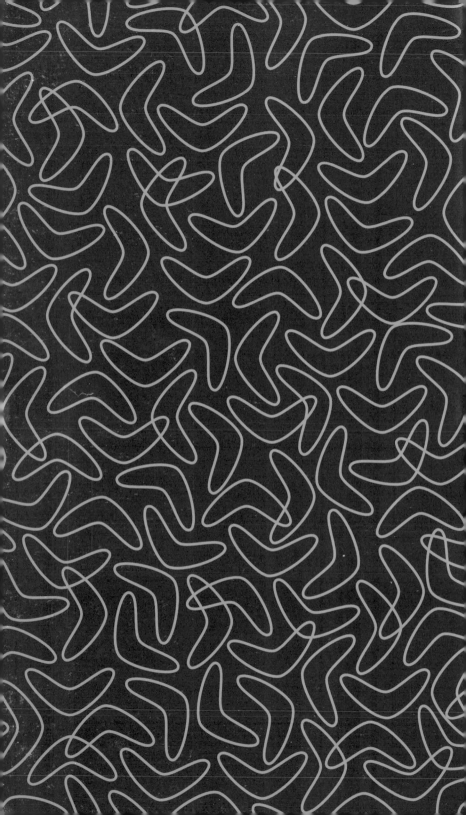